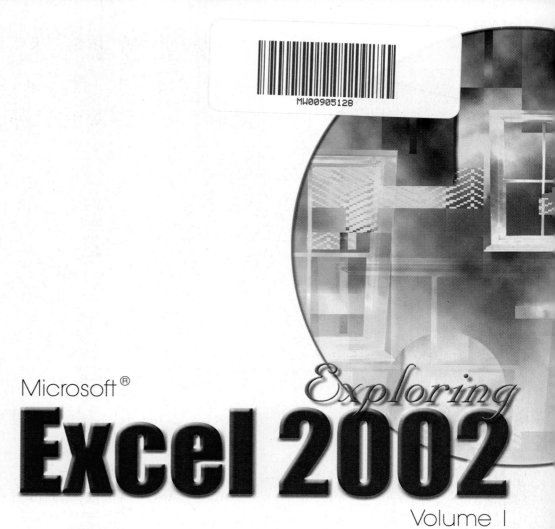

Microsoft®

Exploring

Excel 2002

Volume I

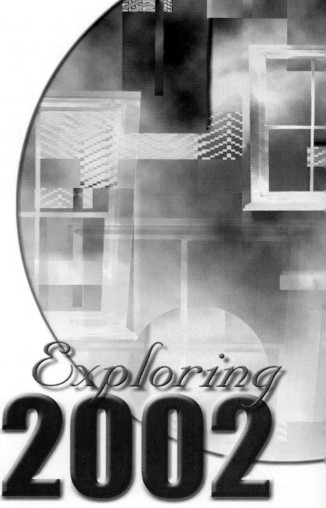

Microsoft®

Exploring

Excel 2002

Volume 1

Robert T. Grauer

University of Miami

Maryann Barber

University of Miami

Prentice
Hall

PRENTICE HALL   *Upper Saddle River, New Jersey 07458*

Senior Acquisitions Editor: David Alexander
VP/Publisher: Natalie Anderson
Managing Editor: Melissa Whitaker
Assistant Editor: Kerri Limpert
Editorial Assistant: Maryann Broadnax
Technical Editor: Cecil Yarbrough
Media Project Manager: Cathleen Profitko
Marketing Assistant: Jason Smith
Production Manager: Gail Steier deAcevedo
Project Manager: Lynne Breitfeller
Production Editor: Greg Hubit
Associate Director, Manufacturing: Vincent Scelta
Manufacturing Buyer: Lynne Breitfeller
Design Manager: Pat Smythe
Interior Design: Jill Yutkowitz
Cover Design: Blair Brown
Cover Illustration: Marjorie Dressler
Composition: GTS
Printer/Binder: Banta Menasha

10 9 8 7 6 5 4 3 2
ISBN 0-13-093440-2

To Marion —
my wife, my lover, and my best friend

Robert Grauer

To Frank —
for giving me the encouragement, love, and the space

Maryann Barber

APPROVED COURSEWARE

What does this logo mean?

It means this courseware has been approved by the Microsoft® Office User Specialist Program to be among the finest available for learning **Excel 2002**. It also means that upon completion of this courseware, you may be prepared to become a Microsoft Office User Specialist.

What is a Microsoft Office User Specialist?

A Microsoft Office User Specialist is an individual who has certified his or her skills in one or more of the Microsoft Office desktop applications of Microsoft Word, Microsoft Excel, Microsoft PowerPoint®, Microsoft Outlook® or Microsoft Access, or in Microsoft Project. The Microsoft Office User Specialist Program typically offers certification exams at the "Core" and "Expert" skill levels.[*] The Microsoft Office User Specialist Program is the only Microsoft approved program in the world for certifying proficiency in Microsoft Office desktop applications and Microsoft Project. This certification can be a valuable asset in any job search or career advancement.

More Information:

To learn more about becoming a Microsoft Office User Specialist, visit www.mous.net

To purchase a Microsoft Office User Specialist certification exam, visit www.DesktopIQ.com

To learn about other Microsoft Office User Specialist approved courseware from Prentice Hall, visit http://www.prenhall.com/phit/mous_frame.html

---

[*]The availability of Microsoft Office User Specialist certification exams varies by application, application version and language. Visit www.mous.net for exam availability.

Microsoft, the Microsoft Office User Specialist Logo, PowerPoint and Outlook are either registered trademarks or trademarks of Microsoft Corporation in the United States and/or other countries.

CONTENTS

PREFACE XI

EXPLORING EXCEL 2002

1

INTRODUCTION TO MICROSOFT® EXCEL: WHAT IS A SPREADSHEET?   1

OBJECTIVES   1
OVERVIEW   1
Introduction to Spreadsheets   2
  The Professor's Grade Book   3
  Row and Column Headings   4
  Formulas and Constants   5
Introduction to Microsoft Excel   6
  Toolbars   7
The File Menu   9
HANDS-ON EXERCISE 1: INTRODUCTION TO MICROSOFT EXCEL   11

Modifying the Worksheet   19
The Page Setup Command   21
HANDS-ON EXERCISE 2: MODIFYING THE WORKSHEET   22

A Better Grade Book   31
Cell Range   32
Copy Command   32
Move Operation   34
Learning by Doing   35
HANDS-ON EXERCISE 3: CREATING A WORKBOOK   36

Formatting   42
Format Cells Command   43
  Alignment   44
  Fonts   44
  Borders, Patterns, and Shading   46
HANDS-ON EXERCISE 4: FORMATTING A WORKSHEET   47

Summary   53
Key Terms   53
Multiple Choice   54
Practice with Excel   56
On Your Own   63

2

GAINING PROFICIENCY: THE WEB AND BUSINESS APPLICATIONS 65

OBJECTIVES 65
OVERVIEW 65
Employee Payroll 66
  Pointing 68
  The Fill Handle 68
  Comments 68
HANDS-ON EXERCISE 1: PAYROLL 69
Excel and the Internet 76
HANDS-ON EXERCISE 2: CREATING A WEB PAGE 78
Web Queries 87
HANDS-ON EXERCISE 3: WEB QUERIES 89
Summary 95
Key Terms 95
Multiple Choice 96
Practice with Excel 98
On Your Own 108

3

SPREADSHEETS IN DECISION MAKING: WHAT IF? 109

OBJECTIVES 109
OVERVIEW 109
Analysis of a Car Loan 110
  PMT Function 112
  FV Function 112
  Inserting a Function 113
  The Goal Seek Command 114
HANDS-ON EXERCISE 1: BASIC FINANCIAL FUNCTIONS 115
Home Mortgages 121
  Relative versus Absolute Address 122
  Mixed References 123
HANDS-ON EXERCISE 2: ADVANCED FINANCIAL FUNCTIONS 124
The Grade Book Revisited 134
  Statistical Functions 135
  Arithmetic Expressions versus Functions 136
  IF Function 137
  VLOOKUP Function 138
Working with Large Spreadsheets 139
  Freezing Panes 139
  Hiding Rows and Columns 139
  Printing a Large Worksheet 139
  AutoFilter Command 142
HANDS-ON EXERCISE 3: THE EXPANDED GRADE BOOK 143
Summary 153
Key Terms 153
Multiple Choice 154
Practice with Excel 156
On Your Own 165

4

GRAPHS AND CHARTS: DELIVERING A MESSAGE   167

OBJECTIVES 167
OVERVIEW 167
Chart Types 168
    Pie Charts 169
    Column and Bar Charts 171
Creating a Chart 174
    The Chart Wizard 176
    Modifying a Chart 178
HANDS-ON EXERCISE 1: THE CHART WIZARD   179

Multiple Data Series 188
    Stacked Column Charts 189
HANDS-ON EXERCISE 2: MULTIPLE DATA SERIES   191

Object Linking and Embedding 197
HANDS-ON EXERCISE 3: OBJECT LINKING AND EMBEDDING   198

Summary 205
Key Terms 205
Multiple Choice 206
Practice with Excel 208
On Your Own 216

ESSENTIALS OF MICROSOFT® WINDOWS®

OBJECTIVES 1
OVERVIEW 1
The Desktop 2
The Common User Interface 5
    Moving and Sizing a Window 7
    Pull-down Menus 7
    Dialog Boxes 8
The Mouse 10
    The Mouse versus the Keyboard 10
The Help Command 11
Formatting a Floppy Disk 11
HANDS-ON EXERCISE 1: WELCOME TO WINDOWS   13

Files and Folders 20
My Computer 22
The Exploring Office Practice Files 22
HANDS-ON EXERCISE 2: THE PRACTICE FILES VIA THE WEB   24

Windows Explorer 33
    Expanding and Collapsing a Drive or Folder 35
HANDS-ON EXERCISE 3: THE PRACTICE FILES VIA A LOCAL AREA NETWORK   36

The Basics of File Management 41
    Moving and Copying a File 41
    Deleting a File 41
    Renaming a File 42

Backup 42
Write Protection 42
Our Next Exercise 42

HANDS-ON EXERCISE 4: FILE MANAGEMENT   43

Summary 51
Key Terms 52
Multiple Choice 52
Practice with Windows 54
On Your Own 63

PREFACE

ABOUT THIS SERIES........

Continuing a tradition of excellence, Prentice Hall is proud to announce the latest update in Microsoft Office texts: the new Exploring Microsoft Office XP series by Robert T. Grauer and Maryann Barber.

The hands-on approach and conceptual framework of this comprehensive series helps students master all aspects of the Microsoft Office XP software, while providing the background necessary to transfer and use these skills in their personal and professional lives.

WHAT'S NEW IN THE EXPLORING OFFICE SERIES FOR XP

The entire Exploring Office series has been revised to include the new features found in the Office XP Suite, which include: Word 2002, Excel 2002, Access 2002, PowerPoint 2002, Publisher 2000, Frontpage 2002, and Outlook 2002.

In addition, this revision features fully revised end-of-chapter material that provides an extensive review of concepts and techniques discussed in the chapter. Many of these exercises feature the World Wide Web and application integration.

Building on the success of the Web site provided for previous editions of this series, Exploring Office XP will introduce the myPHLIP Companion Web site, a site customized for each instructor that includes on-line, interactive study guides, data file downloads, current news feeds, additional case studies and exercises, and other helpful information. Start out at www.prenhall.com/grauer to explore these resources!

Organization of the Exploring Office Series for XP

The new Exploring Microsoft Office XP series includes four combined Office XP texts from which to choose:

- ■ *Volume I* is MOUS certified in each of the major applications in the Office suite (Word, Excel, Access, and PowerPoint). Three additional modules (Essential Computer Concepts, Essentials of Windows, and Essentials of the Internet) are also included.

- ■ *Volume II* picks up where Volume I left off, covering the advanced topics for the individual applications. A VBA primer has been added.

- ■ The *Brief Microsoft Office XP* edition provides less coverage of the individual applications than Volume I (a total of 8 chapters as opposed to 14). The supplementary modules (Windows, Internet, and Concepts) are not included.

- ■ A new volume, *Getting Started with Office XP*, contains the first chapter from each application (Word, Excel, Access, and PowerPoint), plus three additional modules: Essentials of Windows, Essentials of the Internet, and Essential Computer Concepts.

Individual texts for Word 2002, Excel 2002, Access 2002, and PowerPoint 2002 provide complete coverage of the application and are MOUS certified. For shorter courses, we have created brief versions of the Exploring texts that give students a four-chapter introduction to each application. Each of these volumes is MOUS certified at the Core level.

To complete the full coverage of this series, custom modules on Microsoft Outlook 2002, Microsoft FrontPage 2002, Microsoft Publisher 2002, and a generic introduction to Microsoft Windows are also available.

APPROVED COURSEWARE

This book has been approved by Microsoft to be used in preparation for Microsoft Office User Specialist exams.

The Microsoft Office User Specialist (MOUS) program is globally recognized as the standard for demonstrating desktop skills with the Microsoft Office suite of business productivity applications (Microsoft Word, Microsoft Excel, Microsoft PowerPoint, Microsoft Access, and Microsoft Outlook). With a MOUS certification, thousands of people have demonstrated increased productivity and have proved their ability to utilize the advanced functionality of these Microsoft applications.

By encouraging individuals to develop advanced skills with Microsoft's leading business desktop software, the MOUS program helps fill the demand for qualified, knowledgeable people in the modern workplace. At the same time, MOUS helps satisfy an organization's need for a qualitative assessment of employee skills.

Customize the Exploring Office Series with Prentice Hall's Right PHit Binding Program

The Exploring Office XP series is part of the Right PHit Custom Binding Program, enabling instructors to create their own texts by selecting modules from Office XP Volume I, Volume II, Outlook, FrontPage, and Publisher to suit the needs of a specific course. An instructor could, for example, create a custom text consisting of the core modules in Word and Excel, coupled with the brief modules for Access and PowerPoint, and a brief introduction to computer concepts.

Instructors can also take advantage of Prentice Hall's Value Pack program to shrinkwrap multiple texts together at substantial savings to the student. A value pack is ideal in courses that require complete coverage of multiple applications.

The **Instructor's CD** that accompanies the Exploring Office series contains:

- Student data disks
- Solutions to all exercises and problems
- PowerPoint lectures
- Instructor's manuals in Word format enable the instructor to annotate portions of the instructor manual for distribution to the class
- A Windows-based test manager and the associated test bank in Word format

Prentice Hall's New MyPHLIP Companion Web site at www.prenhall.com/grauer offers current events, exercises, and downloadable supplements. This site also includes an on-line study guide containing true/false, multiple choice, and essay questions.

WebCT www.prenhall.com/webct

GOLD LEVEL CUSTOMER SUPPORT available exclusively to adopters of Prentice Hall courses, is provided free-of-charge upon adoption and provides you with priority assistance, training discounts, and dedicated technical support.

Blackboard www.prenhall.com/blackboard

Prentice Hall's abundant on-line content, combined with Blackboard's popular tools and interface, result in robust Web-based courses that are easy to implement, manage, and use—taking your courses to new heights in student interaction and learning.

CourseCompass www.coursecompass.com

CourseCompass is a dynamic, interactive on-line course management tool powered by Blackboard. This exciting product allows you to teach with marketing-leading Pearson Education content in an easy-to-use customizable format.

Exploring Microsoft Office assumes no prior knowledge of the operating system. A 64-page section introduces the reader to the Essentials of Windows and provides an overview of the operating system. Students are shown the necessary file-management operations to use Microsoft Office successfully.

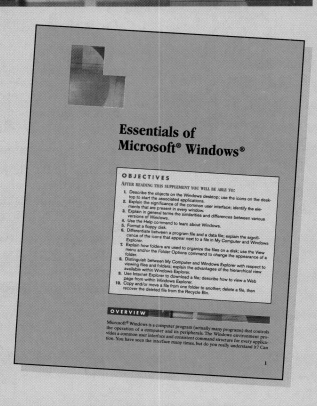

In-depth tutorials throughout all the Office XP applications enhance the conceptual introduction to each task and guide the student at the computer. Every step in every exercise has a full-color screen shot to illustrate the specific commands. Boxed tips provide alternative techniques and shortcuts and/or anticipate errors that students may make.

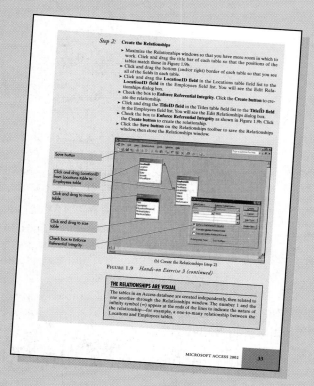

The authors have created an entirely new set of end-of-chapter exercises for every chapter in all of the applications. These new exercises have been written to provide the utmost in flexibility, variety, and difficulty.

Web-based Practice exercises and On Your Own exercises are marked by an icon in the margin and allow further exploration and practice via the World Wide Web.

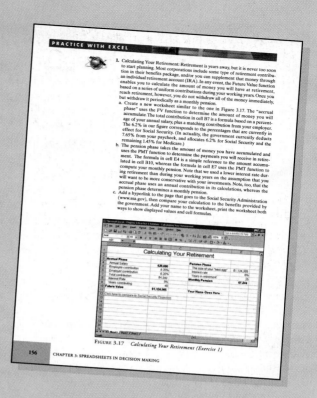

Integration Exercises are marked by an icon in the margin. These exercises take advantage of the Microsoft Office Suite's power to use multiple applications in one document, spreadsheet, or presentation.

Builds On Exercises require students to use selected application files as the starting point in later exercises, thereby introducing new information to students only as needed.

The end-of-chapter material includes multiple-choice questions for self-evaluation plus additional "on your own" exercises to encourage the reader to further explore the application.

ACKNOWLEDGMENTS

We want to thank the many individuals who have helped to bring this project to fruition. David Alexander, senior editor at Prentice Hall, has provided new leadership in extending the series to Office XP. Cathi Profitko did an absolutely incredible job on our Web site. Melissa Whitaker coordinated the myriad details of production and the certification process. Greg Christofferson was instrumental in the acquisition of supporting software. Lynne Breitfeller was the project manager and manufacturing buyer. Greg Hubit has been masterful as the external production editor for every book in the series. Cecil Yarbrough did an outstanding job in checking the manuscript for technical accuracy. Chuck Cox did his usual fine work as copyeditor. Kerri Limpert was the supplements editor. Cindy Stevens, Tom McKenzie, and Michael Olmstead wrote the instructor manuals. Patricia Smythe developed the innovative and attractive design. We also want to acknowledge our reviewers who, through their comments and constructive criticism, greatly improved the series.

Lynne Band, Middlesex Community College
Don Belle, Central Piedmont Community College
Stuart P. Brian, Holy Family College
Carl M. Briggs, Indiana University School of Business
Kimberly Chambers, Scottsdale Community College
Alok Charturvedi, Purdue University
Jerry Chin, Southwest Missouri State University
Dean Combellick, Scottsdale Community College
Cody Copeland, Johnson County Community College
Larry S. Corman, Fort Lewis College
Janis Cox, Tri-County Technical College
Martin Crossland, Southwest Missouri State University
Paul E. Daurelle, Western Piedmont Community College
Carolyn DiLeo, Westchester Community College
Judy Dolan, Palomar College
David Douglas, University of Arkansas
Carlotta Eaton, Radford University
Judith M. Fitspatrick, Gulf Coast Community College
James Franck, College of St. Scholastica
Raymond Frost, Central Connecticut State University
Midge Gerber, Southwestern Oklahoma State University
James Gips, Boston College
Vernon Griffin, Austin Community College
Ranette Halverson, Midwestern State University
Michael Hassett, Fort Hays State University
Mike Hearn, Community College of Philadelphia
Wanda D. Heller, Seminole Community College
Bonnie Homan, San Francisco State University
Ernie Ivey, Polk Community College
Mike Kelly, Community College of Rhode Island
Jane King, Everett Community College

Rose M. Laird, Northern Virginia Community College
John Lesson, University of Central Florida
David B. Meinert, Southwest Missouri State University
Alan Moltz, Naugatuck Valley Technical Community College
Kim Montney, Kellogg Community College
Bill Morse, DeVry Institute of Technology
Kevin Pauli, University of Nebraska
Mary McKenry Percival, University of Miami
Delores Pusins, Hillsborough Community College
Gale E. Rand, College Misericordia
Judith Rice, Santa Fe Community College
David Rinehard, Lansing Community College
Marilyn Salas, Scottsdale Community College
John Shepherd, Duquesne University
Barbara Sherman, Buffalo State College
Robert Spear, Prince George's Community College
Michael Stewardson, San Jacinto College—North
Helen Stoloff, Hudson Valley Community College
Margaret Thomas, Ohio University
Mike Thomas, Indiana University School of Business
Suzanne Tomlinson, Iowa State University
Karen Tracey, Central Connecticut State University
Antonio Vargas, El Paso Community College
Sally Visci, Lorain County Community College
David Weiner, University of San Francisco
Connie Wells, Georgia State University
Wallace John Whistance-Smith, Ryerson Polytechnic University
Jack Zeller, Kirkwood Community College

A final word of thanks to the unnamed students at the University of Miami, who make it all worthwhile. Most of all, thanks to you, our readers, for choosing this book. Please feel free to contact us with any comments and suggestions.

Robert T. Grauer
rgrauer@miami.edu
www.bus.miami.edu/~rgrauer
www.prenhall.com/grauer

Maryann Barber
mbarber@miami.edu
www.bus.miami.edu/~mbarber

CHAPTER 1

Introduction to Microsoft® Excel: What Is a Spreadsheet?

OBJECTIVES

AFTER READING THIS CHAPTER YOU WILL BE ABLE TO:

1. Describe a spreadsheet and suggest several potential applications; explain how the rows and columns of a spreadsheet are identified.
2. Distinguish between a formula and a constant; explain the use of a predefined function within a formula.
3. Open an Excel workbook; insert and delete rows and columns of a worksheet; save and print the modified worksheet.
4. Describe the three-dimensional nature of an Excel workbook; distinguish between a workbook and a worksheet.
5. Print a worksheet to show either the displayed values or the cell contents; use the Page Setup command to modify the appearance of the printed worksheet.
6. Copy and/or move cells within a worksheet; differentiate between relative, absolute, and mixed references.
7. Format a worksheet to include boldface, italics, shading, and borders; change the font and/or alignment of a selected entry.

OVERVIEW

The spreadsheet is the PC application that is used most frequently by business managers and executives. This chapter provides a broad-based introduction to spreadsheets in general and to Microsoft Excel in particular. A spreadsheet (also called a worksheet) is stored within a workbook, which in turn may contain multiple worksheets. The chapter discusses how the rows and columns of a spreadsheet are labeled and the difference between a formula and a constant.

All of the illustrations in this chapter are set in the context of a professor's grade book that computes the semester averages for his or her students. You will learn how students can be inserted or removed from the worksheet and how changing a student's grade automatically recalculates the dependent values in the worksheet. We also show you how to create a new workbook, how to move and copy formulas within the worksheet, and how to format the worksheet.

The hands-on exercises in the chapter enable you to apply all of the material at the computer, and are indispensable to the learn-by-doing philosophy we follow throughout the text. As you do the exercises, you may recognize many commands from other Office applications, all of which share a common user interface and consistent command structure.

INTRODUCTION TO SPREADSHEETS

A *spreadsheet* is the computerized equivalent of an accountant's ledger. As with the ledger, it consists of a grid of rows and columns that enables you to organize data in a readily understandable format. Figures 1.1a and 1.1b show the same information displayed in ledger and spreadsheet format, respectively.

"What is the big deal?" you might ask. The big deal is that after you change an entry (or entries), the spreadsheet will, automatically and almost instantly, recompute all of the formulas. Consider, for example, the profit projection spreadsheet shown in Figure 1.1b. As the spreadsheet is presently constructed, the unit price is $20 and the projected sales are 1,200 units, producing gross sales of $24,000 ($20/unit × 1,200 units). The projected expenses are $19,200, which yields a profit of $4,800 ($24,000 − $19,200). If the unit price is increased to $22 per unit, the spreadsheet recomputes the formulas, adjusting the values of gross sales and net profit. The modified spreadsheet of Figure 1.1c appears automatically.

With a calculator and bottle of correction fluid or a good eraser, the same changes could also be made to the ledger. But imagine a ledger with hundreds of entries and the time that would be required to make the necessary changes to the ledger by hand. The same spreadsheet will be recomputed automatically by the computer. And the computer will not make mistakes. Herein lie the advantages of a spreadsheet—the ability to make changes, and to have the computer carry out the recalculation faster and more accurately than could be accomplished manually.

(a) The Accountant's Ledger

FIGURE 1.1   *The Accountant's Ledger*

Unit price is
increased to $22

Formulas recompute
automatically

	A	B
1	Profit Projection	
2		
3	Unit Price	$20
4	Unit Sales	1,200
5	Gross Sales	$24,000
6		
7	Expenses	
8	Production	$10,000
9	Distribution	$1,200
10	Marketing	$5,000
11	Overhead	$3,000
12	Total Expenses	$19,200
13		
14	Net Profit	$4,800

(b) Original Spreadsheet

	A	B
1	Profit Projection	
2		
3	Unit Price	$22
4	Unit Sales	1,200
5	Gross Sales	$26,400
6		
7	Expenses	
8	Production	$10,000
9	Distribution	$1,200
10	Marketing	$5,000
11	Overhead	$3,000
12	Total Expenses	$19,200
13		
14	Net Profit	$7,200

(c) Modified Spreadsheet

FIGURE 1.1   *The Accountant's Ledger (continued)*

The Professor's Grade Book

A second example of a spreadsheet, one with which you can easily identify, is that of a professor's grade book. The grades are recorded by hand in a notebook, which is nothing more than a different kind of accountant's ledger. Figure 1.2 contains both manual and spreadsheet versions of a grade book.

Figure 1.2a shows a handwritten grade book as it has been done since the days of the little red schoolhouse. For the sake of simplicity, only five students are shown, each with three grades. The professor has computed class averages for each exam, as well as a semester average for every student. The final counts *twice* as much as either test; for example, Adams's average is equal to $(100+90+81+81)/4 = 88$. This is the professor's grading scheme and it is incorporated into the manual grade book and equivalent spreadsheet.

Figure 1.2b shows the grade book as it might appear in a spreadsheet, and is essentially unchanged from Figure 1.2a. Walker's grade on the final exam in Figure 1.2b is 90, giving him a semester average of 85 and producing a class average on the final of 75.2 as well. Now consider Figure 1.2c, in which the grade on Walker's final has been changed to 100, causing Walker's semester average to change from 85 to 90, and the class average on the final to go from 75.2 to 77.2. As with the profit projection, a change to any entry within the grade book automatically recalculates all other dependent formulas as well. Hence, when Walker's final exam was regraded, all dependent formulas (the class average for the final as well as Walker's semester average) were recomputed.

As simple as the idea of a spreadsheet may seem, it provided the first major reason for managers to have a personal computer on their desks. Essentially, anything that can be done with a pencil, a pad of paper, and a calculator can be done faster and far more accurately with a spreadsheet. The spreadsheet, like the personal computer, has become an integral part of every type of business. Indeed, it is hard to imagine that these calculations were ever done by hand. The spreadsheet has become an integral part of corporate culture.

	TEST 1	TEST 2	FINAL	AVERAGE
ADAMS	100	90	81	88
BAKER	90	76	87	85
GLASSMAN	90	78	78	81
MOLDOF	60	60	40	50
WALKER	80	80	90	85
CLASS AVERAGE	84.0	76.8	75.2	
NOTE: FINAL COUNTS DOUBLE				

(a) The Professor's Grade Book

	A	B	C	D	E
1	Student	Test 1	Test 2	Final	Average
2					
3	Adams	100	90	81	88.0
4	Baker	90	76	87	85.0
5	Glassman	90	78	78	81.0
6	Moldof	60	60	40	50.0
7	Walker	80	80	90	85.0
8					
9	Class Average	84.0	76.8	75.2	

(b) Original Grades

	A	B	C	D	E
1	Student	Test 1	Test 2	Final	Average
2					
3	Adams	100	90	81	88.0
4	Baker	90	76	87	85.0
5	Glassman	90	78	78	81.0
6	Moldof	60	60	40	50.0
7	Walker	80	80	100	90.0
8					
9	Class Average	84.0	76.8	77.2	

(c) Modified Spreadsheet

FIGURE 1.2 *The Professor's Grade Book*

Row and Column Headings

A spreadsheet is divided into rows and columns, with each row and column assigned a heading. Rows are given numeric headings ranging from 1 to 65,536 (the maximum number of rows allowed). Columns are assigned alphabetic headings from column A to Z, then continue from AA to AZ and then from BA to BZ and so on, until the last of 256 columns (column IV) is reached.

The intersection of a row and column forms a *cell*, with the number of cells in a spreadsheet equal to the number of rows times the number of columns. The professor's grade book in Figure 1.2, for example, has 5 columns labeled A through E, 9 rows numbered from 1 to 9, and a total of 45 cells. Each cell has a unique *cell reference*; for example, the cell at the intersection of column A and row 9 is known as cell A9. The column heading always precedes the row heading in the cell reference.

Formulas and Constants

Figure 1.3 is an alternate view of the professor's grade book that shows the cell contents rather than the computed values. Cell E3, for example, does not contain the number 88 (Adams's average for the semester), but rather the formula to compute the average from the exam grades. Indeed, it is the existence of the formula that lets you change the value of any cell containing a grade for Adams (cells B3, C3, or D3), and have the computed average in cell E3 change automatically.

To create a spreadsheet, one goes from cell to cell and enters either a constant or a formula. A *constant* is an entry that does not change. It may be a number, such as a student's grade on an exam, or it may be descriptive text (a label), such as a student's name. A *formula* is a combination of numeric constants, cell references, arithmetic operators, and/or functions (described below) that displays the result of a calculation. You can *edit* (change) the contents of a cell by returning to the cell and reentering the constant or formula.

A formula always begins with an equal sign. Consider, for example, the formula in cell E3, =(B3+C3+2*D3)/4, which computes Adams's semester average. The formula is built in accordance with the professor's rules for computing a student's semester average, which counts the final twice as much as the other tests. Excel uses symbols +, −, *, /, and ^ to indicate addition, subtraction, multiplication, division, and exponentiation, respectively, and follows the normal rules of arithmetic precedence. Any expression in parentheses is evaluated first, then within an expression exponentiation is performed first, followed by multiplication or division in left to right order, then finally addition or subtraction.

The formula in cell E3 takes the grade on the first exam (in cell B3), plus the grade on the second exam (in cell C3), plus two times the grade on the final (in cell D3), and divides the result by four. Thus, should any of the exam grades change, the semester average (a formula whose results depend on the individual exam grades) will also change. This, in essence, is the basic principle behind the spreadsheet and explains why, when one number changes, various other numbers throughout the spreadsheet change as well.

A formula may also include a *function*, or predefined computational task, such as the AVERAGE function in cells B9, C9, and D9. The function in cell B9, for example, =AVERAGE(B3:B7), is interpreted to mean the average of all cells starting at cell B3 and ending at cell B7 and is equivalent to the formula =(B3+B4+B5+B6+B7)/5. You can appreciate that functions are often easier to use than the corresponding formulas, especially with larger spreadsheets (and classes with many students). Excel contains a wide variety of functions that help you to create very powerful spreadsheets. Financial functions, for example, enable you to calculate the interest payments on a car loan or home mortgage.

Constant (entry that does not change)   Function (predefined computational task)   Formula (displays the result of a calculation)

	A	B	C	D	E
1	Student	Test 1	Test 2	Final	Average
2					
3	Adams	100	90	81	=(B3+C3+2*D3)/4
4	Baker	90	76	87	=(B4+C4+2*D4)/4
5	Glassman	90	78	78	=(B5+C5+2*D5)/4
6	Moldof	60	60	40	=(B6+C6+2*D6)/4
7	Walker	80	80	90	=(B7+C7+2*D7)/4
8					
9	Class Average	=AVERAGE(B3:B7)	=AVERAGE(C3:C7)	=AVERAGE(D3:D7)	

FIGURE 1.3   *The Professor's Grade Book (cell formulas)*

Figure 1.4 displays the professor's grade book as it is implemented in Microsoft Excel. Microsoft Excel is a Windows application, and thus shares the common user interface with which you are familiar. (It's even easier to learn Excel if you already know another Office application such as Microsoft Word.) You should recognize, therefore, that the desktop in Figure 1.4 has two open windows—an application window for Microsoft Excel and a document window for the workbook, which is currently open.

Each window has its own Minimize, Maximize (or Restore), and Close buttons. Both windows have been maximized and thus the title bars have been merged into a single title bar that appears at the top of the application window. The title bar reflects the application (Microsoft Excel) as well as the name of the workbook (Grade Book) on which you are working. A menu bar appears immediately below the title bar. Two toolbars, which are discussed in depth on page 8, appear below the menu bar. Vertical and horizontal scroll bars appear at the right and bottom of the document window. The Windows taskbar appears at the bottom of the screen and shows the open applications. The Ask a Question list box appears to the right of the menu bar and provides instant access to the Help facility.

The terminology is important, and we distinguish between spreadsheet, worksheet, and workbook. Excel refers to a spreadsheet as a *worksheet*. Spreadsheet is a generic term; *workbook* and *worksheet* are unique to Excel. An Excel *workbook* contains one or more worksheets. The professor's grades for this class are contained in the CIS120 worksheet within the Grade Book workbook. This workbook also contains additional worksheets (CIS223 and CIS316) as indicated by the worksheet tabs at the bottom of the window. These worksheets contain the professor's grades for other courses that he or she is teaching this semester.

Name of workbook		
Menu bar		
Standard toolbar		
Formatting toolbar		
Name box		
Formula bar		
Active cell		
Worksheet tabs		
Status bar		
Task bar		

FIGURE 1.4 *The Professor's Grade Book*

Figure 1.4 resembles the grade book shown earlier, but it includes several other elements that enable you to create and/or edit the worksheet. The heavy border around cell E3 indicates that it (cell E3) is the *active cell*. Any entry made at this time is made into the active cell, and any commands that are executed affect the contents of the active cell. The active cell can be changed by clicking a different cell, or by using the arrow keys to move to a different cell.

The displayed value in cell E3 is 88.0, but as indicated earlier, the cell contains a formula to compute the semester average rather than the number itself. The contents of the active cell, =(B3+C3+2*D3)/4, are displayed in the *formula bar* near the top of the worksheet. The cell reference for the active cell, cell E3 in Figure 1.4, appears in the *Name box* at the left of the formula bar.

The *status bar* at the bottom of the worksheet keeps you informed of what is happening as you work within Excel. It displays information about a selected command or an operation in progress.

THE EXCEL WORKBOOK

An Excel workbook is the electronic equivalent of the three-ring binder. A workbook contains one or more worksheets (or chart sheets), each of which is identified by a tab at the bottom of the workbook. The worksheets in a workbook are normally related to one another; for example, each worksheet may contain the sales for a specific division within a company. The advantage of a workbook is that all of its worksheets are stored in a single file, which is accessed as a unit.

Toolbars

Excel provides several different ways to accomplish the same task. Commands may be accessed from a pull-down menu, from a shortcut menu (which is displayed by pointing to an object and clicking the right mouse button), and/or through keyboard equivalents. Commands can also be executed from one of many *toolbars* that appear immediately below the menu bar. The Standard and Formatting toolbars are displayed by default. The toolbars appear initially on the same line, but can be separated as described in the hands-on exercise that follows.

The *Standard toolbar* contains buttons corresponding to the most basic commands in Excel—for example, opening and closing a workbook, printing a workbook, and so on. The icon on the button is intended to be indicative of its function (e.g., a printer to indicate the Print command). You can also point to the button to display a *ScreenTip* showing the name of the button.

The *Formatting toolbar* appears under the Standard toolbar, and provides access to common formatting operations such as boldface, italics, or underlining. It also enables you to change the alignment of entries within a cell and/or change the font or color. The easiest way to master the toolbars is to view the buttons in groups according to their general function, as shown in Figure 1.5.

The toolbars may appear overwhelming at first, but there is absolutely no need to memorize what the individual buttons do. That will come with time. Indeed, if you use another office application such as Microsoft Word, you may already recognize many of the buttons on the Standard and Formatting toolbars. Note, too, that many of the commands in the pull-down menus are displayed with an image that corresponds to a button on a toolbar.

Opens a new workbook; opens an existing workbook; saves a workbook; sends a workbook via e-mail; or executes a search

Prints the workbook; previews the workbook prior to printing; checks the spelling

Cuts or copies the selecton to the clipboard; pastes the clipboard contents; copies the formatting of the selected cells

Undoes or redoes a previously executed command

Inserts a hyperlink; sums the suggested range; performs an ascending or descending sort

Starts the Chart Wizard; displays the Drawing toolbar

Changes the magnification

Displays the Office Assistant

(a) The Standard Toolbar

Changes the font or point size

Toggles boldface, italics, and underline on and off

Aligns left, center, right; merges cells and centers

Applies accounting, percentage, or comma formatting; increases or decreases the number of decimals

Decreases or increases the indent

Applies a border format; applies a background color; applies a font color

(b) The Formatting Toolbar

FIGURE 1.5   *Toolbars*

The *File menu* is a critically important menu in virtually every Windows application. It contains the Save and Open commands to save a workbook on disk, then subsequently retrieve (open) that workbook at a later time. The File menu also contains the *Print command* to print a workbook, the *Close command* to close the current workbook but continue working in the application, and the *Exit command* to quit the application altogether.

The *Save command* copies the workbook that you are working on (i.e., the workbook that is currently in memory) to disk. The command functions differently the first time it is executed for a new workbook, in that it displays the Save As dialog box as shown in Figure 1.6a. The dialog box requires you to specify the name of the workbook, the drive (and an optional folder) in which the workbook is to be stored, and its file type. All subsequent executions of the command save the workbook under the assigned name, replacing the previously saved version with the new version.

The *file name* (e.g., My First Spreadsheet) can contain up to 255 characters including spaces, commas, and/or periods. (Periods are discouraged, however, since they are too easily confused with DOS extensions.) The Save In list box is used to select the drive (which is not visible in Figure 1.6a) and the optional folder (e.g., Exploring Excel). The *Places bar* provides shortcuts to any of its folders without having to search through the Save In list box. Click the Desktop icon, for example, and the file is saved on the Windows desktop. You can also use the Favorites folder, which is accessible from every application in Office XP.

The *file type* defaults to an Excel 2002 workbook. You can, however, choose a different format to maintain compatibility with earlier versions of Microsoft Excel. You can also save any Excel workbook as a Web page or HTML document.

The *Save As command* saves a copy of an existing workbook under a different name, and/or a different file type, and is useful when you want to retain a copy of the original workbook. The Save As command results in two copies of the workbook. The original workbook is kept on disk under the original name. A copy of the workbook is saved on disk under the new name and remains in memory.

The *Open command* is the opposite of the Save command as it brings a copy of an existing workbook into memory, enabling you to work with that workbook. The Open command displays the Open dialog box in which you specify the file name, the drive (and optionally the folder) that contains the file, and the file type. Microsoft Excel will then list all files of that type on the designated drive (and folder), enabling you to open the file you want.

The Save and Open commands work in conjunction with one another. The Save As dialog box in Figure 1.6a, for example, saves the file My First Spreadsheet in the Exploring Excel folder. The Open dialog box in Figure 1.6b loads that file into memory so that you can work with the file, after which you can save the revised file for use at a later time.

The toolbars in the Save As and Open dialog boxes have several buttons in common that facilitate the execution of either command. The Views button lets you display the files in one of four different views. The Details view shows the file size as well as the date and time a file was last modified. The Preview view shows the beginning of a workbook, without having to open the workbook. The List view displays only the file names, and thus lets you see more files at one time. The Properties view shows information about the workbook including the date of creation and number of revisions.

Other buttons provide limited file management without having to go to My Computer or Windows Explorer. You can, for example, delete a file, create a new folder, or start your Web browser from either dialog box. The Tools button provides access to additional commands that are well worth exploring.

Drive/Folder in which
file is to be stored

Places bar

Views button

File name

File type

(a) Save As Dialog Box (Details View)

Drive/Folder in which
file is stored

Views button

File to be opened

File type

(b) Open Dialog Box (Details View)

FIGURE 1.6   *The Save and Open Commands*

SORT BY NAME, DATE, OR FILE SIZE

The files in the Save As and Open dialog boxes can be displayed in ascending
or descending sequence by name, date modified, or size. Change to the Details
view, then click the heading of the desired column; for example, click the
Modified column to list the files according to the date they were last changed.
Click the column heading a second time to reverse the sequence—that is, to
switch from ascending to descending, and vice versa.

INTRODUCTION TO MICROSOFT EXCEL

Objective   To start Microsoft Excel; to open, modify, and print an existing workbook. Use Figure 1.7 as a guide in the exercise.

Step 1:   **Welcome to Windows**

➤ Turn on the computer and all of its peripherals. The floppy drive should be empty prior to starting your machine. This ensures that the system starts by reading from the hard disk, which contains the Windows files, as opposed to a floppy disk, which does not.

➤ Your system will take a minute or so to get started, after which you should see the desktop in Figure 1.7a. Do not be concerned if the appearance of your desktop is different from ours.

➤ You may also see a Welcome to Windows dialog box with commands to take a tour of the operating system. If so, click the appropriate button(s) or close the dialog box.

➤ You should be familiar with basic file management and very comfortable moving and copying files from one folder to another. If not, you may want to review the material in the Essentials of Windows section of this text.

➤ You are ready to download the practice files you will need for the hands-on exercises that appear throughout the text.

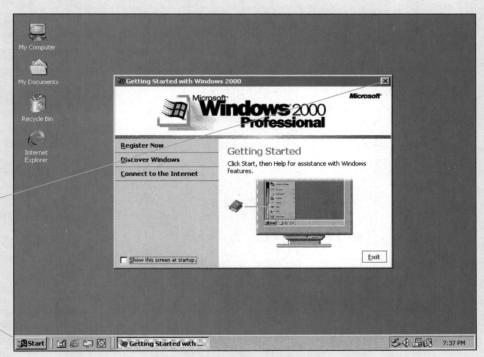

Click the Close button to close the dialog box

Click the Start button to display the Start menu

(a) Welcome to Windows (step 1)

FIGURE 1.7   *Hands-on Exercise 1*

Step 2: **Obtain the Practice Files**

➤ We have created a series of practice files (also called a "data disk") for you to use throughout the text. The files may be on a network drive, in which case you use Windows Explorer to copy the files from the network to a floppy disk.

➤ You can also download the files from our Website provided you have an Internet connection. Start Internet Explorer, then go to the Exploring Windows Series home page at **www.prenhall.com/grauer**.

- Click the book for **Office XP**, which takes you to the Office XP home page. Click the **Student Resources tab** (at the top of the window) to go to the Student Resources page as shown in Figure 1.7b.
- Click the link to **Student Data Disk** (in the left frame), then scroll down the page until you can select Excel 2002. Choose **Exploring Excel 2002** if you have the individual Excel text. Choose **Excel 2002 Volume I** if you are using *Exploring Microsoft Office Volume I*. Click the link to download the file.
- You will see the File Download dialog box asking what you want to do. The option button to save this program to disk is selected. Click **OK**. The Save As dialog box appears.
- Click the down arrow in the Save In list box to select the drive and folder where you want to save the file. It's best to save the file to the Windows desktop or to a temporary folder on drive C.
- Double click the file after it has been downloaded to your PC, then follow the onscreen instructions.

➤ Check with your instructor for additional information.

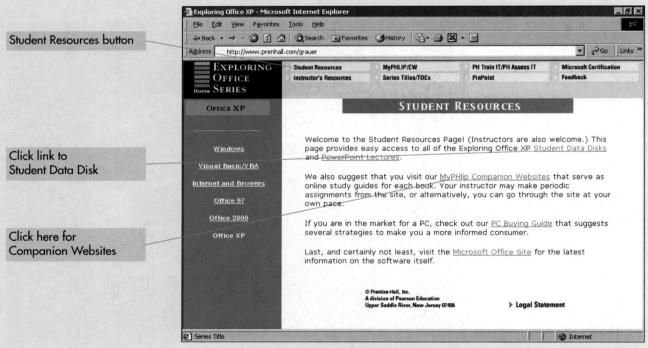

(b) Obtain the Practice Files (step 2)

FIGURE 1.7 *Hands-on Exercise 1 (continued)*

Step 3: **Start Excel**

➤ Click the **Start button** to display the Start menu. Click (or point to) the **Programs menu**, then click **Microsoft Excel** to start the program. Close the task pane if it is open.

➤ Click and drag the Office Assistant out of the way. (The Office Assistant is illustrated in step 8 of this exercise.)

➤ If necessary, click the **Maximize button** in the application window so that Excel takes the entire desktop as shown in Figure 1.7c. Click the **Maximize button** in the document window (if necessary) so that the document window is as large as possible.

Click and drag Office Assistant out of way

(c) Start Excel (step 3)

FIGURE 1.7 *Hands-on Exercise 1 (continued)*

ABOUT THE ASSISTANT

The Assistant is very powerful and hence you want to experiment with various ways to use it. To ask a question, click the Assistant's icon to toggle its balloon on or off. To change the way in which the Assistant works, click the Options button within the balloon and experiment with the various check boxes to see their effects. If you find the Assistant distracting, click and drag the character out of the way or hide it altogether by pulling down the Help menu and clicking the Hide the Office Assistant command. Pull down the Help menu and click the Show the Office Assistant command to return the Assistant to the desktop.

Step 4: **Open the Workbook**

➤ Pull down the **File menu** and click **Open** (or click the **Open button** on the Standard toolbar). You should see a dialog box similar to the one in Figure 1.7d.

➤ Click the **drop-down arrow** on the Views button, then click **Details** to change to the Details view. Click and drag the vertical border between two columns to increase (or decrease) the size of a column.

➤ Click the **drop-down arrow** on the Look In list box. Click the appropriate drive, drive C or drive A, depending on the location of your data. Double click the **Exploring Excel folder** to make it the active folder (the folder from which you will retrieve and into which you will save the workbook).

➤ Click the **down scroll arrow** if necessary in order to click **Grade Book** to select the professor's grade book. Click the **Open command button** to open the workbook and begin the exercise.

(d) Open the Workbook (step 4)

FIGURE 1.7 *Hands-on Exercise 1 (continued)*

SEPARATE THE TOOLBARS

You may see the Standard and Formatting toolbars displayed on one row to save space within the application window. If so, we suggest that you separate the toolbars, so that you see all of the buttons on each. Click the down arrow at the end of any visible toolbar to display toolbar options, then click the option to show the buttons on two rows. Click the down arrow a second time to show the buttons on one row if you prefer this configuration.

Step 5: **The Save As Command**

➤ Pull down the **File menu**. Click **Save As** to display the dialog box shown in Figure 1.7e.

➤ Enter **Finished Grade Book** as the name of the new workbook. (A file name may contain up to 255 characters. Spaces and commas are allowed in the file name.)

➤ Click the **Save button**. Press the **Esc key** or click the **Close button** if you see a Properties dialog box.

➤ There are now two identical copies of the file on disk: "Grade Book" and "Finished Grade Book," which you just created. The title bar shows the latter name, which is the workbook currently in memory.

➤ You will work with "Finished Grade Book," but can always return to the original "Grade Book" if necessary.

(e) Save As Command (step 5)

FIGURE 1.7 *Hands-on Exercise 1 (continued)*

QUIT WITHOUT SAVING

There will be times when you do not want to save the changes to a workbook—for example, when you have edited it beyond recognition and wish you had never started. The Undo command, useful as it is, reverses only the last operation and is of no use if you need to cancel all changes. Pull down the File menu and click the Close command, then click No in response to the message asking whether to save the changes. Pull down the File menu, click the file's name at the bottom of the menu to reopen the file, then begin all over.

Step 6: **The Active Cell, Formula Bar, and Worksheet Tabs**

➤ You should see the workbook in Figure 1.7f. Click in **cell B3**, the cell containing Adams's grade on the first test. Cell B3 is now the active cell and is surrounded by a heavy border. The Name box indicates that cell B3 is the active cell, and its contents are displayed in the formula bar.

➤ Click in **cell B4** (or press the **down arrow key**) to make it the active cell. The Name box indicates cell B4 while the formula bar indicates a grade of 90.

➤ Click in **cell E3**, the cell containing the formula to compute Adams's semester average; the worksheet displays the computed average of 88.0, but the formula bar displays the formula, =(B3+C3+2*D3)/4, to compute that average based on the test grades.

➤ Click the **CIS223 tab** to view a different worksheet within the same workbook. This worksheet contains the grades for a different class.

➤ Click the **CIS316 tab** to view this worksheet. Click the **CIS120 tab** to return to this worksheet and continue with the exercise.

(f) The Active Cell, Formula Bar, and Worksheet Tabs (step 6)

FIGURE 1.7 *Hands-on Exercise 1 (continued)*

THE MENUS MAY CHANGE

Office XP gives you the option of displaying short menus (ending in a double arrow to show additional commands) as opposed to complete menus with all commands. We prefer the complete menus because that is the way you learn an application, but the settings may be different on your system. Pull down the Tools menu, click the Customize command to display the Customize dialog box, click the Options tab, and clear the box that menus show recently used commands first.

Step 7: **Experiment (What If?)**

➤ Click in **cell C4**, the cell containing Baker's grade on the second test. Enter a corrected value of **86** (instead of the previous entry of 76). Press **enter** (or click in another cell).

➤ The effects of this change ripple through the worksheet, automatically changing the computed value for Baker's average in cell E4 to 87.5. The class average on the second test in cell C9 changes to 78.8.

➤ Change Walker's grade on the final from 90 to **100**. Press **enter** (or click in another cell). Walker's average in cell E7 changes to 90.0, while the class average in cell D9 changes to 77.2.

➤ Your worksheet should match Figure 1.7g. Save the workbook.

Change test score to 86

Change grade on final to 100

Walker's Average changes to 90.0

Class Average changes to 77.2

(g) Experiment (What If?) (step 7)

FIGURE 1.7 *Hands-on Exercise 1 (continued)*

THE UNDO AND REDO COMMANDS

The Undo Command lets you undo the last several changes to a workbook. Click the down arrow next to the Undo button on the Standard toolbar to display a reverse-order list of your previous commands, then click the command you want to undo, which also cancels all of the preceding commands. Undoing the fifth command in the list, for example, will also undo the preceding four commands. The Redo command redoes (reverses) the last command that was undone. It, too, displays a reverse-order list of commands, so that redoing the fifth command in the list will also redo the preceding four commands.

Step 8: **The Office Assistant**

➤ If necessary, pull down the **Help menu** and click the command to **Show the Office Assistant**. You may see a different character than the one we have selected. Click the Assistant, then enter the question, **How do I use the Office Assistant?** as shown in Figure 1.7h.

➤ Click the **Search button** in the Assistant's balloon to look for the answer. The size of the Assistant's balloon expands as the Assistant suggests several topics that may be appropriate.

➤ Select (click) any topic, which in turn displays a Help window with multiple links associated with the topic you selected.

➤ Read the displayed information and explore Help, then close the Help window when you are finished.

➤ Pull down the **File menu** and click **Exit** to close Excel if you do not wish to continue with the next exercise at this time. Save the workbook if you are prompted.

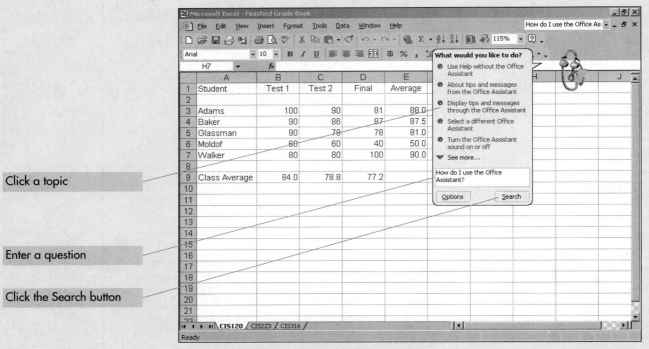

Click a topic

Enter a question

Click the Search button

(h) The Office Assistant (step 8)

FIGURE 1.7 *Hands-on Exercise 1 (continued)*

ABOUT MICROSOFT EXCEL

Pull down the Help menu and click About Microsoft Excel to display the specific release number as well as other licensing information, including the Product ID. This Help screen also contains two very useful command buttons, System Info and Technical Support. The first button displays information about the hardware installed on your system, including the amount of memory and available space on the hard drive. The Technical Support button provides information on obtaining technical assistance.

We trust that you completed the hands-on exercise without difficulty and that you are more confident in your ability than when you first began. The exercise was not complicated, but it did accomplish several objectives and set the stage for a second exercise, which follows shortly.

Consider now Figure 1.8, which contains a modified version of the professor's grade book. Figure 1.8a shows the grade book at the end of the first hands-on exercise and reflects the changes made to the grades for Baker and Walker. Figure 1.8b shows the worksheet as it will appear at the end of the second exercise. Several changes bear mention:

1. One student has dropped the class and two other students have been added. Moldof appeared in the original worksheet in Figure 1.8a, but has somehow managed to withdraw; Coulter and Courier did not appear in the original grade book but have been added to the worksheet in Figure 1.8b.
2. A new column containing the students' majors has been added.

The implementation of these changes is accomplished through a combination of the **Insert command** (to add individual cells, rows, or columns) and/or the **Delete command** (to remove individual cells, rows, or columns). Execution of either command automatically adjusts the cell references in existing formulas to reflect the insertion or deletion of the various cells. The Insert and Delete commands can also be used to insert or delete a worksheet. The professor could, for example, add a new sheet to a workbook to include grades for another class and/or delete a worksheet for a class that was no longer taught. We focus initially, however, on the insertion and deletion of rows and columns within a worksheet.

	A	B	C	D	E
1	Student	Test 1	Test 2	Final	Average
2					
3	Adams	100	90	81	88.0
4	Baker	90	86	87	87.5
5	Glassman	90	78	78	81.0
6	Moldof	60	60	40	50.0
7	Walker	80	80	100	90.0
8					
9	Class Average	84.0	78.8	77.2	

Moldof will be dropped from class

(a) After Hands-on Exercise 1

	A	B	C	D	E	F
1	Student	Major	Test 1	Test 2	Final	Average
2						
3	Adams	CIS	100	90	81	88.0
4	Baker	MKT	90	86	87	87.5
5	Coulter	ACC	85	95	100	95.0
6	Courier	FIN	75	75	85	80.0
7	Glassman	CIS	90	78	78	81.0
8	Walker	CIS	80	80	100	90.0
9						
10	Class Average		86.7	84.0	88.5	

A new column has been added (Major)

Two new students have been added

Moldof has been deleted

(b) After Hands-on Exercise 2

FIGURE 1.8 *The Modified Grade Book*

Figure 1.9 displays the cell formulas in the professor's grade book and corresponds to the worksheets in Figure 1.8. The "before" and "after" worksheets reflect the insertion of a new column containing the students' majors, the addition of two new students, Coulter and Courier, and the deletion of an existing student, Moldof.

Let us consider the formula to compute Adams's semester average, which is contained in cell E3 of the original grade book, but in cell F3 in the modified grade book. The formula in Figure 1.9a referenced cells B3, C3, and D3 (the grades on test 1, test 2, and the final). The corresponding formula in Figure 1.9b reflects the fact that a new column has been inserted, and references cells C3, D3, and E3. The change in the formula is made automatically by Excel, without any action on the part of the user other than to insert the new column. The formulas for all other students have been adjusted in similar fashion.

Some students (all students below Baker) have had a further adjustment to reflect the addition of the new students through insertion of new rows in the worksheet. Glassman, for example, appeared in row 5 of the original worksheet, but appears in row 7 of the revised worksheet. Hence the formula to compute Glassman's semester average now references the grades in row 7, rather than in row 5 as in the original worksheet.

Finally, the formulas to compute the class averages have also been adjusted. These formulas appeared in row 9 of Figure 1.9a and averaged the grades in rows 3 through 7. The revised worksheet has a net increase of one student, which automatically moves these formulas to row 10, where the formulas are adjusted to average the grades in rows 3 through 8.

Formula references grades in B3, C3, and D3

Function references grades in rows 3–7

	A	B	C	D	E
1	Student	Test1	Test2	Final	Average
2					
3	Adams	100	90	81	=(B3+C3+2*D3)/4
4	Baker	90	86	87	=(B4+C4+2*D4)/4
5	Glassman	90	78	78	=(B5+C5+2*D5)/4
6	Moldof	60	60	40	=(B6+C6+2*D6)/4
7	Walker	80	80	100	=(B7+C7+2*D7)/4
8					
9	Class Average	=AVERAGE(B3:B7)	=AVERAGE(C3:C7)	=AVERAGE(D3:D7)	

(a) Before

	A	B	C	D	E	F
1	Student	Major	Test1	Test2	Final	Average
2						
3	Adams	CIS	100	90	81	=(C3+D3+2*E3)/4
4	Baker	MKT	90	86	87	=(C4+D4+2*E4)/4
5	Coulter	ACC	85	95	100	=(C5+D5+2*E5)/4
6	Courier	FIN	75	75	85	=(C6+D6+2*E6)/4
7	Glassman	CIS	90	78	78	=(C7+D7+2*E7)/4
8	Walker	CIS	80	80	100	=(C8+D8+2*E8)/4
9						
10	Class Average		=AVERAGE(C3:C8)	=AVERAGE(D3:D8)	=AVERAGE(E3:E8)	

Function changes to reference grades in rows 3–8 (due to addition of 2 new students and deletion of 1)

Formula changes to reference grades in C3, D3, and E3 due to addition of new column

(b) After

FIGURE 1.9   *The Insert and Delete Commands*

The **Page Setup command** gives you complete control of the printed worksheet as illustrated in Figure 1.10. Many of the options may not appear important now, but you will appreciate them as you develop larger and more complicated worksheets later in the text.

The Page tab in Figure 1.10 determines the orientation and scaling of the printed page. **Portrait orientation** ($8\frac{1}{2} \times 11$) prints vertically down the page. **Landscape orientation** ($11 \times 8\frac{1}{2}$) prints horizontally across the page and is used when the worksheet is too wide to fit on a portrait page. The option buttons indicate mutually exclusive items, one of which *must* be selected; that is, a worksheet must be printed in either portrait or landscape orientation. Option buttons are also used to choose the scaling factor. You can reduce (enlarge) the output by a designated scaling factor, or you can force the output to fit on a specified number of pages. The latter option is typically used to force a worksheet to fit on a single page.

The Margins tab not only controls the margins, but will also center the worksheet horizontally and/or vertically. The Margins tab also determines the distance of the header and footer from the edge of the page.

The Header/Footer tab lets you create a header (and/or footer) that appears at the top (and/or bottom) of every page. The pull-down list boxes let you choose from several preformatted entries, or alternatively, you can click the appropriate command button to customize either entry.

The Sheet tab offers several additional options. The Gridlines option prints lines to separate the cells within the worksheet. The Row and Column Headings option displays the column letters and row numbers. Both options should be selected for most worksheets. Information about the additional entries can be obtained by clicking the Help button.

The Print Preview command button is available from all four tabs within the Page Setup dialog box. The command shows you how the worksheet will appear when printed and saves you from having to rely on trial and error.

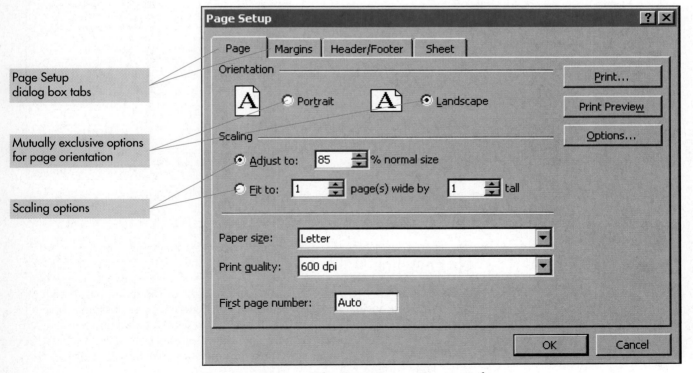

Page Setup dialog box tabs

Mutually exclusive options for page orientation

Scaling options

FIGURE 1.10 *The Page Setup Command*

MODIFYING A WORKSHEET

Objective   To open an existing workbook; to insert and delete rows and columns in a worksheet; to print cell formulas and displayed values; to use the Page Setup command. Use Figure 1.11 as a guide.

Step 1:   **Open an Existing Workbook**

➤ Start Excel. If necessary, pull down the **View menu** and click the **Task Pane command** to display the task pane as shown in Figure 1.11a. You should see the Finished Grade Book from the previous exercise since the most recently used workbooks are listed automatically.

➤ Click the link to the **Finished Grade Book workbook**. (Click the link to **More Workbooks** if the workbook is not listed to display the Open dialog box where you can select the drive and folder to locate your workbook.)

➤ The task pane closes automatically after the workbook has been opened.

Ask a Question list box

Task pane

Click link to
Finished Grade Book

Click to display the
open dialog box

(a) Open an Existing Workbook (step 1)

FIGURE 1.11   *Hands-on Exercise 2*

ASK A QUESTION

Click in the "Ask a Question" list box to the right of the menu bar, type a question, press enter, and Excel returns a list of Help topics. Click any topic that appears promising to open the Help window with detailed information. You can ask multiple questions during an Excel session, then click the down arrow in the list box to return to an earlier question, which will return you to the Help topics.

Step 2: **Delete a Row**

> Click any cell in **row 6** (the row you will delete). Pull down the **Edit menu**. Click **Delete** to display the dialog box in Figure 1.11b. Click **Entire row**. Click **OK** to delete row 6.
> Moldof has disappeared from the grade book, and the class averages (now in row 8) have been updated automatically.
> Pull down the **Edit menu** and click **Undo Delete** (or click the **Undo button** on the Standard toolbar) to reverse the last command.
> The row for Moldof has been put back into the worksheet.
> Click any cell in **row 6**, and this time delete the entire row for good.
> Save the workbook.

Undo button

Click a cell in row 6

Click Entire row

(b) Delete a Row (step 2)

FIGURE 1.11   *Hands-on Exercise 2 (continued)*

INSERT COMMENT COMMAND

You can add a comment, which displays a ScreenTip when you point to the cell, to any cell in a worksheet to explain a formula or other piece of information associated with that cell. Click in the cell that is to hold the comment, pull down the Insert menu, and click Comment to display a box in which you enter the comment. Click outside the box when you have completed the entry. Point to the cell (which should have a tiny red triangle) and you will see the comment you just created.

Step 3: **Insert a Row**

➤ Click any cell in **row 5** (the row containing Glassman's grades). Pull down the **Insert menu**. Click **Rows** to add a new row above the current row.

➤ A new row is inserted into the worksheet with the same formatting as in the row above. (Thus, you can ignore the Format Painter button, which allows you to change the formatting.) Row 5 is now blank, and Glassman is now in row 6.

➤ Enter the data for the new student in row 5 as shown in Figure 1.11c. Click in **cell A5**. Type **Coulter**. Press the **right arrow key** or click in **cell B5**. Enter the test grades of 85, 95, 100 in cells B5, C5, and D5, respectively.

➤ Enter the formula to compute the semester average, **=(B5+C5+2*D5)/4**. Be sure to begin the formula with an equal sign. Press **enter**.

➤ Click the **Save button** on the Standard toolbar, or pull down the **File menu** and click **Save** to save the changes made to this point.

Save button

Enter data for
new student (Coulter)

Glassman is now in row 6

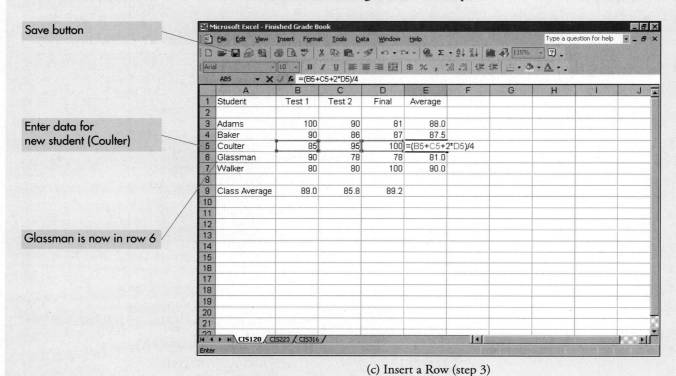

(c) Insert a Row (step 3)

FIGURE 1.11 *Hands-on Exercise 2 (continued)*

CORRECTING MISTAKES

The fastest way to change the contents of an existing cell is to double click in the cell in order to make the changes directly in the cell rather than on the formula bar. Use the mouse or arrow keys to position the insertion point at the point of correction. Press the Ins key to toggle between insert and overtype and/or use the Backspace or Del key to erase a character. Press the Home and End keys to move to the first and last characters in the cell, respectively.

Step 4: **The AutoComplete Feature**

➤ Point to the row heading for **row 6** (which now contains Glassman's grades), then click the **right mouse button** to select the row and display a shortcut menu. Click **Insert** to insert a new row 6, which moves Glassman to row 7 as shown in Figure 1.11d.

➤ Click in **cell A6**. Type **C**, the first letter in "Courier," which also happens to be the first letter in "Coulter," a previous entry in column A. If the AutoComplete feature is on (see boxed tip), Coulter's name will be automatically inserted in cell A6 with "oulter" selected.

➤ Type **ourier** (the remaining letters in "Courier," which replace "oulter."

➤ Enter Courier's grades in the appropriate cells (75, 75, and 85 in cells B6, C6, and D6, respectively). Click in **cell E6**. Enter the formula to compute the semester average, **=(B6+C6+2*D6)/4**. Press **enter**.

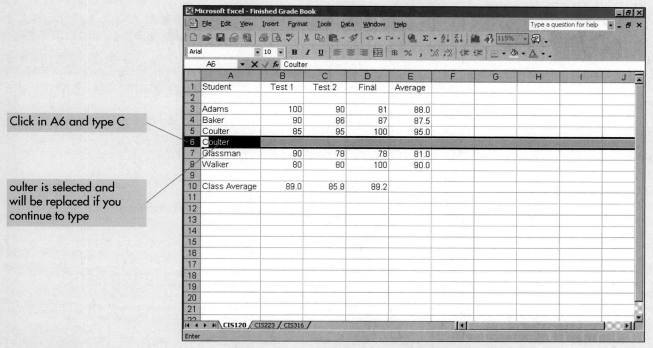

Click in A6 and type C

oulter is selected and will be replaced if you continue to type

(d) The AutoComplete Feature (step 4)

FIGURE 1.11 *Hands-on Exercise 2 (continued)*

AUTOCOMPLETE

As soon as you begin typing a label into a cell, Excel searches for and (automatically) displays any other label in that column that matches the letters you typed. It's handy if you want to repeat a label, but it can be distracting if you want to enter a different label that just happens to begin with the same letter. To turn the feature on (off), pull down the Tools menu, click Options, then click the Edit tab. Check (clear) the box to enable the AutoComplete feature.

Step 5:   **Insert a Column**

➤ Point to the column heading for column B, then click the **right mouse button** to display a shortcut menu as shown in Figure 1.11e.

➤ Click **Insert** to insert a new column, which becomes the new column B. All existing columns have been moved to the right.

➤ Click in **cell B1**. Type **Major**.

➤ Click in **cell B3**. Enter **CIS** as Adams's major. Press the **down arrow** to move automatically to the major for the next student.

➤ Type **MKT** in cell B4. Press the **down arrow**. Type **ACC** in cell B5. Press the **down arrow**. Type **FIN** in cell B6.

➤ Press the **down arrow** to move to cell B7. Type **C** (AutoComplete will automatically enter "IS" to complete the entry). Press the **down arrow** to move to cell B8. Type **C** (the AutoComplete feature again enters "IS"), then press **enter** to complete the entry.

(e) Insert a Column (step 5)

FIGURE 1.11   *Hands-on Exercise 2 (continued)*

INSERTING AND DELETING INDIVIDUAL CELLS

You can insert and/or delete individual cells as opposed to an entire row or column. To insert a cell, click in the cell to the left or above where you want the new cell to go, pull down the Insert menu, then click Cells to display the Insert dialog box. Click the appropriate option button to shift cells right or down and click OK. To delete a cell or cells, select the cell(s), pull down the Edit menu, click the Delete command, then click the option button to shift cells left or up. See practice exercise 2 at the end of the chapter.

Step 6:   **Display the Cell Formulas**

➤ Pull down the **Tools menu**. Click **Options** to display the Options dialog box. Click the **View tab**. Check the box for **Formulas**. Click **OK**. (You can also press Ctrl+~ to toggle between cell formulas and displayed values.)

➤ The worksheet should display the cell formulas as shown in Figure 1.11f. If necessary, click the **right scroll arrow** on the horizontal scroll bar until column F, the column containing the formulas to compute the semester averages, comes into view.

➤ If necessary (i.e., if the formulas are not completely visible), double click the border between the column headings for columns F and G. This increases the width of column F to accommodate the widest entry in that column.

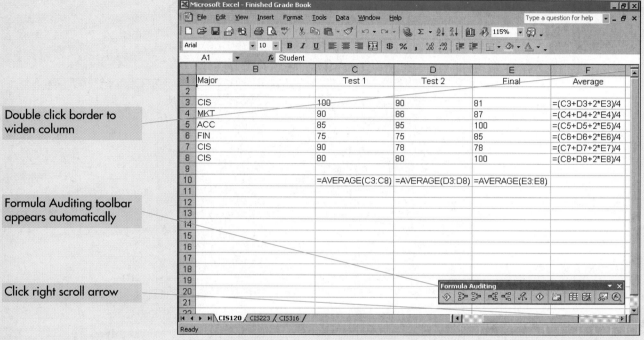

(f) Display the Cell Formulas (step 6)

FIGURE 1.11   *Hands-on Exercise 2 (continued)*

THE FORMULA AUDITING TOOLBAR

The Formula Auditing Toolbar appears automatically any time the display is changed to show cell formulas rather than displayed values. The toolbar is designed to help you detect and correct errors in cell formulas. Click in any cell, then click the Trace Precedents button to show the cells that are used to evaluate the formula in the selected cell. You can also click in any cell and use the Trace Dependents button to show those cells whose formula references the selected cell. Click the Remove All Arrows button to erase the arrows from the display.

Step 7: **The Page Setup Command**

➤ Pull down the **File menu**. Click the **Page Setup command** to display the Page Setup dialog box as shown in Figure 1.11g.
- Click the **Page tab**. Click the **Landscape option button**. Click the option button to **Fit to 1 page**.
- Click the **Margins tab**. Check the box to center the worksheet horizontally.
- Click the **Header/Footer tab**. Click the **drop-down arrow** on the Footer list box. Scroll to the top of the list and click **(none)** to remove the footer.
- Click the **Sheet tab**. Check the boxes to print Row and Column Headings and Gridlines.

➤ Click **OK** to exit the Page Setup dialog box.

➤ Save the workbook.

Print Preview button

Click Page tab

Click Landscape

Click Fit to 1 page

(g) The Page Setup Command (step 7)

FIGURE 1.11   *Hands-on Exercise 2 (continued)*

KEYBOARD SHORTCUTS—THE DIALOG BOX

Press Tab or Shift+Tab to move forward (backward) between fields in a dialog box, or press the Alt key plus the underlined letter to move directly to an option. Use the space bar to toggle check boxes on or off and the up (down) arrow keys to move between options in a list box. Press enter to activate the highlighted command button and Esc to exit the dialog box without accepting the changes. These are universal shortcuts and apply to any Windows application.

Step 8: **The Print Preview Command**

➤ Pull down the **File menu** and click **Print Preview** (or click the **Print Preview button** on the Standard toolbar).

➤ Your monitor should match the display in Figure 1.11h. (The Page Setup dialog box is also accessible from this screen.)

➤ Click the **Print command button** to display the Print dialog box, then click **OK** to print the worksheet.

➤ Press **Ctrl+~** to switch to displayed values rather than cell formulas. Click the **Print button** on the Standard toolbar to print the worksheet without displaying the Print dialog box.

Click Print command button

Click Setup to display the Page Setup dialog box.

(h) The Print Preview Command (step 8)

FIGURE 1.11 *Hands-on Exercise 2 (continued)*

FIND AND REPLACE

Anyone familiar with a word processor takes the Find and Replace command for granted, but many people are surprised to learn that the same commands are also found in Excel. The commands are found in the Edit menu and provide the same options as in Microsoft Word. You can replace text and/or formatting throughout a worksheet. See practice exercise 4 at the end of the chapter.

Step 9: **Insert and Delete a Worksheet**

➤ Pull down the **Insert menu** and click the **Worksheet command** to insert a new worksheet. The worksheet is inserted as Sheet1.

➤ Click in cell **A1**, type **Student**, and press **enter**. Enter the labels and student data as shown in Figure 1.11i. Enter the formulas to calculate the students' semester averages in column D. (The midterm and final count equally.)

➤ Enter the formulas in row 7 to compute the class averages on each exam. If necessary, click and drag the column border between columns A and B to widen column A.

➤ Double click the name of the worksheet (Sheet1) to select the name. Type a new name, **CIS101**, to replace the selected text and press **enter**. If necessary, click and drag the worksheet tab to the beginning of the workbook.

➤ Click the worksheet tab for **CIS223**. Pull down the **Edit menu** and click the **Delete Sheet command**. Click **Delete** when you are warned that the worksheet will be permanently deleted.

➤ Save the workbook. Print the new worksheet. Exit Excel.

Pull down Insert menu to insert new sheet

Click tab, then pull down Edit menu to delete sheet

Double click worksheet tab to rename sheet

Click and drag to move the worksheet.

(i) Insert and Delete a Worksheet (step 9)

FIGURE 1.11   *Hands-on Exercise 2 (continued)*

MOVING, COPYING, AND RENAMING WORKSHEETS

The fastest way to move a worksheet is to click and drag the worksheet tab. You can copy a worksheet in similar fashion by pressing and holding the Ctrl key as you drag the worksheet tab. To rename a worksheet, double click its tab to select the current name, type the new name, and press the enter key.

Figure 1.12 contains a much improved version of the professor's grade book. The most *obvious* difference is in the appearance of the worksheet, as a variety of formatting commands have been used to make it more attractive. The exam scores and semester averages are centered under the appropriate headings. The exam weights are formatted with percentages, and all averages are displayed with exactly one decimal point. Boldface and italics are used for emphasis. Shading and borders are used to highlight various areas of the worksheet. The title has been centered over the worksheet and is set in a larger typeface.

The most *significant* differences, however, are that the weight of each exam is indicated within the worksheet, and that the formulas to compute the students' semester averages reference these cells in their calculations. The professor can change the contents of the cells containing the exam weights and see immediately the effect on the student averages.

The isolation of cells whose values are subject to change is one of the most important concepts in the development of a spreadsheet. This technique lets the professor explore alternative grading strategies. He or she may notice, for example, that the class did significantly better on the final than on either of the first two exams. The professor may then decide to give the class a break and increase the weight of the final relative to the other tests. But before the professor says anything to the class, he or she wants to know the effect of increasing the weight of the final to 60%. What if the final should count 70%? The effect of these and other changes can be seen immediately by entering the new exam weights in the appropriate cells at the bottom of the worksheet.

Title is centered in larger font size; it is also in boldface and italics

Formatting includes boldface, shading, and borders

Exam weights are used to calculate the semester average

	A	B	C	D	E
1	*CIS120 - Spring Semester*				
2					
3	**Student**	**Test 1**	**Test 2**	**Final**	**Average**
4	Costa, Frank	70	80	90	82.5
5	Ford, Judd	70	85	80	78.8
6	Grauer, Jessica	90	80	98	91.5
7	Howard, Lauren	80	78	98	88.5
8	Krein, Darren	85	70	95	86.3
9	Moldof, Adam	75	75	80	77.5
10					
11	**Class Averages**	**78.3**	**78.0**	**90.2**	
12					
13	**Exam Weights**	**25%**	**25%**	**50%**	

FIGURE 1.12   *A Better Grade Book*

ISOLATE ASSUMPTIONS

The formulas in a worksheet should always be based on cell references rather than on specific values—for example, B13 or $B$13 rather than .25. The cells containing these values should be clearly labeled and set apart from the rest of the worksheet. You can then vary the inputs (or *assumptions* on which the worksheet is based) to see the effect within the worksheet. The chance for error is also minimized because you are changing the contents of a single cell rather than changing the multiple formulas that reference those values.

Every command in Excel operates on a rectangular group of cells known as a *range*. A range may be as small as a single cell or as large as the entire worksheet. It may consist of a row or part of a row, a column or part of a column, or multiple rows and/or columns. The cells within a range are specified by indicating the diagonally opposite corners, typically the upper-left and lower-right corners of the rectangle. Many different ranges could be selected in conjunction with the worksheet of Figure 1.12. The exam weights, for example, are found in the range B13:D13. The students' semester averages are found in the range E4:E9. The student data is contained in the range A4:E9.

The easiest way to select a range is to click and drag—click at the beginning of the range, then press and hold the left mouse button as you drag the mouse to the end of the range where you release the mouse. Once selected, the range is highlighted and its cells will be affected by any subsequent command. The range remains selected until another range is defined or until you click another cell anywhere on the worksheet.

COPY COMMAND

The *Copy command* duplicates the contents of a cell, or range of cells, and saves you from having to enter the contents of every cell individually. Figure 1.13 illustrates how the command can be used to duplicate the formula to compute the class average on the different tests. The cell that you are copying from, cell B11, is called the *source range*. The cells that you are copying to, cells C11 and D11, are the *destination range*. The formula is not copied exactly, but is adjusted as it is copied, to compute the average for the pertinent test.

The formula to compute the average on the first test was entered in cell B11 as =AVERAGE(B4:B9). The range in the formula references the cell seven rows above the cell containing the formula (i.e., cell B4 is seven rows above cell B11) as well as the cell two rows above the formula (i.e., cell B9). When the formula in cell B11 is copied to C11, it is adjusted so that the cells referenced in the new formula are in the same relative position as those in the original formula; that is, seven and two rows above the formula. The formula in cell C11 becomes =AVERAGE(C4:C9). The formula in cell D11 becomes =AVERAGE(D4:D9).

	A	B	C	D	E
1			*CIS120 - Spring Semester*		
2					
3	Student	Test 1	Test 2	Final	Average
4	Costa, Frank	70	80	90	=$B$13*B4+$C$13*C4+$D$13*D4
5	Ford, Judd	70	85	80	=$B$13*B5+$C$13*C5+$D$13*D5
6	Grauer, Jessica	90	80	98	=$B$13*B6+$C$13*C6+$D$13*D6
7	Howard, Lauren	80	78	98	=$B$13*B7+$C$13*C7+$D$13*D7
8	Krein, Darren	85	70	95	=$B$13*B8+$C$13*C8+$D$13*D8
9	Moldof, Adam	75	75	80	=$B$13*B9+$C$13*C9+$D$13*D9
10					
11	Class Averages	=AVERAGE(B4:B9)	=AVERAGE(C4:C9)	=AVERAGE(D4:D9)	
12					
13	Exam Weights	25%	25%	50%	

Formula was entered in B11

Relative addresses adjust when formula is copied

Absolute addresses stay the same when formula is copied

Relative addresses adjust when formula is copied

FIGURE 1.13   *The Copy Command*

Figure 1.13 also illustrates how the Copy command is used to copy the formula for a student's semester average, from cell E4 (the source range) to cells E5 through E9 (the destination range). This is slightly more complicated than the previous example because the formula is based on a student's grades, which vary from one student to the next, and on the exam weights, which do not. The cells referring to the student's grades should adjust as the formula is copied, but the addresses referencing the exam weights should not.

The distinction between cell references that remain constant versus cell references that change is made by means of a dollar sign. An **absolute reference** remains constant throughout the copy operation and is specified with a dollar sign in front of the column and row designation, for example, $B$13. A **relative reference**, on the other hand, adjusts during a copy operation and is specified without dollar signs; for example, B4. (A **mixed reference** uses a single dollar sign to make the column absolute and the row relative; for example, $A5. Alternatively, you can make the column relative and the row absolute as in A$5.)

Consider, for example, the formula to compute a student's semester average as it appears in cell E4 of Figure 1.13:

=$B$13*B4+$C$13*C4+$D$13*D4

Final exam grade is in cell D4 and is a *relative reference*

Weight for final exam is in cell D13 and is an *absolute reference*

Test 2 grade is in cell C4 and is a *relative reference*

Weight for test 2 is in cell C13 and is an *absolute reference*

Test 1 grade is in cell B4 and is a *relative reference*

Weight for Test 1 is in cell B13 and is an *absolute reference*

The formula in cell E4 uses a combination of relative and absolute addresses to compute the student's semester average. Relative addresses are used for the exam grades (found in cells B4, C4, and D4) and change automatically when the formula is copied to the other rows. Absolute addresses are used for the exam weights (found in cells B13, C13, and D13) and remain constant.

The copy operation is implemented by using the **clipboard** common to all Windows applications and a combination of the Copy and Paste commands from the Edit menu. (Office 2002 also supports the Office Clipboard that can hold 24 separate items. All references to the "clipboard" in this chapter, however, are to the Windows clipboard.) The contents of the source range are copied to the clipboard, from where they are pasted to the destination range. The contents of the clipboard are replaced with each subsequent Copy command but are unaffected by the Paste command. Thus, you can execute the Paste command several times in succession to paste the contents of the clipboard to multiple locations.

MIXED REFERENCES

Most spreadsheets can be developed using only absolute or relative references such as $A1$1 or A, respectively. Mixed references, where only the row ($A1) or column (A$1) changes, are more subtle, and thus are typically not used by beginners. Mixed references are necessary in more sophisticated worksheets and add significantly to the power of Excel.

The ***move operation*** is not used in the grade book, but its presentation is essential for the sake of completeness. The move operation transfers the contents of a cell (or range of cells) from one location to another. After the move is completed, the cells where the move originated (that is, the source range) are empty. This is in contrast to the Copy command, where the entries remain in the source range and are duplicated in the destination range.

A simple move operation is depicted in Figure 1.14a, in which the contents of cell A3 are moved to cell C3, with the formula in cell C3 unchanged after the move. In other words, the move operation simply picks up the contents of cell A3 (a formula that adds the values in cells A1 and A2) and puts it down in cell C3. The source range, cell A3, is empty after the move operation has been executed.

Figure 1.14b depicts a situation where the formula itself remains in the same cell, but one of the values it references is moved to a new location; that is, the entry

Source range is empty after move

	A	B	C
1	5		
2	2		
3	=A1+A2		

	A	B	C
1	5		
2	2		
3			=A1+A2

(a) Example 1 (only cell A3 is moved)

Cell reference is adjusted to follow moved entry

	A	B	C
1	5		
2	2		
3	=A1+A2		

	A	B	C
1			5
2	2		
3	=C1+A2		

(b) Example 2 (only cell A1 is moved)

Both cell references adjust to follow moved entries

	A	B	C
1	5		
2	2		
3	=A1+A2		

	A	B	C
1			5
2			2
3			=C1+C2

(c) Example 3 (all three cells in column A are moved)

Cell reference adjusts to follow moved entry

Moved formula is unchanged

	A	B	C
1	5	=A3*4	
2	2		
3	=A1+A2		

	A	B	C
1	5	=C3*4	
2	2		
3			=A1+A2

(d) Example 4 (dependent cells)

FIGURE 1.14 *The Move Command*

	A	B	C
1	5	=$A$3*4	
2	2		
3	=$A$1+$A$2		

	A	B	C
1		=$C$3*4	5
2			2
3			=$C$1+$C$2

(e) Example 5 (absolute cell addresses)

FIGURE 1.14   *The Move Command (continued)*

in A1 is moved to C1. The formula in cell A3 is adjusted to follow the moved entry to its new location; that is, the formula is now =C1+A2.

The situation is different in Figure 1.14c as the contents of all three cells—A1, A2, and A3—are moved. After the move has taken place, cells C1 and C2 contain the 5 and the 2, respectively, with the formula in cell C3 adjusted to reflect the movement of the contents of cells A1 and A2. Once again the source range (A1:A3) is empty after the move is completed.

Figure 1.14d contains an additional formula in cell B1, which is *dependent* on cell A3, which in turn is moved to cell C3. The formula in cell C3 is unchanged after the move because *only* the formula was moved, *not* the values it referenced. The formula in cell B1 changes because cell B1 refers to an entry (cell A3) that was moved to a new location (cell C3).

Figure 1.14e shows that the specification of an absolute reference has no meaning in a move operation, because the cell addresses are adjusted as necessary to reflect the cells that have been moved. Moving a formula that contains an absolute reference does not adjust the formula. Moving a value that is specified as an absolute reference, however, adjusts the formula to follow the cell to its new location. Thus all of the absolute references in Figure 1.14e are changed to reflect the entries that were moved.

The move operation is a convenient way to improve the appearance of a worksheet after it has been developed. It is subtle in its operation, and we suggest you think twice before moving cell entries because of the complexities involved.

The move operation is implemented by using the Windows clipboard and a combination of the Cut and Paste commands from the Edit menu. The contents of the source range are transferred to the clipboard, from which they are pasted to the destination range. (Executing a Paste command after a Cut command empties the clipboard. This is different from pasting after a Copy command, which does not affect the contents of the clipboard.)

LEARNING BY DOING

As we have already indicated, there are many different ways to accomplish the same task. You can execute commands using a pull-down menu, a shortcut menu, a toolbar, or the keyboard. In the exercise that follows we emphasize pull-down menus (the most basic technique) but suggest various shortcuts as appropriate.

Realize, however, that while the shortcuts are interesting, it is far more important to focus on the underlying concepts in the exercise, rather than specific key strokes or mouse clicks. The professor's grade book was developed to emphasize the difference between relative and absolute cell references. The grade book also illustrates the importance of isolating assumptions so that alternative strategies (e.g., different exam weights) can be considered.

CREATING A WORKBOOK

Objective To create a new workbook; to copy formulas containing relative and absolute references. Use Figure 1.15 as a guide in doing the exercise.

Step 1: **Create a New Workbook**

➤ Click the **Start button**, click (or point to) the **Programs command,** then click **Microsoft Excel** to start the program. If Excel is already open, click the **New button** on the Standard toolbar (or click **Blank Workbook** in the task pane) to open a new workbook.

➤ Click and drag the Office Assistant out of the way or hide it altogether. (Pull down the **Help menu** and click **Hide the Office Assistant**.)

➤ If necessary, separate the Standard and Formatting toolbars. Pull down the **View menu**, click **Toolbars**, click **Customize**, and click the **Options tab**. Check the box that indicates the Standard and Formatting toolbars should be displayed on two rows.

➤ Close the task pane. Click in cell **A1**. Enter the title of the worksheet, **CIS120 - Spring Semester.**

➤ Enter the column headings in row 3 as in Figure 1.15a. Click in cell **A3** and type **Student**, then press the **right arrow key** to move to cell **B3**. Type **Test 1**.

➤ Press the **right arrow key** to move to cell **C3**. Type **Test 2**. Enter the words **Final** and **Average** in cells D3 and E3, respectively. Your worksheet should match Figure 1.15a.

(a) Create a New Workbook (step 1)

FIGURE 1.15 *Hands-on Exercise 3*

Step 2: **Save the Workbook**

➤ Pull down the **File menu** and click **Save** (or click the **Save button** on the Standard toolbar) to display the Save As dialog box as shown in Figure 1.15b. (The Save As dialog box always appears the first time you save a workbook, so that you can give the workbook a name.)

➤ Click the **drop-down arrow** on the Save In list box. Click the appropriate drive, drive C or drive A, depending on where you are saving your Excel workbooks.

➤ Double click the **Exploring Excel folder** to make it the active folder (the folder in which you will save the document).

➤ Click and drag **Book1** (the default entry) in the File name text box to select it, then type **Better Grade Book** as the name of the workbook. Click **Save** or press the **enter key**. The title bar changes to reflect the name of the workbook.

Save button

Click drop-down arrow to select drive/folder

Click to create a new folder

Enter file name

(b) Save the Workbook (step 2)

FIGURE 1.15 *Hands-on Exercise 3 (continued)*

CREATE A NEW FOLDER

Do you work with a large number of different workbooks? If so, it may be useful to store those workbooks in different folders, perhaps one folder for each subject you are taking. Pull down the File menu, click the Save As command to display the Save As dialog box, then click the Create New Folder button to display the associated dialog box. Enter the name of the folder, then click OK. Once the folder has been created, use the Look In box to change to that folder the next time you open that workbook. See practice exercise 7 at the end of the chapter.

Step 3: **Enter Student Data and Literal Information**

➤ Click in cell **A4** and type **Costa, Frank**, then enter Frank's grades on the two tests and the final as shown in Figure 1.15c. Do *not* enter Frank's semester average in cell E4 as that will be entered as a formula.

➤ If necessary, click and drag the border between columns A and B so that you can read Frank Costa's complete name. Check that you entered the data for this student correctly. If you made a mistake, return to the cell and retype the entry.

➤ Enter the names and grades for the other students in rows 5 through 9. Do *not* enter the student averages.

➤ Complete the entries in column A by typing **Class Averages** and **Exam Weights** in cells **A11** and **A13**, respectively.

➤ Enter the exam weights in row 13. Click in cell **B13** and enter **.25**, press the **right arrow key** to move to cell **C13** and enter **.25**, then press the **right arrow key** to move to cell **D13** and enter **.5**. Press **enter**.

➤ Do *not* be concerned that the exam weights do not appear as percentages as they will be formatted in a later exercise. Save the workbook.

Click and drag to change column width

Enter data for students

Enter exam weights

(c) Enter Student Data and Literal Information (step 3)

FIGURE 1.15 *Hands-on Exercise 3 (continued)*

COLUMN WIDTHS AND ROW HEIGHTS

Drag the border between column headings to change the column width; for example, to increase (decrease) the width of column A, drag the border between column headings A and B to the right (left). Double click the right boundary of a column heading to change the column width to accommodate the widest entry in that column. Use the same techniques to change the row heights. See practice exercise 2 at the end of the chapter.

Step 4: **Compute the Student Semester Averages**

➤ Click in cell **E4** and type the formula **=$B$13*B4+$C$13*C4+$D$13*D4** to compute the semester average for the first student. Press **enter**. Check that the displayed value in cell E4 is 82.5 as shown in Figure 1.15d.

➤ Click in cell **E4** to make this the active cell, then click the **Copy button** on the Standard toolbar. A moving border will surround cell E4 indicating that its contents have been copied to the clipboard.

➤ Click and drag to select cells **E5** through **E9** as the destination range. Click the **Paste button** to copy the contents of the clipboard to the destination range. Ignore the Paste Options button that appears automatically any time the Paste command is executed.

➤ Press **Esc** to remove the moving border around cell E4. The Paste Options button also disappears.

➤ Click in cell **E5** and look at the formula. The cells that reference the grades have changed to B5, C5, and D5. The cells that reference the exam weights— $B$13, $C$13, and $D$13—are the same as in cell E4.

➤ Save the workbook.

Copy button

Paste button

Formula bar displays formula

Click in E4 and enter formula; cell displays computed result

(d) Compute the Student Semester Averages (step 4)

FIGURE 1.15   *Hands-on Exercise 3 (continued)*

THE PASTE OPTIONS BUTTON

The Paste Options button (includes options from the Paste Special command and) provides flexibility when you paste the contents of the clipboard into a worksheet. Press Esc to ignore the options and you automatically paste both the cell formulas and associated formatting. Alternatively, you can click the down arrow to display options to copy values rather than formulas with or without formatting, Formatting is discussed in detail later in the chapter.

Step 5: **Compute the Class Averages**

➤ Click in cell **B11** and type the formula **=AVERAGE(B4:B9)** to compute the class average on the first test. Press the **enter key** when you have completed the formula.

➤ Point to cell B11, then click the **right mouse button** to display a context-sensitive menu, then click the **Copy command**. You should see a moving border around cell B11, indicating that the contents of this cell have been copied to the clipboard.

➤ Click and drag to select cells **C11** and **D11** as shown in Figure 1.15e. Click the **Paste button** on the standard toolbar to copy the contents of the clipboard to the destination range. Press **Esc** to remove the moving border.

➤ Click anywhere in the worksheet to deselect cells C11 through D11. Cells C11 and D11 should contain 78 and 90.16667, the class averages on Test 2 and the Final, respectively. Do not worry about formatting at this time.

➤ Save the workbook.

Paste button

Enter formula
=AVERAGE(B4:B9) in B11

Click and drag to
select C11:D11

(e) Compute the Class Averages (step 5)

FIGURE 1.15 *Hands-on Exercise 3 (continued)*

TWO DIFFERENT CLIPBOARDS

The Office clipboard holds a total of up to 24 objects from multiple applications, as opposed to the Windows clipboard, which stores only the results of the last Cut or Copy command. Thus, each time you execute a Cut or Copy command, the contents of the Windows clipboard are replaced, whereas the copied object is added to the objects already in the Office clipboard. To display the Office clipboard, open the task pane, click the down arrow and select clipboard. Leave the clipboard open as you execute multiple cut and copy operations to observe what happens.

Step 6: **Change the Exam Weights**

➤ Change the entries in cells **B13** and **C13** to **.20** and the entry in cell **D13** to **.60**. The semester average for every student changes automatically; for example, Costa and Moldof change to 84 and 78, respectively, as shown in Figure 1.15f.

➤ The professor decides this does not make a significant difference and wants to go back to the original weights. Click the **Undo button** three times to reverse the last three actions. You should see .25, .25, and .50 in cells B13, C13, and D13, respectively.

➤ Click in cell **A15** and type the label **Grading Assistant**. Press **enter**. Type your name in cell **A16**, so that you will get credit for this assignment.

➤ Save the workbook. You do not need to print the workbook yet, since we will do that at the end of the next exercise, after we have formatted the workbook.

➤ Exit Excel if you are not ready to begin the next exercise at this time.

Undo button

Change entries in B13:D13

Semester averages recalculate automatically

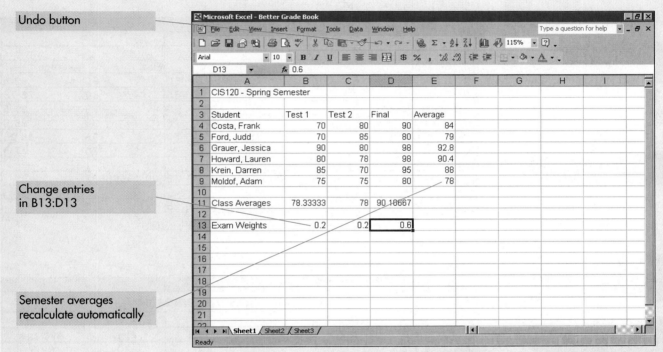

(f) Change the Exam Weights (step 6)

FIGURE 1.15   *Hands-on Exercise 3 (continued)*

CHANGE THE ZOOM SETTING

You can increase or decrease the size of a worksheet as it appears on the monitor by clicking the down arrow on the zoom box and selecting an appropriate percentage. If you are working with a large spreadsheet and cannot see it at one time on the screen, choose a number less than 100%. Conversely, if you find yourself squinting because the numbers are too small, select a percentage larger than 100%. Changing the magnification on the screen does not affect printing; that is, worksheets are always printed at 100% unless you change the scaling within the Page Setup command.

Figure 1.16a shows the grade book as it exists at the end of the third hands-on exercise, without concern for its appearance. Figure 1.16b shows the grade book as it will appear at the end of the next exercise after it has been formatted. The differences between the two are due entirely to formatting. Consider:

- The exam weights are formatted as percentages in Figure 1.16b, as opposed to decimals in Figure 1.16a. The class and semester averages are displayed with a single decimal place in Figure 1.16b.
- Boldface and italics are used for emphasis, as are shading and borders.
- Exam grades and computed averages are centered under their respective headings, as are the exam weights.
- The worksheet title is centered across all five columns.

Class Averages are not uniformly formatted

Percentages are not formatted

	A	B	C	D	E
1	CIS120 - Spring Semester				
2					
3	Student	Test 1	Test 2	Final	Average
4	Costa, Frank	70	80	90	82.5
5	Ford, Judd	70	85	80	78.75
6	Grauer, Jessica	90	80	98	91.5
7	Howard, Lauren	80	78	98	88.5
8	Krein, Darren	85	70	95	86.25
9	Moldof, Adam	75	75	80	77.5
10					
11	Class Averages	78.33333333	78	90.16666667	
12					
13	Exam Weights	0.25	0.25	0.5	

(a) At the End of Hands-on Exercise 3

Title is centered across columns; font is larger and both bold and italics

Shading, borders, and boldface are used for emphasis

Test grades are centered in columns

Uniform number of decimal places

Percent formatting has been applied

	A	B	C	D	E
1	CIS120 - Spring Semester				
2					
3	Student	Test 1	Test 2	Final	Average
4	Costa, Frank	70	80	90	82.5
5	Ford, Judd	70	85	80	78.8
6	Grauer, Jessica	90	80	98	91.5
7	Howard, Lauren	80	78	98	88.5
8	Krein, Darren	85	70	95	86.3
9	Moldof, Adam	75	75	80	77.5
10					
11	Class Averages	78.3	78.0	90.2	
12					
13	Exam Weights	25%	25%	50%	

(b) At the End of Hands-on Exercise 4

FIGURE 1.16 *Developing the Grade Book*

The *Format Cells command* controls the formatting for numbers, alignment, fonts, borders, and patterns (color). Execution of the command produces a tabbed dialog box in which you choose the particular formatting category, then enter the desired options. All formatting is done within the context of *select-then-do*. You select the cells to which the formatting is to apply, then you execute the Format Cells command (or click the appropriate button on the Formatting toolbar).

Once a format has been assigned to a cell, the formatting remains in the cell and is applied to all subsequent values that are entered into that cell. You can, however, change the formatting by executing a new formatting command. You can also remove the formatting by using the Clear command in the Edit menu. Note, too, that changing the format of a number changes the way the number is displayed, but does not change its value. If, for example, you entered 1.2345 into a cell, but displayed the number as 1.23, the actual value (1.2345) would be used in all calculations involving that cell. The numeric formats are shown in Figure 1.17a and described below.

- *General format* is the default format for numeric entries and displays a number according to the way it was originally entered. Numbers are shown as integers (e.g., 123), decimal fractions (e.g., 1.23), or in scientific notation (e.g., 1.23E+10) if the number exceeds 11 digits.
- *Number format*, which displays a number with or without the 1000 separator (e.g., a comma) and with any number of decimal places. Negative numbers can be displayed with parentheses and/or can be shown in red.
- *Currency format*, which displays a number with the 1000 separator and an optional dollar sign (which is placed immediately to the left of the number). Negative values can be preceded by a minus sign or displayed with parentheses and/or can be shown in red.
- *Accounting format*, which displays a number with the 1000 separator, an optional dollar sign (at the left border of the cell, which vertically aligns the dollar signs within a column), negative values in parentheses, and zero values as hyphens.
- *Date format*, which displays the date in different ways, such as March 4, 2001, 3/4/01, or 4-Mar-01.
- *Time format*, which displays the time in different formats, such as 10:50 PM or the equivalent 22:50 (24-hour time).
- *Percentage format*, whereby the number is multiplied by 100 for display purposes only, a percent sign is included, and any number of decimal places can be specified.
- *Fraction format*, which displays a number as a fraction, and is appropriate when there is no exact decimal equivalent. A fraction is entered into a cell by preceding the fraction with an equal sign—for example, = ⅓.
- *Scientific format*, which displays a number as a decimal fraction followed by a whole number exponent of 10; for example, the number 12345 would appear as 1.2345E+04. The exponent, +04 in the example, is the number of places the decimal point is moved to the left (or right if the exponent is negative). Very small numbers have negative exponents.
- *Text format*, which left aligns the entry and is useful for numerical values that have leading zeros and should be treated as text, such as ZIP codes.
- *Special format*, which displays a number with editing characters, such as hyphens in a Social Security number or parentheses around the area code of a telephone number.
- *Custom format*, which allows you to develop your own formats.

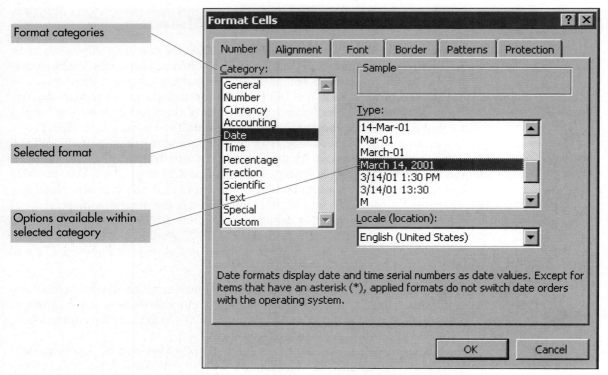

Format categories

Selected format

Options available within selected category

(a) The Number Tab

FIGURE 1.17 *The Format Cells Command*

Alignment

The contents of a cell (whether text or numeric) may be aligned horizontally and/or vertically as indicated by the dialog box of Figure 1.17b. The default horizontal *alignment* is general, which left-aligns text and right-aligns date and numbers. You can also center an entry across a range of selected cells (or *merge cells*), as in the professor's grade book, which centered the title in cell A1 across columns A through E. Clear the box to merge cells if you want to *split cells* that have been previously merged. The Fill option duplicates the characters in the cell across the entire width of that cell.

Vertical alignment is important only if the row height is changed and the characters are smaller than the height of the row. Entries may be vertically aligned at the top, center, or bottom (the default) of a cell.

It is also possible to wrap the text within a cell to emulate the word wrap of a word processor. You select multiple cells and merge them together. And finally, you can achieve some interesting effects by rotating text up to 90° in either direction.

Fonts

You can use the same fonts in Excel as you can in any other Windows application. All fonts are WYSIWYG (What You See Is What You Get), meaning that the worksheet you see on the monitor will match the printed worksheet.

Any entry in a worksheet may be displayed in any font, style, or point size as indicated by the dialog box of Figure 1.17c. The example shows Arial, Bold Italic, and 14 points, and corresponds to the selection for the worksheet title in the improved grade book. Special effects, such as subscripts or superscripts, are also possible. You can even select a different color, but you will need a color printer to see the effect on the printed page. The Preview box shows the text as it will appear in the worksheet.

Horizontal alignment options

Vertical alignment options

Click to wrap text in cell

Click to merge selected cells; clear to split cells

Enter degrees to rotate text

(b) The Alignment Tab

List of available styles

List of available fonts

List of available sizes

Preview of font

(c) Font Tab

FIGURE 1.17   *The Format Cells Command (continued)*

Borders, Patterns, and Shading

The **Border tab** in Figure 1.17d enables you to create a border around a cell (or cells) for additional emphasis. You can outline the entire selection, or you can choose the specific side or sides; for example, thicker lines on the bottom and right sides produce a drop shadow, which is very effective. You can also specify a different line style and/or a different color for the border, but you will need a color printer to see the effect on the printed output.

The **Patterns tab** (not shown in the figure) lets you choose a different color in which to shade the cell and further emphasize its contents. The Pattern drop-down list box lets you select an alternate pattern, such as dots or slanted lines.

Preset borders

Preview of borders

List of available line styles

Line color options

(d) The Border Tab

FIGURE 1.17 *The Format Cells Command (continued)*

USE RESTRAINT

More is not better, especially in the case of too many typefaces and styles, which produce cluttered worksheets that impress no one. Limit yourself to a maximum of two typefaces per worksheet, but choose multiple sizes and/or styles within those typefaces. Use boldface or italics for emphasis, but do so in moderation, because if you emphasize too many elements, the effect is lost.

FORMATTING A WORKSHEET

Objective   To format a worksheet using boldface, italics, shading, and borders; to change the font and/or alignment of a selected entry. Use Figure 1.18 as a guide in the exercise.

Step 1:   **Center the Title**

> ➤ Open **Better Grade Book** from the previous exercise. Click in cell **A1** to select the cell containing the title of the worksheet. Click the **Bold button** on the Formatting toolbar to boldface the title. Click the **Italics button** to italicize the title.
> ➤ Click in cell **A15** and click the **Bold button**. Click the **Bold button** a second time, and the boldface disappears. Click the **Bold button** again, and you are back to boldface. The same is true of the Italics button; that is, the Bold and Italics buttons function as toggle switches.
> ➤ Click in cell **A1**. Click the **down arrow** on the Font size list box and change the size to **14** to further accentuate the title.
> ➤ Click and drag to select cells **A1** through **E1**, which represents the width of the entire worksheet. Click the **Merge and Center button** on the Formatting toolbar as shown in Figure 1.18a to center the title across the width of your worksheet.
> ➤ Save the workbook.

(a) Center the Title (step 1)

FIGURE 1.18   *Hands-on Exercise 4*

Step 2:   **Format the Exam Weights**

➤ Click and drag to select cells **B13** through **D13**. Pull down the **Format menu**, then click the **Cells command** to display the dialog box in Figure 1.18b.

➤ If necessary, click the **Number tab**. Click **Percentage** in the Category list box. Click the **down spin arrow** in the Decimal Places box to select **zero decimals**, then click **OK**. The exam weights are displayed with percent signs and no decimal places.

➤ You can also use the buttons on the Formatting toolbar to accomplish the same formatting. First remove the formatting by clicking the **Undo button** on the Standard toolbar to cancel the formatting command.

➤ Check that cells B13 through D13 are still selected. Click the **Percent Style button** on the Formatting toolbar. (You can also pull down the **Format menu**, click the **Style command**, then choose the **Percent Style** from the Style Name list box.) Once again cells B13 through D13 are displayed in percent.

➤ Save the workbook.

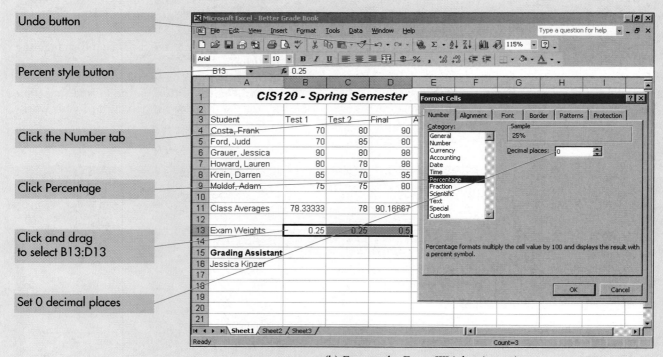

Undo button

Percent style button

Click the Number tab

Click Percentage

Click and drag to select B13:D13

Set 0 decimal places

(b) Format the Exam Weights (step 2)

FIGURE 1.18   *Hands-on Exercise 4 (continued)*

THE MENU OR THE TOOLBAR

The Formatting toolbar is often the easiest way to implement a variety of formatting operations. There are buttons for boldface, italics, and underlining (each of which functions as a toggle switch). There are also buttons for alignment (including merge and center), currency, percent, and comma formats, together with buttons to increase or decrease the number of decimal places. You can find various buttons to change the font, point size, color, and borders.

Step 3: **Format the Class Averages**

➤ Click and drag to select cells **B11 through D11**. Now press and hold the **Ctrl key** as you click and drag to select cells **E4 through E9**. Using the Ctrl key in this way allows you to select noncontiguous (nontouching) cells as shown in Figure 1.18c.
➤ Format the selected cells using the Formatting toolbar or the Format menu:
  • To use the Format menu, pull down the **Format menu**, click **Cells**, click the **Number tab**, then click **Number** in the Category list box. Click the **down spin arrow** in the Decimal Places text box to reduce the decimal places to one. Click **OK**.
  • To use the Formatting toolbar, click the appropriate button repeatedly to increase or decrease the number of decimal places to one.
➤ Click and drag to select cells **B3 through E13**. Click the **Center button** to center the numeric data in the worksheet under the respective column headings.
➤ Save the workbook.

(c) Format the Class Averages (step 3)

FIGURE 1.18 *Hands-on Exercise 4 (continued)*

CLEAR THE FORMATS, BUT KEEP THE CONTENTS

You can clear the formatting in a cell and retain the contents, and/or you can clear contents but retain the formatting. Click and drag over the cell(s) for which the command is to apply, then pull down the Edit menu, click the Clear command, and choose the appropriate option—for example, the option to clear Formats. Click the tiny square immediately below the name box (to the left of the header for column A) to select the entire worksheet, then clear the formats for the worksheet. You can then repeat the steps in this exercise to practice the various formatting commands.

Step 4:   **Borders and Color**

➤ Click and drag to select cells **A3 through E3**. Press and hold the **Ctrl key** as you click and drag to select the range **A11:E11**.

➤ Continue to press the **Ctrl key** as you click and drag to select cells **A13:E13**. All three cell ranges should be selected, which means that any formatting command you execute will apply to all of the selected cells.

➤ Pull down the **Format menu** and click **Cells** (or point to any of the selected cells and click the **right mouse button** to display a shortcut menu, then click **Format Cells**). Click the **Border tab** to display the dialog box in Figure 1.18d.

➤ Choose a line width from the Style section. Click the **Top** and **Bottom** boxes in the Border section. Click **OK** to exit the dialog box.

➤ Check that all three ranges are still selected (A3:E3, A11:E11, *and* A13:E13). Click the **down arrow** on the **Fill Color button** on the Formatting toolbar. Click **yellow** (or whatever color appeals to you).

➤ Click the **Bold button** on the Formatting toolbar. Click outside the selected cells to see the effects of the formatting change. Save the workbook.

Bold button

Fill Color button

Click and drag to select A3:E3

Press the Ctrl key as you click and drag to select A11:E11 and then A13:E13

Click the Border tab

Click the Top Border box

Click the Bottom Border box

(d) Borders and Color (step 4)

FIGURE 1.18   *Hands-on Exercise 4 (continued)*

USE A PEN TO DRAW THE BORDER

You can draw borders of any thickness or color around the cells in a worksheet using a "pen" as opposed to a menu command. Click the down arrow on the Borders button on the Standard toolbar, then click the Draw Borders command to change the mouse pointer to a pen and simultaneously display the Borders toolbar. Click the Line Color or Line Style buttons to change the appearance of the border, then draw the borders directly in the worksheet. Close the Borders toolbar when you are finished.

Step 5: **The Completed Worksheet**

➤ Check that your worksheet matches ours as shown in Figure 1.18e. Pull down the **File menu**. Click **Page Setup** to display the Page Setup dialog box.
- Click the **Margins tab**. Check the box to center the worksheet horizontally.
- Click the **Sheet tab**. Check the boxes to print Row and Column Headings and Gridlines.
- Click the **Header/Footer tab**. If necessary, click the **drop-down arrow** on the Header list box. Scroll to the top of the list and click **(none)** to remove the header. Click the **drop-down arrow** on the Footer list box. Scroll to the top of the list and click **(none)** to remove the footer. Click **OK**.

➤ Click the **Print Preview button** to preview the worksheet before printing:
- If you are satisfied with the appearance of the worksheet, click the **Print button** within the Preview window, then click **OK** to print the worksheet.
- If you are not satisfied with the appearance of the worksheet, click the **Setup button** within the Preview window to make the necessary changes.

➤ Save the workbook.

Print Preview button

Your name goes here

(e) The Completed Worksheet (step 5)

FIGURE 1.18 *Hands-on Exercise 4 (continued)*

FIND-AND-REPLACE FORMATTING

You can use the Find and Replace command to replace formatting as well as text. Pull down the Edit menu and click the Replace command to display the Find and Replace dialog box, then click the options button to display a Format button next to both text boxes. Click the Format button next to the Find text box and specify Bold as the Font style. Click the Format button next to the Replace text box and choose Italic. Now click the Replace All button to replace all bold with Italics. Try this within the grade book. See practice exercise 4 at the end of the chapter.

Step 6: **Print the Cell Formulas**

➤ Pull down the **Tools menu**, click **Options**, click the **View tab**, check the box for **Formulas**, then click **OK** (or use the keyboard shortcut **Ctrl+˜**). The worksheet should display the cell formulas.

➤ If necessary, click the arrow to the right of the horizontal scroll box so that column E, the column containing the cell formulas, comes into view.

➤ Double click the border between the column headings for columns E and F to increase the width of column E to the widest entry in the column.

➤ Pull down the **File menu**. Click **Page Setup** to display the Page Setup dialog box. Click the **Page tab**. Click the **Landscape** orientation **button**. Click the option button to **Fit to 1 Page**. Click **OK** to exit the Page Setup dialog box.

➤ Click the **Print Preview button** to preview the worksheet before printing as shown in Figure 1.18f. Click the **Zoom button** to increase/decrease the size of the worksheet as necessary. If you are not satisfied with the appearance of the worksheet, click the **Setup button** within the Preview window to make the necessary changes. Print the worksheet.

➤ Pull down the **File menu**. Click **Exit**. Click **No** if prompted to save changes.

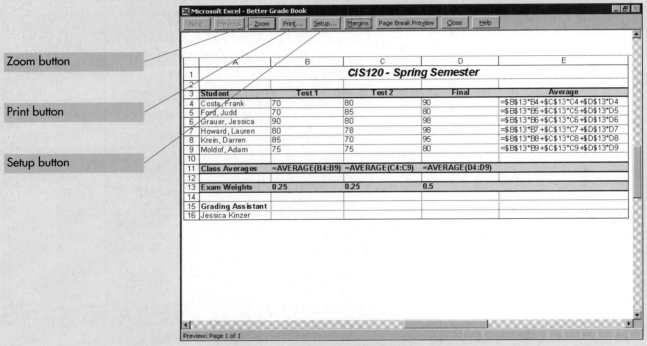

(f) Print the Cell Formulas (step 6)

FIGURE 1.18 *Hands-on Exercise 4 (continued)*

CLICK AND DRAG TO CORRECT A CELL FORMULA

Press Ctrl+˜ to display the cell formulas, then click in any cell that contains a formula. Look closely and you will see that each cell reference in that formula appears in a different color that corresponds to the border color of the referenced cell. To change a cell reference in the formula (e.g., from A4 to B4), drag the color-coded border surrounding cell A4 (the reference you want to change) to cell B4 (the new reference).

A spreadsheet is the computerized equivalent of an accountant's ledger. It is divided into rows and columns, with each row and column assigned a heading. The intersection of a row and column forms a cell. Spreadsheet is a generic term. Workbook and worksheet are Excel specific. An Excel workbook contains one or more worksheets.

Every cell in a worksheet (spreadsheet) contains either a formula or a constant. A formula begins with an equal sign and is a combination of numeric constants, cell references, arithmetic operators, and/or functions. A constant is an entry that does not change and may be numeric or descriptive text.

The Insert and Delete commands add or remove individual cells, rows, or columns of a worksheet. The commands are also used to insert or delete worksheets within a workbook. The Open command brings a workbook from disk into memory. The Save command copies the workbook in memory to disk.

The Page Setup command provides complete control over the printed page, enabling you to print a worksheet with or without gridlines or row and column headings. The Page Setup command also controls margins, headers and footers, centering the worksheet on a page, and orientation. The Print Preview command shows the worksheet as it will print and should be used prior to printing.

All worksheet commands operate on a cell or group of cells known as a range. A range is selected by dragging the mouse to highlight the range; the range remains selected until another range is selected or you click another cell in the worksheet. Noncontiguous (nonadjacent) ranges may be selected in conjunction with the Ctrl key.

The formulas in a cell or range of cells may be copied or moved anywhere within a worksheet. An absolute reference remains constant throughout a copy operation whereas a relative address is adjusted for the new location. Absolute and relative references have no meaning in a move operation.

Formatting is done within the context of select-then-do; that is, select the cell or range of cells, then execute the appropriate command. The Format Cells command controls the formatting for numbers, alignment, font, borders, and patterns (colors). The Formatting toolbar simplifies the formatting process.

KEY TERMS

Absolute reference (p. 33)
Accounting format (p. 43)
Active cell (p. 7)
Alignment (p. 44)
Assumptions (p. 31)
Border tab (p. 46)
Cell (p. 4)
Cell reference (p. 4)
Clipboard (p. 33)
Close command (p. 9)
Constant (p. 5)
Copy command (p. 32)
Currency format (p. 43)
Custom format (p. 43)
Date format (p. 43)
Delete command (p. 19)
Destination range (p. 32)
Edit (p. 5)
Exit command (p. 9)
File menu (p. 9)
File name (p. 9)
File type (p. 9)

Format Cells command (p. 43)
Formatting toolbar (p. 7)
Formula (p. 5)
Formula bar (p. 7)
Fraction format (p. 43)
Function (p. 5)
General format (p. 43)
Insert command (p. 19)
Landscape orientation (p. 21)
Merge cells (p. 44)
Mixed reference (p. 33)
Move operation (p. 34)
Name box (p. 7)
Number format (p. 43)
Office Assistant (p. 18)
Open command (p. 9)
Page Setup command (p. 21)
Patterns tab (p. 46)
Percentage format (p. 43)
Places bar (p. 9)
Portrait orientation (p. 21)

Print command (p. 9)
Range (p. 32)
Relative reference (p. 33)
Save command (p. 9)
Save As command (p. 9)
Scientific format (p. 43)
Select-then-do (p. 43)
Source range (p. 32)
Special format (p. 43)
Split cells (p. 44)
Spreadsheet (p. 2)
Standard toolbar (p. 7)
Status bar (p. 7)
Task pane (p. 22)
Text format (p. 43)
Time format (p. 43)
Toolbars (p. 7)
Undo command (p. 17)
Workbook (p. 6)
Worksheet (p. 6)

1. Which of the following is true?
   (a) A worksheet contains one or more workbooks
   (b) A workbook contains one or more worksheets
   (c) A spreadsheet contains one or more worksheets
   (d) A worksheet contains one or more spreadsheets

2. The cell at the intersection of the second column and third row is cell:
   (a) B3
   (b) 3B
   (c) C2
   (d) 2C

3. What is the effect of typing F5+F6 into a cell *without* a beginning equal sign?
   (a) The entry is equivalent to the formula =F5+F6
   (b) The cell will display the contents of cell F5 plus cell F6
   (c) The entry will be treated as a text entry and display F5+F6 in the cell
   (d) The entry will be rejected by Excel which will signal an error message

4. The Open command:
   (a) Brings a workbook from disk into memory
   (b) Brings a workbook from disk into memory, then erases the workbook on disk
   (c) Stores the workbook in memory on disk
   (d) Stores the workbook in memory on disk, then erases the workbook from memory

5. The Save command:
   (a) Brings a workbook from disk into memory
   (b) Brings a workbook from disk into memory, then erases the workbook on disk
   (c) Stores the workbook in memory on disk
   (d) Stores the workbook in memory on disk, then erases the workbook from memory

6. In the absence of parentheses, the order of operation is:
   (a) Exponentiation, addition or subtraction, multiplication or division
   (b) Addition or subtraction, multiplication or division, exponentiation
   (c) Multiplication or division, exponentiation, addition or subtraction
   (d) Exponentiation, multiplication or division, addition or subtraction

7. Cells A1, A2, and A3 contain the values 10, 20, and 40, respectively, what value will be displayed in a cell containing the cell formula =A1/A2*A3+1?
   (a) 1.125
   (b) 21
   (c) 20.125
   (d) Impossible to determine

8. The entry =AVERAGE(A4:A6):
   (a) Is invalid because the cells are not contiguous
   (b) Computes the average of cells A4 and A6
   (c) Computes the average of cells A4, A5, and A6
   (d) None of the above

9. Which of the following was suggested with respect to printing a workbook?
   (a) Print the displayed values only
   (b) Print the cell formulas only
   (c) Print both the displayed values and cell formulas
   (d) Print neither the displayed values nor the cell formulas

10. Which options are mutually exclusive in the Page Setup menu?
   (a) Portrait and landscape orientation
   (b) Cell gridlines and row and column headings
   (c) Left and right margins
   (d) All of the above

11. What is the end result of clicking in a cell, then clicking the Italics button on the Formatting toolbar twice in a row?
   (a) The cell contents are displayed in Italics
   (b) The cell contents are displayed in ordinary (nonitalicized) type
   (c) The cell contents are unchanged and appear exactly as they did prior to clicking the Italics button twice in a row
   (d) Impossible to determine

12. Which of the following best describes the formula used to compute a student's semester average, when the weights of each exam are isolated at the bottom of a spreadsheet?
   (a) The student's individual grades are entered as absolute references and the exam weights are entered as relative references
   (b) The student's individual grades are entered as relative references and the exam weights are entered as absolute references
   (c) All cell references are relative
   (d) All cell references are absolute

13. Cell B11 contains the formula, =SUM (B3:B9). What will the contents of cell C11 be if the formula in cell B11 is copied to cell C11?
   (a) =SUM (C3:C9)
   (b) =SUM (B3:B9)
   (c) =SUM ($B$3:$B$9)
   (d) =SUM ($C$3:$C$9)

14. Cell E6 contains the formula, =B6*$B$12+C6*$C$12+D6*$D$12. What will be the formula in cell E7 if the contents of cell E6 are copied to that cell?
   (a) =B7*$B$12+C7*$C$12+D7*$D$12
   (b) =B7*$B$13+C7*$C$13+D7*$D$13
   (c) =B6*$B$13+C6*$C$13+D6*$D$13
   (d) None of the above

15. A formula containing the reference =D$5 is copied to a cell one column over and two rows down. How will the entry appear in its new location?
   (a) =E5
   (b) =E$5
   (c) =E$6
   (d) =$E5

ANSWERS

1. b	**6.** d	**11.** c
2. a	**7.** b	**12.** b
3. c	**8.** c	**13.** a
4. a	**9.** c	**14.** a
5. c	**10.** a	**15.** b

1. **Isolate Assumptions:** Figure 1.19 displays a new grade book with a different grading scheme. Students take three exams worth 100 points each, submit a term paper and various homework assignments worth 50 points each, then receive a grade for the semester based on their total points. The maximum points possible is 400. A student's semester average is computed by dividing his or her total points by this number.

   a. Open the partially completed workbook, *Chapter 1 Practice 1*, in the Exploring Excel folder. Click in cell G4 and enter a formula to compute Anderson's total points. Click in cell H4 and enter a formula that will compute Anderson's semester average. Be sure this formula includes an absolute reference to cell B16.

   b. Click and drag to select the formulas in cells G4 and H4, then copy these formulas to cells G5 through H12.

   c. Click in cell B14 and enter a formula that will compute the class average on the first exam. Copy this formula to cells C14 to H14.

   d. Format the worksheet appropriately. (You need not copy our formatting exactly.) Add your name as the grading assistant, then print the worksheet twice, once to show displayed values and once to show the cell formulas. Use landscape printing and be sure that the worksheet fits on one sheet of paper.

   e. The professor is concerned about the grades being too low and wants to introduce a curve. He does this by reducing the point threshold on which the students' semester averages are based. Click in cell B16 and change the threshold to 350, which automatically raises the average of every student.

   f. Print the displayed values that reflect the change in part (e). Can you see the value of isolating the assumptions within a worksheet?

   g. Add a cover page, then submit the complete assignment (four pages in all counting the cover page) to your instructor.

FIGURE 1.19 *Isolate Assumptions (Exercise 1)*

2. **Formatting and Cell Movement:** Figure 1.20 provides practice with formatting and basic cell operations (inserting and deleting cells, moving cells, splitting and/or merging cells). Open the partially completed *Chapter 1 Practice 2 workbook*, then follow the instructions in the individual cells to create the workbook in Figure 1.20. Cell B3, for example, asks you to italicize the text in green. The formatting is easy, but inserting and deleting cells is a little trickier since it can affect cells that have been merged together. You will find it easier, therefore, if you follow the instructions to split the cells first (cell A14 in the finished workbook), then merge the cells at the end of the exercise. Print the completed workbook for your instructor. Use landscape orientation so that the worksheet fits on one page.

	A	B
1	**Your Name in 16-Point White Text on Blue Background**	
2		
3	Center black text with yellow background	*Italicize this text in green*
4	This is red text underlined	**Boldface this text in violet**
5	*Italicize in Times New Roman and center*	This was **moved** from cell B2 to B5
6	**Boldface** the first word only	*Boldface and Italicize in Orange Arial*
7	**Indent this text and color it bold green**	Right align blue text
8	Format the cell on the right as currency with two decimals	$ 123.45
9	Format the cell on the right as percent with one decimal	98.7%
10	Format the cell on the right as a fraction	3/4
11	Format the cell on the right as date to include the printed month	March 23, 2001
12	Format the cell on the right as a social security number	111-22-3333
13	Delete the cell that originally above this cell change to blue text.	
14	**Split the text** originally in this merged cell into two cells. Type "Do this first" in 18-point blue text in the resulting blank cell on the right. Change **row height** to 42. **Wrap text**.	**Do this first**
15	**Insert this cell** two rows above the last row in column A	Change the width of column B to 35
16	Change the width of column A to 55	
17	**Do this last.** Merge and center the two cells in this row. Change the row height to 27. Wrap the text in the merged cells. Change the font to red. This was a great exercise. I can move, insert, and delete individual cells.	

FIGURE 1.20 *Formatting and Cell Movement (Exercise 2)*

3. **The Movies:** Figure 1.21 displays a spreadsheet that is used to compute the weekly revenue for a chain of movie theatres. Open the partially completed version of this spreadsheet in *Chapter 1 Practice 3*, then proceed as follows:
   a. Click in cell D4 and enter a formula, using a combination of relative and absolute references, to compute the ticket revenues for the first theatre.
   b. Click in cells E4 and F4 to enter the appropriate formulas in these cells for the first theatre. Copy the formulas in cells D4, E4, and F4 to the appropriate rows for the other theatres.
   c. Click in cell B9 and enter the function to compute the total number of evening tickets that were sold. Copy this formula to the appropriate cells in row 9 to compute the other totals.
   d. Format the completed worksheet as appropriate. Print the worksheet twice, once to show the displayed values and once to show the cell contents. Submit both printouts to your instructor as proof you did this exercise.

4. **Judson Ford Realty:** The worksheet in Figure 1.22 displays the sales for Judson Ford Realty for the month of October. You can open a partially completed version of this worksheet in *Chapter 1 Practice 4*, but it is up to you to complete the worksheet so that it matches Figure 1.22..
   a. The price per square foot is the selling price divided by the square feet.

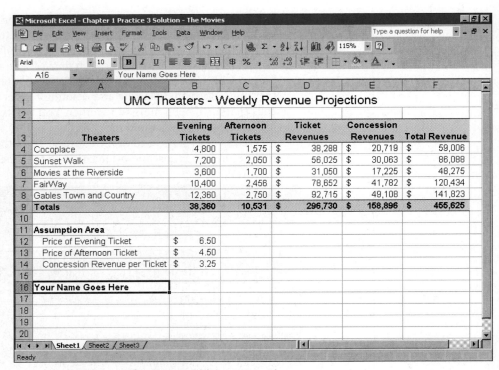

FIGURE 1.21 *The Movies (Exercise 3)*

Microsoft Excel - Chapter 1 Practice 3 Solution - The Movies

Cell A16: Your Name Goes Here

UMC Theaters - Weekly Revenue Projections

	Theaters	Evening Tickets	Afternoon Tickets	Ticket Revenues	Concession Revenues	Total Revenue
4	Cocoplace	4,800	1,575	$ 38,288	$ 20,719	$ 59,006
5	Sunset Walk	7,200	2,050	$ 56,025	$ 30,063	$ 86,088
6	Movies at the Riverside	3,600	1,700	$ 31,050	$ 17,225	$ 48,275
7	FairWay	10,400	2,456	$ 78,652	$ 41,782	$ 120,434
8	Gables Town and Country	12,360	2,750	$ 92,715	$ 49,108	$ 141,823
9	**Totals**	**38,360**	**10,531**	**$ 296,730**	**$ 158,896**	**$ 455,625**

Assumption Area

Price of Evening Ticket	$	6.50
Price of Afternoon Ticket	$	4.50
Concession Revenue per Ticket	$	3.25

Your Name Goes Here

Microsoft Excel - Chapter 1 Practice 4 Solution - Judson Ford Realty

Judson Ford Realty - October Sales

	Property	Size (square feet)	Asking Price	Selling Price	Price Per Square Foot	Commission	Net to Home Owner
4	122 West 75 Street	4,000	$ 450,000	$ 350,000	$ 87.50	$ 12,250	$ 337,750
5	4567 S.W. 95 Street	5,750	$ 750,000	$ 648,500	$ 112.78	$ 22,698	$ 625,803
6	123 Alamo Road	3,000	$ 350,000	$ 275,000	$ 91.67	$ 9,625	$ 265,375
7	9000 Brickell Avenue	2,500	$ 275,000	$ 250,000	$ 100.00	$ 8,750	$ 241,250
8	5596 Powerline Road	2,250	$ 189,000	$ 189,000	$ 84.00	$ 6,615	$ 182,385
9	8900 N.W. 89 Street	4,200	$ 456,000	$ 390,000	$ 92.86	$ 13,650	$ 376,350
10	75 Maynada Avenue	2,475	$ 300,000	$ 265,000	$ 107.07	$ 9,275	$ 255,725
11							
12	**Totals:**		**$ 2,770,000**	**$ 2,367,500**		**$ 82,863**	**$ 2,284,638**
13							
14	**Commission %:**	**3.50%**				**Realtor:** Your Name Goes Here	

Notes:
1. The commission is paid on the actual selling price, not the asking price
2. The price per square foot is based on the actual selling price, not the asking price
3. The net to the home owner is the actual selling price minus the commission

FIGURE 1.22 *Judson Ford Realty (Exercise 4)*

b. The realtor's commission is a percentage of the selling price and is based on the commission percentage in cell B14.

c. The net to the homeowner is the selling price minus the commission.

d. Compute the totals for the agency as shown in row 12. Format the worksheet in an appropriate fashion. You need not match our formatting exactly.

e. Use the Find and Replace command to change the text in the various addresses. Change all occurrences of "Str" to "Street", "Rd" to "Road", and "Ave" to "Avenue". You also need to replace the Courier New font with Arial throughout the worksheet.

f. Add your name in cell F14, then print the worksheet to show both displayed values and cell formulas. Create a cover sheet, then submit the assignment to your instructor.

5. The Solar System: The potential uses of a spreadsheet are limited only by your imagination as can be seen by Figure 1.23, which displays a spreadsheet with information about our solar system. Open the partially completed version of the workbook in *Chapter 1 Practice 5*, then complete the worksheet by developing the formulas for the first planet, copying those formulas to the remaining rows in the worksheet, then formatting appropriately.

a. Click in cell C15 and enter your weight on earth. You can specify your weight in pounds rather than kilograms.

b. Click in cell C16 and enter the function =Pi() as shown in Figure 1.23. The displayed value for the cell shows the value of Pi to several decimal places.

c. Click in cell D4 and enter the formula to compute the diameter of the first planet (Mercury). The diameter of a planet is equal to twice its radius.

d. Click in cell E4 and enter the formula to compute the circumference of a planet. The circumference is equal to the diameter times the constant Pi.

e. Click in cell F4 and enter the formula to compute the surface area, which is equal to four times Pi times the radius squared.

Microsoft Excel - Chapter 1 Practice 5 and 6 Solution - The Solar System

	A	B	C	D	E	F	G
1				The Solar System			
2							
3	Planet	Radius (km)	Gravity	Diameter (km)	Circumference (km)	Area (sq km)	Weight (lbs)
4	Mercury	2,440	0.378	4,880	15,331	74,815,144	57
5	Venus	6,052	0.905	12,104	38,026	460,264,737	136
6	Earth	6,378	1	12,756	40,074	511,185,933	150
7	Mars	3,397	0.379	6,794	21,344	145,011,003	57
8	Jupiter	71,492	2.529	142,984	449,197	64,228,053,050	379
9	Saturn	60,268	1.066	120,536	378,675	45,643,971,258	160
10	Uranus	25,559	0.903	51,118	160,592	8,209,138,445	135
11	Neptune	24,766	1.096	49,532	155,609	7,707,643,182	164
12	Pluto	1,137	0.069	2,274	7,144	16,245,414	10
13							
14	Constants and Assumptions				Prepared by		
15	Weight on Earth (lbs)		150		Your name goes here		
16	The constant **Pi**		3.14159265				
17	**Notes:**				The data is taken from a Web site by Bill Arnett		
18	1. The diameter of a sphere is twice the radius						
19	2. The circumference of a sphere is **Pi** times the diameter						
20	3. The surface area of a sphere is 4 **Pi** times the radius squared						
21	4. Your weight is equal to the gravity of the planet times your weight on Earth						

FIGURE 1.23 *The Solar System (Exercise 5)*

f. Click in cell G4 and enter the formula to compute your weight on Mercury, which is your weight on earth times the relative gravity of Mercury compared to that of earth.

g. Copy the formulas in row 4 to the remainder of the worksheet, then format the worksheet appropriately. You need not copy our formatting exactly. Add your name in cell E16 as indicated.

h. The worksheet contains a hyperlink to a Web site by Bill Arnett, which has additional information about the planets. If you click the hyperlink within Excel your browser will open automatically, and you will be connected to the site, provided you have an Internet connection.

i. Print the worksheet two ways, once with displayed values, and once to show the cell contents. Use landscape orientation and appropriate scaling so that the worksheet fits on a single page.

BUILDS ON

PRACTICE
EXERCISE 5
PAGE 59

6. Worksheet References: Figure 1.24 displays a second worksheet within the workbook for our solar system from the previous exercise. The worksheet in Figure 1.24 uses the English system (e.g., miles) as opposed to the metric system (kilometers). It's up to you to develop the appropriate conversion.

a. Open the completed workbook from the previous exercise, then click the English tab to display the worksheet in Figure 1.24. The radius of the individual planets is not entered directly into this worksheet, but is calculated from the metric worksheet.

b. Click in cell B4 and enter the formula =Metric!B4*English!$C$17. The names of the worksheets, Metric and English, are followed by exclamation points to indicate which worksheet is to be used. Cell C17 in the English worksheet contains the conversion factor to change kilometers to miles.

c. Copy the formula in cell B4 to the remaining rows in column B. The worksheet references are absolute and will not change when the formula is copied. Cell B4 is a relative reference, however, and will be modified to reflect the appropriate row as the formula is copied. The reference to cell C17, $C$17, is absolute and remains constant throughout.

FIGURE 1.24   *Worksheet References (Exercise 6)*

d. Develop the remaining formulas in row 4 using the information from the previous exercise. Copy these formulas to the remaining rows in the worksheet, then format the worksheet appropriately.

e. Print the worksheet twice, once to show displayed values, and once to show cell formulas.

7. **Student Budget:** Figure 1.25 displays a hypothetical budget for a nine-month academic year. You can use the partially completed version of this worksheet in the *Chapter 1 Practice 7* workbook, or you can create your own. If you use our file, then the totals in your worksheet should correspond exactly to those in Figure 1.25, whereas if you create your own budget, the numbers will differ. In any event, we would like you to show at least one month where you run a deficit. Negative numbers should be formatted to appear in red.

Substitute your name for Maryann's, then complete the worksheet and format it appropriately. Print the worksheet two ways, to show both displayed values and cell formulas, then submit both pages to your instructor. Be sure to use the Page Setup command to specify landscape printing, and appropriate scaling so that the entire worksheet fits on a single page.

Use this exercise to practice your file-mangement skills by saving the solution in a new folder. Complete the exercise, then pull down the File menu and click the Save As command to display the Save As dialog box. Change to the Exploring Excel folder, click the New Folder button on the toolbar, then create a new folder as shown in Figure 1.25.

FIGURE 1.25 *Student Budget (Exercise 7)*

8. **The Housing Office:** Open the partially completed workbook in *Chapter 1 Practice 8*, then complete the workbook to match Figure 1.26. You can modify the formatting, but the displayed values should be the same. Pay special attention to the formula for the meal plan revenue (cell G4 for the first residence hall), which uses a combination of relative and absolute addresses. Note, too, that each double room has two students, each of whom is required to pay for the meal plan. Place your name somewhere in the worksheet, then print the worksheet two ways, to show both displayed values and cell formulas.

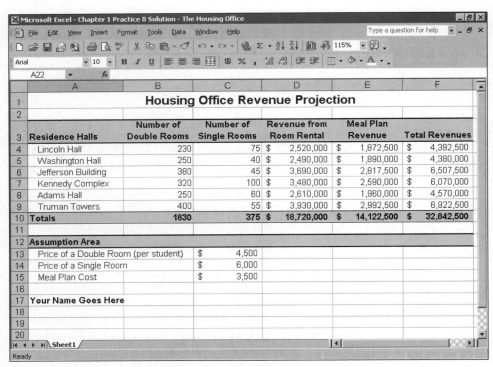

FIGURE 1.26   *The Housing Office (Exercise 8)*

 9. E-mail Your Homework: It's easy to send an Excel workbook as an attached file as shown in Figure 1.27, but we suggest you check with your professor first. He or she may prefer that you print the assignment, rather than mail it and/or e-mail may not be available to you. If e-mail is an option, start your e-mail program and create a message to your instructor. Click the Insert (or Attach) button to select the file, then click the Send button to mail the message.

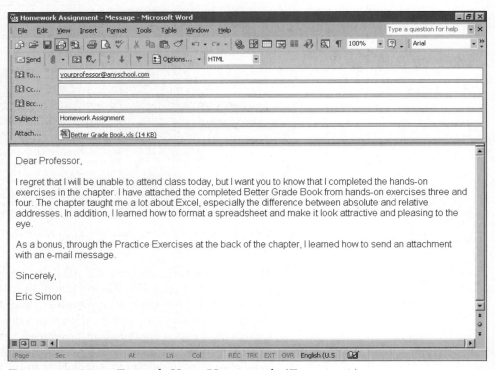

FIGURE 1.27   *E-mail Your Homework (Exercise 9)*

The MyPHLIP Web Site

Every text in the *Exploring Office XP* series has a corresponding MyPHLIP (Prentice Hall Learning on the Internet Partnership) Web site, where you will find a variety of student resources as well as online review questions for each chapter. Go to www.prenhall.com/myphlip and follow the instructions. The first time at the site you will be prompted to register by supplying your e-mail address and choosing a password. Next, you choose the discipline (CIS/MIS) and a book (e.g., *Exploring Microsoft Office XP, Volume I*). Your professor will tell you whether he or she has created an online syllabus, in which case you should click the link to find your professor after adding the book. Either way, the next time you return to the site, you will be taken directly to your text. Select any chapter, click "Go", then use the review questions as directed.

Residential Colleges

Congratulations! You have been recommended for a work-study assignment in the Office of Housing. Your supervisor has collected data on the number of students living in each dorm, and further, has divided that data according to the year in school. Your job is to open the partially completed *Residential Colleges* workbook, and compute the total number of students living in each dorm, as well as the total number of students for each year. In addition, you are to determine the percentage of the dormitory population for year in school.

The Cost of Smoking

Smoking is hazardous to your health as well as your pocketbook. A one-pack-a-day habit, at $3/pack, will cost you more than $1,000 per year. For the same money you could buy 20 concert tickets at $50 each, or more than 700 gallons of gas at $1.50 per gallon. Open the partially completed *Cost of Smoking* workbook and compute the number of various items that you could buy over the course of a year in lieu of cigarettes.

Accuracy Counts

The *Underbid* workbook on the data disk was the last assignment completed by your predecessor prior to his unfortunate dismissal. The worksheet contains a significant error, which caused your company to underbid a contract and assume a subsequent loss of $100,000. As you look for the error, don't be distracted by the attractive formatting. The shading, lines, and other touches are nice, but accuracy is more important than anything else. Write a memo to your instructor describing the nature of the error.

Two Different Clipboards

The Office clipboard is different from the Windows clipboard, but both clipboards share some functionality. Thus, whenever you copy an object to the Windows clipboard, it can also be copied to the Office clipboard, where the last 24 copied objects are retained. This is in contrast to the Windows clipboard, where each copy operation replaces the clipboard in its entirety. Experiment with the Office clipboard from different applications, then summarize your findings in a brief note to your instructor. Explain how the Office clipboard can be accessed from the task pane in Excel and/or an icon that appears on the Windows taskbar.

The Office Assistant

The Office Assistant monitors your work and offers advice throughout a session. You can tell that the Assistant has a suggestion when you see a light bulb on the Office Assistant button on the Standard toolbar or in the Office Assistant window. You can read the suggestions as they occur and/or review them at the end of a session. Redo one or more of the exercises in this chapter, but this time pay attention to the Assistant. Write a brief note to your instructor describing three tips (shortcuts) offered by the Assistant. (You should, however, reset the Assistant before you begin, or else the Assistant will not repeat tips that were offered in a previous session.) Start the Assistant, click the Options button, click the Options tab, then click the button to Reset tips.

Planning for Disaster

This case has nothing to do with spreadsheets per se, but it is perhaps the most important case of all, as it deals with the question of backup. Do you have a backup strategy? Do you even know what a backup strategy is? You had better learn, because sooner or later you will wish you had one. You will erase a file, be unable to read from a floppy disk, or worse yet suffer a hardware failure in which you are unable to access the hard drive. The problem always seems to occur the night before an assignment is due. Describe in 250 words or less the backup strategy you plan to implement in conjunction with your work in this class.

The Threat of Virus Infection

A computer virus is an actively infectious program that attaches itself to other programs and alters the way a computer works. Some viruses do nothing more than display an annoying message at an inopportune time. Most, however, are more harmful, and in the worst case erase all files on the disk. Use your favorite search engine to research the subject of computer viruses in order to answer the following questions: When is a computer subject to infection by a virus? What precautions does your school or university take against the threat of virus infection in its computer lab? What precautions, if any, do you take at home? Can you feel confident that your machine will not be infected if you faithfully use a state-of-the-art antivirus program that was purchased in January 2001?

CHAPTER 2

Gaining Proficiency: The Web and Business Applications

OBJECTIVES

AFTER READING THIS CHAPTER YOU WILL BE ABLE TO:

1. Gain proficiency in the use of relative and absolute references to create a spreadsheet; explain the importance of isolating the assumptions in a worksheet.
2. Use the fill handle to copy a cell formula to a range of adjacent cells.
3. Use pointing to enter a formula; explain the advantage of pointing over explicitly typing cell references.
4. Insert a hyperlink into an Excel worksheet.
5. Save a worksheet as a Web page; explain how the concept of "round trip HTML" applies to editing a Web page.
6. Import data from a Web query into an Excel workbook; explain how to refresh the query to obtain current information.
7. Describe the Today( ) function and its use in date arithmetic.

OVERVIEW

This chapter provides practice in creating a variety of spreadsheets using combinations of relative, absolute, and mixed references. The distinction between the different types of references, coupled with the importance of isolating the assumptions on which a worksheet is based, are two of the most basic concepts in spreadsheet design. You simply cannot use Excel effectively unless you are comfortable with this material.

The chapter also introduces several new capabilities to increase your proficiency in Excel. We begin with pointing, a preferred way to enter a cell formula, and present the fill handle to facilitate copying a formula to other rows or columns within a worksheet. We introduce the Today( ) function and the use of date arithmetic. We also discuss the various Web capabilities that are built into Excel. You will learn how to add a hyperlink to a worksheet and how to save a worksheet as a Web page for viewing in a browser such as Internet Explorer or Netscape Navigator. You will also learn how to create a Web query to download information from the Web directly into an Excel worksheet.

All of this is accomplished through three diverse examples, each of which is a typical illustration of how spreadsheets are used in business. As always, the hands-on exercises provide the opportunity to apply the concepts at the computer.

EMPLOYEE PAYROLL

The spreadsheet in Figure 2.1 shows how Excel can be used to compute a simple payroll. Figure 2.1a shows the displayed values and Figure 2.1b contains the underlying formulas. The concepts necessary to develop the spreadsheet were presented in the previous chapter. The intent here is to reinforce the earlier material, with emphasis on the use of *relative* and *absolute references* in the various cell formulas.

The calculation of an individual's gross pay depends on the employment practices of the organization. The formula used in the worksheet is simply an algebraic statement of how employees are paid, in this example, straight time for regular hours, and time-and-a-half for each hour of overtime. The first employee, Adams, earns $400 for 40 regular hours (40 hours at $10/hour) plus $60 for overtime (4 overtime hours × $10/hour × 1.5 for overtime). The formula to compute Adams' gross pay is entered into cell E2 as follows:

Gross Pay = Regular Hours * Hourly Rate + Overtime Hours * Hourly Rate * 1.5

Relative reference to cell B2

Regular reference to cell D2

Relative reference to cell B2

Relative reference to cell C2

Entered into cell E2 as =C2*B2+D2*B2*1.5

The cell references in the formula are relative references, which means that they will change when copied to another cell. Thus, you can copy the formula in cell E2 to the other rows in column E to compute the gross pay for the other employees. The formula in cell E3, for example, becomes C3*B3+D3*B3*1.5, as can be seen from the displayed formulas in Figure 2.1b.

The withholding tax is computed by multiplying an individual's gross pay by the withholding tax rate. (This is an approximate calculation because the true withholding tax rate is implemented on a sliding scale; that is, the more an individual earns, the higher the tax rate. We use a uniform rate, however, to simplify the example.) The formula in cell F2 to compute the withholding tax uses a combination of relative and absolute references as follows:

Withholding Tax = Gross Pay * Withholding Rate

Absolute reference to cell C11

Relative reference to cell E2

Entered into cell F2 as =E2*$C$11

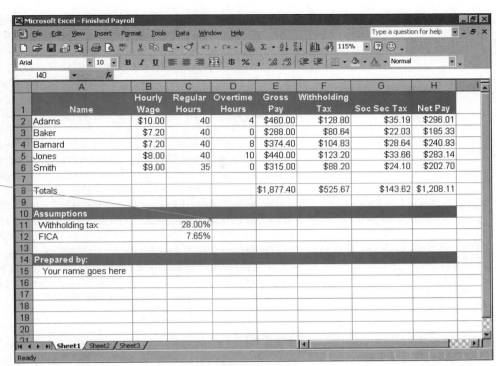

Red triangle indicates a comment

(a) Displayed Values

Formula uses relative references

Formula uses relative and absolute references

Comment is visible when you point to the cell

Formula Auditing toolbar is visible with cell formulas

(b) Cell Formulas

FIGURE 2.1 *Payroll*

It is important to emphasize that the formula to compute the withholding tax contains an absolute reference to the tax rate (cell C11), as opposed to the actual constant (.28 in this example). The distinction may seem trivial, but most assuredly it is not, as two important objectives are achieved. First, the user sees those factors that affect the results of the spreadsheet in a separate assumption area (e.g., the withholding rate). Second, the user can change the value in one place, cell C11, then have the change automatically reflected in the calculations for all of the employees. The calculation of the employee's Social Security tax in cell G2 is performed in similar fashion and includes an absolute reference to cell C12.

The remaining formulas in the worksheet are also straightforward. An employee's net pay is computed by subtracting the deductions (the withholding tax and the Social Security tax) from the gross pay. Thus the net pay for the first employee is entered in cell H2 using the formula $=E2-(F2+G2)$. The cell references are relative, which enables us to copy the formula to the remaining rows in column H, and thus calculate the net pay for the other employees.

The employee totals for gross pay, withholding tax, social security tax, and net pay are computed using the SUM function in the appropriate cells in row 8. The formula to compute the gross pay, $=SUM(E2:E6)$, is entered into cell E8, after which it is copied to the remaining cells in row 8.

Pointing

Any cell reference can be entered into a formula by typing the address explicitly into a cell. Entering addresses in this way is not recommended, however, because it is all too easy to make a mistake, such as typing A40 when you really mean A41. *Pointing* to the cell is a more accurate method, since you use the mouse (or arrow keys) to select the cell directly when you build the formula. In essence you 1) Click in the cell that will contain the formula, 2) Type an equal sign to begin entering the formula, and 3) Click in the cell you want to reference. You then type any arithmetic operator, then continue pointing to additional cells using the steps we just described. And finally, you press the enter key to complete the formula. It's easier than it sounds and you get to practice in our next exercise.

The Fill Handle

There are several ways to copy the contents of a cell. You can use the Copy and Paste buttons on the Standard toolbar, the associated keyboard shortcuts, and/or the corresponding commands in the Edit menu. You can also use the *fill handle*, a tiny black square that appears in the lower-right corner of a selected cell. All you do is 1) Select the cell or cells to be copied, 2) Point to the fill handle for the selected cell(s), which changes the mouse pointer to a thin crosshair, 3) Click and drag the fill handle over the destination range, and 4) Release the mouse to complete the operation. (The fill handle can be used to copy only to adjacent cells.) Again, it's easier than it sounds, and as you may have guessed, it's time for our next hands-on exercise in which you build the payroll worksheet in Figure 2.1.

Comments

The *Insert Comment command* creates the equivalent of a screen tip that displays information about the worksheet. Cell C11 in Figure 2.1a contains a tiny red triangle to indicate the presence of a comment, which appears as a screen tip when you point to the cell, as shown in Figure 2.1b. (An option can be set to display the comment permanently, but most people opt for just the triangle.) Comments may be subsequently edited, or deleted altogether if they are no longer appropriate.

HANDS-ON EXERCISE 1

PAYROLL

Objective Develop a spreadsheet for a simplified payroll to illustrate relative and absolute references. Use pointing to enter formulas and the fill handle to copy formulas. Use Figure 2.2 as a guide in the exercise.

Step 1: **Compute the Gross Pay**

➤ Start Excel. Open the **Payroll workbook** in the **Exploring Excel folder** to display the worksheet in Figure 2.2a.

➤ Save the workbook as **Finished Payroll** so that you may return to the original workbook if necessary.

➤ Click in cell **E2**, the cell that contains the gross pay for the first employee. Press the **equal sign** on the keyboard to begin pointing, click in cell **C2** (which produces a moving border around the cell), press the **asterisk key**, then click in cell **B2**. You have entered the first part of the formula to compute an employee's gross pay.

➤ Press the **plus sign**, click in cell **D2**, press the **asterisk**, click in cell **B2**, press the **asterisk**, type **1.5**, then press **enter**. You should see 460 as the displayed value for cell E2.

➤ Click in cell **E2**, then check to be sure that the formula you entered matches the formula in the formula bar in Figure 2.2a. If necessary, click in the formula bar and make the appropriate changes so that you have the correct formula in cell E2.

➤ Save the workbook.

Formula entered in E2 is displayed in formula bar

Click in E2

Labels are entered for you

	A	B	C	D	E	F	G	H
1	Name	Hourly Wage	Regular Hours	Overtime Hours	Gross Pay	Withholding Tax	Soc Sec Tax	Net Pay
2	Adams	10	40	4	460			
3	Baker	7.2	40	0				
4	Barnard	7.2	40	8				
5	Jones	8	40	10				
6	Smith	9	35	0				
7								
8	Totals							
9								
10	Assumptions							
11	Withholding tax		0.28					
12	FICA		0.0765					
13								
14	Prepared by:							

E2 =C2*B2+D2*B2*1.5

(a) Compute the Gross Pay (step 1)

FIGURE 2.2 *Hands-on Exercise 1*

Step 2: Complete the Calculations

➤ Click in cell **F2**, the cell that contains the withholding tax for the first employee. Press the **equal sign** on the keyboard to begin pointing, then click in cell **E2**, the cell that contains the employee's gross pay.

➤ Press the **asterisk key**, then click in cell **C11**, the cell that contains the withholding tax. Cell F2 should now contain the formula, =E2*C11, but this is not quite correct.

➤ Check that the insertion point (the flashing vertical line) is within (or immediately behind) the reference to cell C11, then press the **F4 key** to change the cell reference to $C$11 as shown in Figure 2.2b.

➤ Press **enter**. The displayed value in cell F2 should be 128.8, corresponding to the withholding tax for this employee.

➤ Use pointing to enter the remaining formulas for the first employee. Click in cell **G2**, then enter the formula **=E2*$C$12**. The displayed value is 35.19, corresponding to the Social Security Tax.

➤ Click in cell **H2**, and enter the formula **=E2−(F2+G2)**. The displayed value is 296.01, corresponding to the net pay for this individual.

➤ Save the workbook.

Enter formula in F2 that references E2 and C11

Moving border indicates cell selected during pointing operation

(b) Complete the Calculations (step 2)

FIGURE 2.2 *Hands-on Exercise 1 (continued)*

THE F4 KEY

The F4 key cycles through relative, absolute, and mixed references. Click on any reference within the formula bar; for example, click on A1 in the formula =A1+A2. Press the F4 key once, and it changes to an absolute reference. Press the F4 key a second time, and it becomes a mixed reference, A$1; press it again, and it is a different mixed reference, $A1. Press the F4 key a fourth time, and return to the original relative reference, A1.

Step 3: **Copy the Formulas**

➤ Click in cell **E2**, then click and drag to select cells **E2:H2**, as shown in Figure 2.2c. Point to the **fill handle** in the lower-right corner of cell H2. The mouse pointer changes to a thin crosshair.

➤ Drag the **fill handle** to cell H6 (the lower-right cell in the range of employee calculations). A dim border appears as you drag the fill handle as shown in Figure 2.2c.

➤ Release the mouse to complete the copy operation. The formulas for the first employee have been copied to the corresponding rows for the other employees.

➤ Click in cell **E3**, the cell containing the gross pay for the second employee. You should see the formula =C3*B3+D3*B3*1.5. Now click in cell **F3**, the cell containing the withholding tax for the second employee.

➤ You should see the formula =E3*$C$11, which contains a relative reference (cell E3) that is adjusted from one row to the next, and an absolute reference (cell $C$11) that remains constant from one employee to the next.

➤ Save the workbook.

Click and drag to select E2:H2

Drag fill handle to H6

(c) Copy the Formulas (step 3)

FIGURE 2.2 *Hands-on Exercise 1 (continued)*

IT'S ONLY ALGEBRA

There are several ways to enter the formula to compute an employee's gross pay. You could, for example, factor out the hourly rate and enter the formula as =B3*(C3+D3*1.5). It doesn't matter how you enter the formula as long as the results are algebraically correct. What is important is the combination of relative and absolute references, so that the formula is copied correctly from one row to the next.

Step 4:   **Compute the Totals**

➤ Click in cell **E8**, the cell that is to contain the total gross pay for all employees. Type the **=sign**, type **SUM(**, then click and drag over cells **E2** through **E6**.

➤ Type a **closing parenthesis**, and then press **enter** to complete the formula. Cell E8 should display the value 1877.4. Now click in cell **E8** and you should see the function, =SUM(E2:E6).

➤ Click and drag the **fill handle** in cell E8 to the remaining cells in this row (cells F8 through H8). Release the mouse to complete the copy operation.

➤ You should see 1208.1069 in cell H8, corresponding to the total net pay for all employees. Click in cell **H8** to view the formula, =SUM(H2:H6), which results from the copy operation.

➤ Save the workbook.

Click and drag over E2:E6

Click in E8
and type =SUM(

(d) Compute the Totals (step 4)

FIGURE 2.2   *Hands-on Exercise 1 (continued)*

FORMULAS VERSUS FUNCTIONS

There are in essence two ways to compute the total gross pay for all employees, using the SUM function, or the equivalent formula (e.g., =E2+E3+E4+E5+E6). The function is preferable for two reasons. First, it's easier to enter, and therefore less prone to error. Second, the function adjusts automatically to include any additional employees that will be entered within the cell range. Try inserting a new employee between the existing employees in rows 3 and 4, then observe how the values for this employee will be included automatically in the computed totals. The function also adjusts for deleted rows, whereas the formula does not.

Step 5:   Format the Spreadsheet

➤ Click in cell **B2**, then click and drag to select cells **B2 through B6**. Press and hold the **Ctrl key** as you click and drag to select cells **E2 through H8** (in addition to the previously selected cells).

➤ Pull down the **Format menu** and click the **Cells command** to display the Format Cells dialog box in Figure 2.2e. Click the **Number tab** and choose **Currency** from the Category list box. Specify **2** as the number of decimal places.

➤ If necessary, choose the **$ sign** as the currency symbol. (Note, too, that you can select a variety of alternative symbols such as the British Pound or the Euro symbol for the European Community.) Click **OK** to accept the settings and close the dialog box.

➤ Click and drag to select cells **C11 and C12**, then click the **Percent Style button** on the Formatting toolbar. Click the **Increase/Decrease Decimals buttons** to format each number to two decimal places.

➤ Save the workbook.

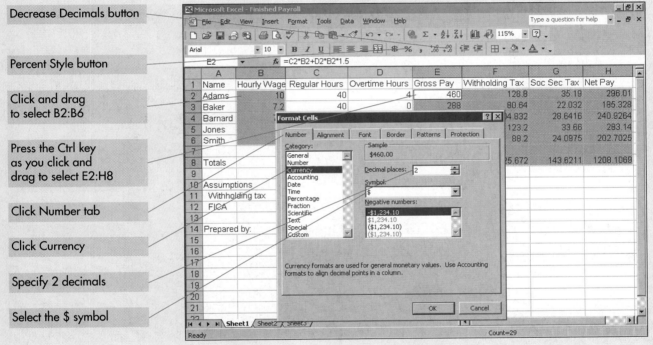

(e) Format the Spreadsheet (step 5)

FIGURE 2.2   *Hands-on Exercise 1 (continued)*

THE FORMAT STYLE COMMAND

A style is a collection of formats such as the font, alignment, and number of decimal places. Common styles, such as percent or currency, are represented by buttons on the Formatting toolbar and are most easily applied by clicking the appropriate tool. You can also apply the style by pulling down the Format menu, clicking the Style command, and selecting the style from the Style Name list box. The latter allows you to modify the definition of existing styles and/or to create a new style.

Step 6: **Complete the Formatting**

➤ Click and drag to select cells **A1 though H1**. Press and hold the **Ctrl key**, then click and drag to select **cells A10 through H10** in addition to the cells in row one. Continue to press and hold the **Ctrl key**, then click and drag to select cells **A14 through H14**.

➤ Click the **Fill Color arrow** on the Formatting toolbar, then select **blue** as the fill color. Click the **Font Color arrow** on the Formatting toolbar, then select **white** as the color for the text. Click the **Bold button** so that the text stands out from the fill color.

➤ Click and drag to select cells **A1 through H1** (which also deselects the cells in rows 10 and 14). Click the **Right mouse button** to display a context-sensitive menu, then click the **Format Cells command** to display the dialog box in Figure 2.2f.

➤ Click the **Alignment tab**, then check the box to **Wrap text** in a cell. Click **OK** to accept the settings and close the dialog box.

➤ Click the **Center button** to center the text as well. Reduce the width of columns C and D. Save the workbook.

Bold button

Click and drag
to select A1:H1

Fill Color button

Font Color button

Press the Ctrl key
as you click and drag
to select A10:H10
and then A14:H14

Wrap text check box

(f) Complete the Formatting (step 6)

FIGURE 2.2   *Hands-on Exercise 1 (continued)*

SORT THE EMPLOYEE LIST

The employees are listed on the worksheet in alphabetical order, but you can rearrange the list according to any other field, such as the net pay. Click a cell containing employee data in the column on which you want to sort, then click the Sort Ascending or Sort Descending button on the Standard toolbar. Click the Undo button if the result is different from what you intended.

Step 7:   **The Completed Workbook**

> ➤ Click in cell **C11**. Pull down the **Insert menu** and click **Comment**, then insert the text of the comment as shown in Figure 2.2g. (The name that appears in the comment box will be different on your system.)
> ➤ Click in any other cell when you have finished inserting the comment. The text of the comment is no longer visible, but you should still see the tiny triangle. Now point to cell C11 and you see the text of the comment.
> ➤ Pull down the **File menu** and click the **Page Setup command** to display the Page Setup dialog box. Click the **Page tab**. Click the **Landscape** option **button**. Click the option to **Fit to 1 page**.
> ➤ Click the **Margins tab**. Check the box to center the worksheet horizontally. Click the **Sheet tab**. Check the boxes to print **Row and Column Headings** and **Gridlines**. Click **OK**. Print the worksheet.
> ➤ Press **Ctrl+~** to show the cell formulas rather than the displayed values. Adjust the column widths as necessary, then print the worksheet a second time.
> ➤ Save the workbook. Close the workbook. Exit Excel.

Print Preview button

Triangle appears to indicate a comment

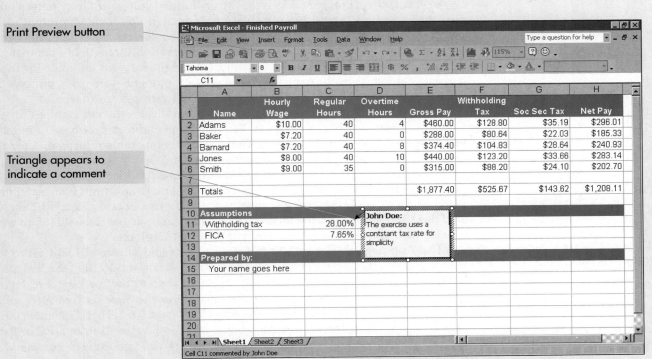

(g) The Completed Workbook (step 7)

FIGURE 2.2   *Hands-on Exercise 1 (continued)*

EDIT AND DELETE COMMENTS

Point to any cell that contains a comment, then click the right mouse button to display a context sensitive menu with commands to edit or delete a comment. (The menu also contains the option to show or hide the comment.) The name that appears within the comment box corresponds to the user name set during installation. Pull down the Tools menu, click the Option command, click the General tab, then go to the User Name area to modify this information.

The *Internet* is closely tied to Microsoft Excel 2002 through three basic capabilities. First, you can insert a *hyperlink* (a reference to another document) into any Excel worksheet, then view the associated document by clicking the link without having to start your Web browser manually. Second, you can save any Excel workbook as a *Web page* (or *HTML document*), which in turn can be displayed through a Web browser. And finally, you can download information from a Web server directly into an Excel workbook through a *Web query* (a capability that we illustrate later in the chapter).

Consider, for example, Figure 2.3a, which contains an Excel worksheet that displays a consolidated statement of earnings for a hypothetical company. The information in this worksheet is typical of what companies publish in their annual report, a document that summarizes the financial performance of a corporation. Every public corporation is required by law to publish this type of information so that investors may evaluate the strength of the company. The annual report is mailed to the shareholders and it is typically available online as well.

The worksheet in Figure 2.3a is easy to create, and you do not have to be a business major to understand the information. Indeed, if you have any intention of investing in the stock market, you should be able to analyze the data in the worksheet, which conveys basic information about the financial strength of a company to potential investors. In essence, the worksheet shows the sales for the company in the current year, subtracts the expenses to obtain the earnings before taxes, displays the income taxes that were paid, then arrives at the net earnings after taxes.

The worksheet also contains a calculation that divides the net earnings for the company by the number of shares to determine the earnings per share (a number that is viewed closely by investors). There is also comparable information for the previous year in order to show the increase or decrease for each item. And finally, the worksheet contains a hyperlink or reference to a specific Web site, such as the home page for the corporation. You can click the link from within Excel, and provided you have an Internet connection, your Web browser will display the associated page. Once you click the link, its color will change, just as it would if you were viewing the page in Netscape Navigator or Internet Explorer.

The Web page in Figure 2.3b is, for all intents and purposes, identical to the worksheet in Figure 2.3a. Look closely, however, and you will see that the Web page in Figure 2.3b is displayed in Internet Explorer, whereas the worksheet in Figure 2.3a is displayed in Microsoft Excel. Excel contains the *Save as Web Page command*, whereby a worksheet is converted to a Web page (or HTML document). The page can be uploaded to the Internet, but it can also be viewed from a PC or local area network, as was done in Figure 2.3b. Use the *Web Page Preview command* in the File menu to view the page, or open the page directly in your browser.

Our next exercise has you create the worksheet in Figure 2.3a, after which you create the HTML document in Figure 2.3b. All applications in Office XP incorporate a concept known as *round trip HTML*, which means that you can subsequently edit the Web page in the application that created it originally. In other words, you start with an Excel worksheet, save it as a Web page, then you can open the Web page and return to Excel in order to edit the document.

WHAT IS HTML?

Most Web documents are written in HTML (HyperText Markup Language), a universal standard that is recognized by both Internet Explorer and Netscape Navigator. The Address bar of a Web browser displays the document name and extension. The latter may appear as either html or htm, depending on how the Web document was created initially. The distinction is immaterial.

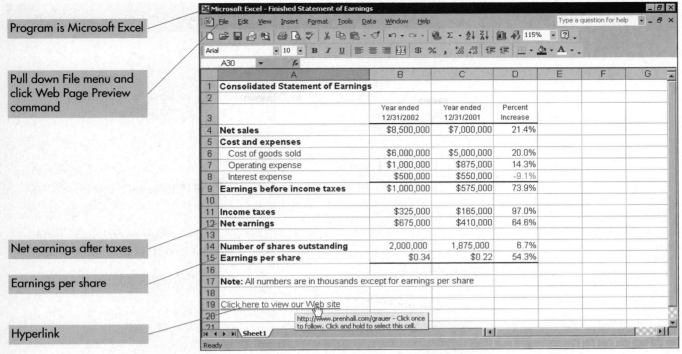

Program is Microsoft Excel

Pull down File menu and click Web Page Preview command

Net earnings after taxes

Earnings per share

Hyperlink

(a) Excel Worksheet

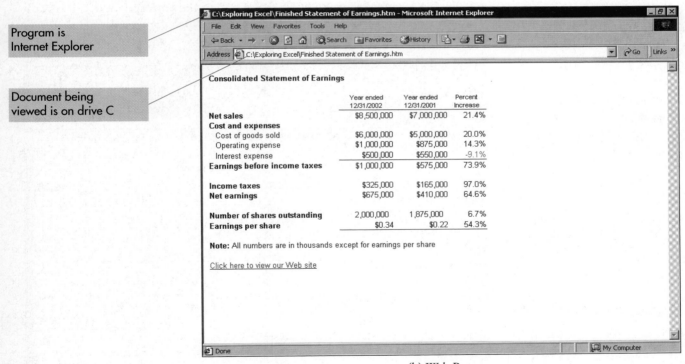

Program is Internet Explorer

Document being viewed is on drive C

(b) Web Page

FIGURE **2.3** *Consolidated Statement of Earnings*

CREATING A WEB PAGE

Objective   To insert a hyperlink into an Excel workbook; to save a workbook as an HTML document, then subsequently edit the Web page. Use Figure 2.4 as a guide in the exercise.

Step 1:   **Compute the Net Earnings**

> ➤ Open the **Statement of Earnings workbook** in the **Exploring Excel** folder. Save the workbook as **Finished Statement of Earnings** so that you can always go back to the original workbook if necessary.
>
> ➤ We have entered the labels and data for you, but you have to create the formulas. Click in cell **B9**. Type an **equal sign**, then click in cell **B4** to begin the pointing operation.
>
> ➤ Type a **minus sign**, type **SUM(**, then click and drag to select cells **B6 through B8** as shown in Figure 2.4a.
>
> ➤ Type a **closing parenthesis**, then press the **enter key** to complete the formula. You should see 1000000 as the displayed value in cell B4.
>
> ➤ Click in cell **B12**, then use pointing to enter the formula for net earnings, **=B9−B11**.
>
> ➤ Click in cell **B15**, then use pointing to enter the formula for earnings per share, **=B12/B14**.
>
> ➤ Copy the formulas in cells B9, B12, and B15 to the corresponding cells in column C. You have to copy the formulas one at a time.
>
> ➤ Save the workbook.

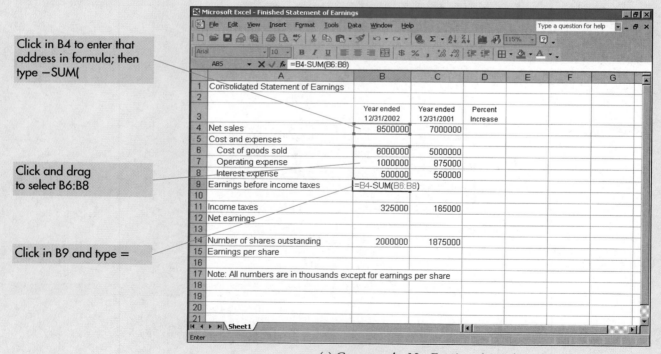

Click in B4 to enter that address in formula; then type −SUM(

Click and drag to select B6:B8

Click in B9 and type =

(a) Compute the Net Earnings (step 1)

FIGURE 2.4   *Hands-on Exercise 2*

Step 2: **Compute the Percent Increases**

➤ Click in cell **D4**, then enter the formula to compute the percent increase from the previous year. Use pointing to enter the formula, **=(B4-C4)/C4**.

➤ You should see .214288 as the displayed value in cell D4 as shown in Figure 2.4b. Do not worry about formatting at this time.

➤ Click in cell **D4**. Click the **Copy button** on the Standard toolbar (or use the **Ctrl+C** keyboard shortcut) to copy the contents of this cell to the clipboard. You should see a moving border around cell D4.

➤ Press and hold the **Ctrl key** to select cells **D6 through D9**, **D11 and D12**, and **D14 and D15** as shown in Figure 2.4b. (We have selected a noncontiguous range of cells, because we do not want to copy the formula to cells D10 or D13.)

➤ Click the **Paste button** on the Standard toolbar (or use the **Ctrl+V** keyboard shortcut) to paste the contents of cell D4 into these cells. Ignore the Paste Options button if it appears.

➤ Press the **Esc key** to remove the moving border around cell D4.

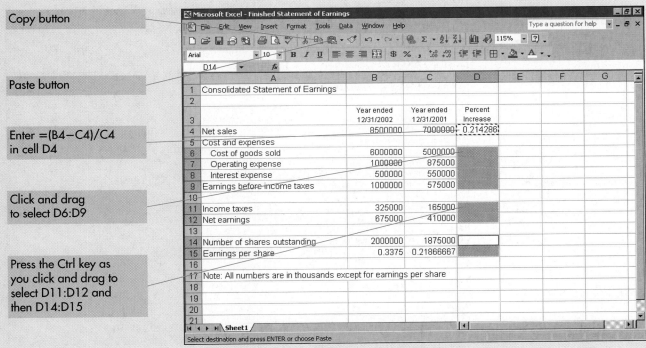

(b) Compute the Percent Increases (step 2)

FIGURE 2.4 *Hands-on Exercise 2 (continued)*

USE POINTING TO ENTER CELL FORMULAS

A cell reference can be typed directly into a formula, or it can be entered more easily through pointing. The latter is also more accurate as you use the mouse or arrow keys to reference cells directly. To use pointing, select (click) the cell to contain the formula, type an equal sign to begin entering the formula, click (or move to) the cell containing the reference, then press the F4 key as necessary to change from relative to absolute references. Type any arithmetic operator to place the cell reference in the formula, then continue pointing to additional cells. Press the enter key to complete the formula.

Step 3: **Format the Worksheet**

➤ Format the worksheet as shown in Figure 2.4c. Click in cell **A1**, then press and hold the **Ctrl key** to select cells **A4**, **A5**, **A9**, **A11**, **A12**, **A14**, **and A15**. Click the **Bold button** on the Formatting toolbar (or use the **Ctrl+B** keyboard shortcut).

➤ Double click in cell **A17**, then click and drag **Note:** within the cell to select this portion of the label. Press **Ctrl+B** to boldface the selected text.

➤ Remember that boldfacing the contents of a cell functions as a toggle switch; that is, click the Boldface button and the text is bold. Click the button a second time and the boldface is removed.

➤ Select cells **B3 through D3**, **B8 through D8**, and **B15 through D15** as shown in Figure 2.4c. Click the **down arrow** on the Borders button on the Formatting toolbar to display the available borders. Click the bottom border icon to implement this formatting in the selected cells.

➤ Complete the formatting in the remainder of the worksheet by using currency, comma, and percent formats as appropriate. Save the workbook.

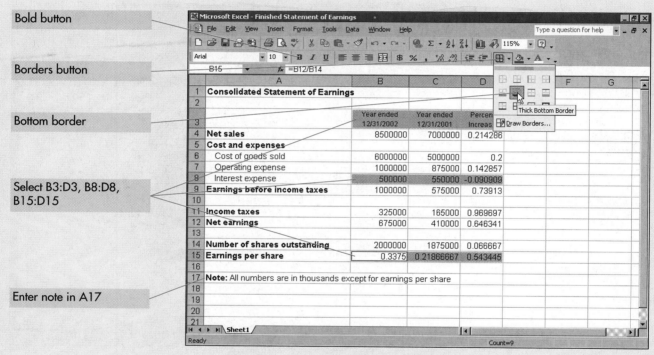

(c) Format the Worksheet (step 3)

FIGURE 2.4 *Hands-on Exercise 2 (continued)*

THE FORMAT PAINTER

The Format Painter copies the formatting of the selected cell to other cells in the worksheet. Click the cell whose formatting you want to copy, then double click the Format Painter button on the Standard toolbar. The mouse pointer changes to a paintbrush to indicate that you can copy the current formatting; just click and drag the paintbrush over the cells that you want to assume the formatting of the original cell. Repeat the painting process as often as necessary, then click the Format Painter button a second time to return to normal editing.

Step 4: **Conditional Formatting**

➤ Click and drag to select cells **D4 through D15**, the cells that contain the percentage increase from the previous year. Pull down the **Format menu** and click the **Conditional Formatting command** to display the Conditional Formatting dialog box.

➤ Check that the Condition 1 list box displays Cell Value Is. Click the **down arrow** in the relationship list box and choose **less than**. Press **Tab** to move to the next list box and enter a **zero** as shown in Figure 2.4d.

➤ Click the **Format button** to display the Format Cells dialog box. Click the **Font tab**, click the **down arrow** on the Color list box and choose **Red**. Click **OK** to close the Format Cells dialog box.

➤ Click **OK** to close the Conditional Formatting dialog box. The decrease in the interest expense should be displayed in red as −9.1%.

➤ Save the workbook.

Condition 1 displays
Cell Value Is

Click drop-down arrow
and select less than

Enter 0

Font tab

Click the Format button

Click drop-down arrow
and select Red

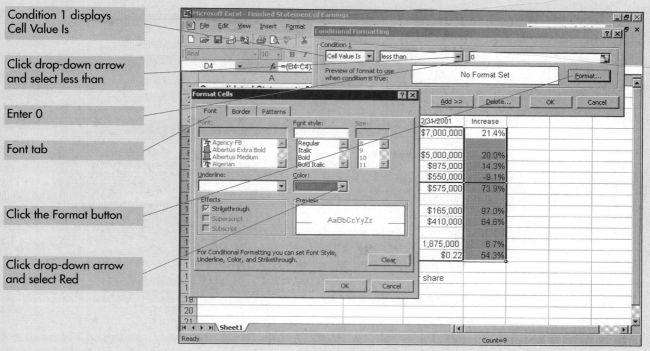

(d) Conditional Formatting (step 4)

FIGURE 2.4 *Hands-on Exercise 2 (continued)*

ADDING MULTIPLE CONDITIONS

Use the Conditional Formatting command to impose additional conditions with alternative formats depending on the value within a cell. You can, for example, display negative values in red (as was done in this example) and positive values (above a certain number) in blue. Pull down the Format menu and click the Conditional Formatting command, then click the Add button within the dialog box to add the additional conditions. Conditional formatting is a lesser-known feature that adds significantly to the appearance of a worksheet.

Step 5: **Insert the Hyperlink**

➤ Click in cell **A19**. Pull down the **Insert menu** and click the **Hyperlink command** (or click the **Insert Hyperlink button** on the Standard toolbar) to display the Insert Hyperlink dialog box in Figure 2.4e. Click in the **Text to display** text box and enter **Click here to view our Web site**.

➤ Click **Existing File or Web Page**, then click the button for **Browsed Pages**, then click in the Address text box (toward the bottom of the dialog box) and enter the Web address such as **www.prenhall.com/grauer** (the http:// is assumed). Click **OK** to accept the settings and close the dialog box.

➤ The hyperlink should appear as an underlined entry in the worksheet. Point to the hyperlink (the Web address should appear as a ScreenTip), then click the link to start your browser and view the Web page. You need an Internet connection to see the actual page.

➤ You are now running two applications, Excel and the Web browser, each of which has its own button on the Windows taskbar. Click the **Excel button** to continue working (and correct the hyperlink if necessary).

➤ Save the workbook.

Insert Hyperlink button

Enter text of hyperlink

Click Browsed Pages button

Enter Web address of site

Click in A19

(e) Insert the Hyperlink (step 5)

FIGURE 2.4 *Hands-on Exercise 2 (continued)*

SELECTING (EDITING) A HYPERLINK

In an ideal world, you will enter all the information for a hyperlink correctly on the first attempt. But what if you make a mistake and need to edit the information? You cannot select a hyperlink by clicking it, because that displays the associated Web page. You can, however, right click the cell containing the hyperlink to display a context-sensitive menu, then click the Edit Hyperlink command to display the associated dialog box in which to make the necessary changes.

Step 6: **Save the Web Page**

➤ Pull down the **File menu** and click the **Save as Web Page command** to display the Save As dialog box in Figure 2.4f. Note the following:

- The Exploring Excel folder is entered automatically as the default folder, since that is the location of the original workbook.
- Finished Statement of Earnings is entered automatically as the name of the Web page, corresponding to the name of the workbook, Finished Statement of Earnings.
- It does not matter whether you save the entire workbook or a single sheet, since the workbook contains only a single sheet. However, you need to specify a single sheet if and when you want to add interactivity (i.e., Excel functionality) when the page is opened through a Web browser.

➤ Click the **Save button**. There are now two versions of the workbook on disk, both with the same name (Finished Statement of Earnings), but with different extensions, html and xls, corresponding to a Web page and Excel workbook, respectively.

➤ Close Microsoft Excel. (We will restart the application later in the exercise.)

Exploring Excel folder is default folder

Options for Entire Workbook or Selected Sheet

File name corresponds to name of workbook

Save button

(f) Save the Web Page (step 6)

FIGURE 2.4 *Hands-on Exercise 2 (continued)*

CHANGE THE DEFAULT FILE LOCATION

The default file location is the folder Excel uses to open and save a workbook unless it is otherwise instructed. To change the default location, pull down the Tools menu, click Options, and click the General tab. Enter the name of the new folder (e.g., C:\Exploring Excel) in the Default File Location text box, then click OK. The next time you access the Open or Save command from the File menu, the Look In text box will reflect the change.

Step 7: **Start Windows Explorer**

> Click the **Start button**, start **Windows Explorer**, then change to the Exploring Excel folder. The location of this folder depends on whether you have your own computer.
>   • If you are working from a floppy disk, select drive A in the left pane.
>   • If you are working on your own computer, select drive C in the left pane, then scroll until you can select the Exploring Excel folder.
> Either way, you should see the contents of the Exploring Excel folder in the right pane as shown in Figure 2.4g. As indicated, there are two versions of the Finished Statement of Earnings, with different icons and file types.
> Right click the file with the Excel icon and file type to display a shortcut menu, then click the **Delete command** to delete this file. You do not need the Excel workbook any longer because you can edit the workbook from the Web page through the concept of round trip HTML.
> Double click the Web page version of the earnings statement to view the document in your default browser.

Double click Web Page version of Finished Statement of Earnings

Select the Exploring Excel folder

Right click the Excel version of Finished Statement of Earnings

Click Delete

(g) Start Windows Explorer (step 7)

FIGURE 2.4   *Hands-on Exercise 2 (continued)*

ROUND TRIP HTML

Each application in Microsoft Office XP lets you open an HTML document in both Internet Explorer and the application that created the Web page initially. In other words, you can start with an Excel worksheet and use the Save as Web Page command to convert the document to a Web page, then view that page in a Web browser. You can then reopen the Web page in Excel (the application that created it initially) with full access to all Excel commands in order to edit the document.

Step 8: **View the Web Page**

➤ You should see the Finished Statement of Earnings displayed within Internet Explorer (or Netscape Navigator) as shown in Figure 2.4h. The Web page looks identical to the worksheet that was displayed earlier in Excel.

➤ Click the hyperlink to view the Web site that was inserted through the Insert Hyperlink command. You should see our Web site (**www.prenhall.com/grauer**) if that was the address you used earlier.

➤ Click the **Back button** on the Standard Buttons toolbar to return to the Finished Earnings Web page. Look carefully at the Address bar and note that unlike other Web documents, this page is displayed from your local system (drive C or drive A), depending on the location of the file.

➤ Click the **Edit with Microsoft Excel button** on the Standard Buttons toolbar to start Excel in order to modify the Web page.

➤ Both applications, Internet Explorer and Microsoft Excel, are open as can be seen by the taskbar, which contains buttons for both.

Program is Internet Explorer

Back button

Address bar indicates page is on local hard drive

Edit with Microsoft Excel button

Click hyperlink

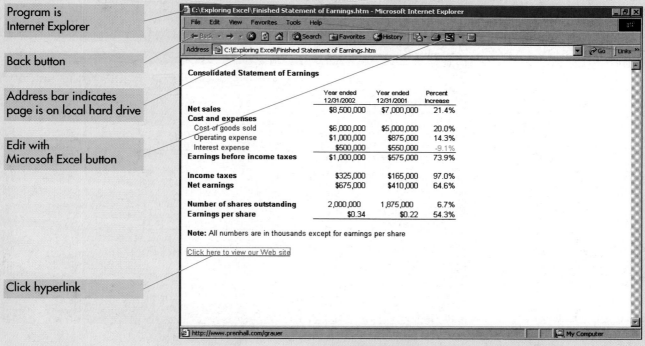

(h) View the Web Page (step 8)

FIGURE 2.4   *Hands-on Exercise 2 (continued)*

MULTITASKING

Multitasking, the ability to run multiple applications at the same time, is one of the primary advantages of the Windows environment. Minimizing an application is different from closing it, and you want to minimize, rather than close, an application to take advantage of multitasking. Closing an application removes it from memory so that you have to restart the application if you want to return to it later in the session. Minimizing, however, leaves the application open in memory, but shrinks its window to a button on the Windows taskbar.

Step 9:   **Edit the Web Page**

➤ You should be back in Microsoft Excel as shown in Figure 2.4i. Click in cell **A21** and enter the label, **Prepared by**, followed by your name.

➤ Save the worksheet.

➤ Click the **Internet Explorer button** on the toolbar to return to your browser. The change you made (the addition of your name) is not yet visible because the browser displays the previous version of the page.

➤ Click the **Refresh button** on the Standard Buttons toolbar to bring in the most current version of the worksheet. Your changes should now be visible.

➤ Pull down the **File menu** (within Internet Explorer) and click the **Print command**, then click the **Print command button** to print the Web page for your instructor.

➤ Close Internet Explorer. Exit Excel if you do not wish to continue with the next exercise at this time.

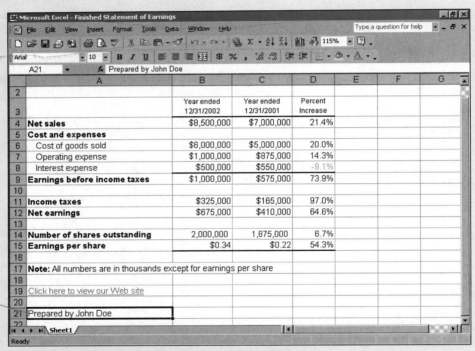

Enter text in A21

(i) Edit the Web Page (step 9)

FIGURE 2.4   *Hands-on Exercise 2 (continued)*

USE A TEMPLATE

A template is a partially completed workbook that is used to create other workbooks. It typically contains formulas and formatting but no specific data. Thus you open a template and enter the information that is specific to your application, then you save the template as an ordinary workbook. Excel provides several business templates. See practice exercise 11 at the end of the chapter.

Our next example is a worksheet to maintain a stock portfolio and compute the gain or loss associated with investment. The worksheet in Figure 2.5 lists several stocks, each with its recognized symbol, and records the purchase price, number of shares, and date of purchase of each investment. This information is "fixed" for each stock at the time of purchase. The worksheet then uses the current (today's) price to determine the gain or loss. It also uses today's date to compute the length of time the investment was held. The interesting thing about the worksheet is that the current price is entered into the worksheet via a Web query, a capability that enables Excel to go to a specific site on the Web to retrieve the information.

The top half of the worksheet is typical of the worksheets we have studied thus far. The bottom portion (from row 14 down) represents the result of the Web query, which is entered into the worksheet via the ***Import External Data command***. Execution of this command prompts you for the location of the result (e.g., cell A14 in Figure 2.5) and the location of the parameters (or stock symbols), for which you want to determine the price (cells A5 through A10 in this example). Excel does the rest and places the results of the query into the worksheet. The results of the query can be continually updated through the ***Refresh command***, which is represented by the exclamation point button on the ***External Data toolbar***.

The worksheet in Figure 2.5 also illustrates the use of ***date arithmetic*** to determine the length of time an investment is held. (This is an important consideration for investors who can reduce their tax liability through a capital gains tax break on investments held for more than one year.) Date arithmetic is made possible through a simple concept by which Excel stores all dates as integers (serial numbers) beginning with January 1, 1900. Thus, January 1, 1900 is stored as the number 1, January 2, 1900 as the number 2, and so on. December 27, 1999 (the purchase date of DIS) is stored as 36521 as can be seen by comparing the contents of cell B5 in Figures 2.5a and 2.5b, respectively.

Current date is displayed

Date is 12/27/99

Stock symbols

Results of Web query

(a) The Excel Worksheet

FIGURE 2.5 *Web Queries*

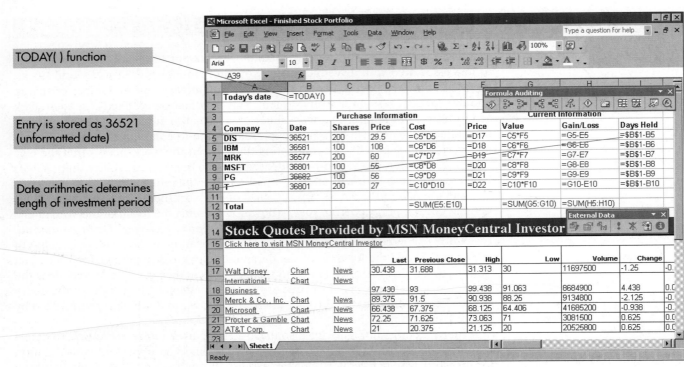

Labels pointing to the figure:

- TODAY( ) function
- Entry is stored as 36521 (unformatted date)
- Date arithmetic determines length of investment period

(b) Cell Formulas

FIGURE 2.5   Web Queries (continued)

The ***Today( ) function*** returns the current date (i.e., the date on which the spreadsheet is opened). If, for example, you entered the Today( ) function into a spreadsheet that was created on May 14, and you opened the spreadsheet a month later, the value of the function would be automatically updated to June 14. The fact that dates are stored as integers enables you to add or subtract two different dates and/or to use a date in any type of arithmetic computation. A person's age can be computed by subtracting the date of birth from today's date, and dividing the result by 365.

In similar fashion, you can subtract the purchase date of an investment from today's date to determine the number of days the investment was held. Look now at the formula in cell I5 of Figure 2.5b, which subtracts the date of purchase (cell B5) from an absolute reference to today's date (cell B1) to compute the length of the investment. The formula in cell I5 (=$B$1 − B5) can then be copied to the remaining rows in column I to determine the length of each investment.

A date is entered in different ways, most easily by typing the date in conventional fashion such as 12/31/99 or 12/31/1999. If you specify a two-digit year, then any year from 00 to 29, is assumed to be in the 21st century; for example, 1/21/00, will be stored as January 21, 2000. (The number 29 is arbitrary and you will have to ask Microsoft why it was chosen.) Any year between 30 and 99 is stored as a date in the 20th century. Thus, 3/23/48 would be stored as March 23, 1948. To avoid confusion, you should enter all four digits of the year—for example, 10/31/2001 for October 31, 2001.

YOU MUST UNDERSTAND THE PROBLEM

The formulas to compute the cost of an investment, its current value, the associated gain or loss, and the number of days the investment was held have nothing to do with Excel per se. Neither did the formulas to compute the gross pay, net pay, and so on in the payroll example. In other words, Excel is a means to an end, rather than an end unto itself, and you must understand the underlying problem if you are to use Excel successfully.

WEB QUERIES

Objective Include a Web query into a worksheet to retrieve current stock prices from the Internet. (The exercise requires an Internet connection.) Use the Today( ) function to illustrate the use of date arithmetic. Use Figure 2.6 as a guide in the exercise.

Step 1: **Open the Stock Portfolio**

➤ Open the **Stock Portfolio workbook** in the **Exploring Excel folder** to display the worksheet in Figure 2.6a.

➤ Save the workbook as **Finished Stock Portfolio** so that you can return to the original workbook if necessary.

➤ Cell **B1** displays today's date 11/13/2000 in our figure, but a different date on your machine. If necessary, click in cell **B1**, and note that it contains the function, =**Today( )**. Thus the displayed value in cell B1 will always reflect the current date.

➤ Click in cell **B5**, the cell containing the date on which the shares in DIS were purchased. The contents of cell B5 are 12/27/1999 (there is no equal sign). This is a "fixed" date and its value will not change from one day to the next.

➤ Pull down the **Data menu**, click **the Import External Data command**, then choose **Import Data command** to display the Select Data Source dialog box in Figure 2.6a.

➤ Choose the **MSN MoneyCentral Investor Stock Quotes** query, then click the **Open button**.

B5 is a fixed date

B1 displays current date (=TODAY( ) function)

Click in B5

Click MSN MoneyCentral Investor Stock Quotes

(a) Open the Stock Portfolio (step 1)

FIGURE 2.6 *Hands-on Exercise 3*

Step 2: **Complete the Web Query**

➤ The Import Data dialog box opens and prompts you for information about the Web query. Click the option button to put the data into the existing worksheet, then click in cell **A14** to indicate the location within the current worksheet. Click **OK**.

➤ Click and drag to select cells A5 through A10, as the cells containing the stock symbols as shown in Figure 2.6b. Check the box to use this value reference for future refreshes. Click **OK**.

➤ Your system will pause as Excel goes to the Web to retrieve the information, provided you have an Internet connection. You should then see the stock quotes provided by MSN Money Central Investor.

➤ Do not be concerned if the column widths change as a result of the query. (You can widen them later.)

➤ Save the workbook.

Cells A5:A10 contain stock symbols

Check box to use this value/reference for future refreshes

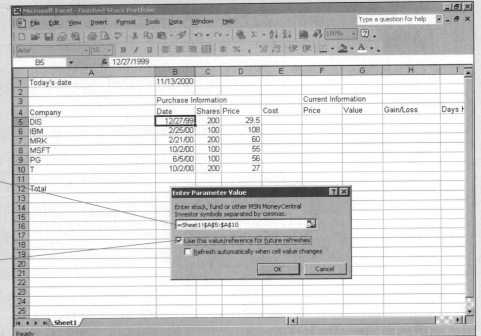

(b) Complete the Web Query (step 2)

FIGURE 2.6 *Hands-on Exercise 3 (continued)*

CREATE A NEW WEB QUERY

Web queries were available in both Office 97 and Office 2000, but were limited in that you had to use existing queries. Office XP, however, makes it easy to create new queries from virtually any Web page. Pull down the Data menu, click the Import External Data command, then click New Web query to display the associated dialog box. Enter the address of any Web page (try your favorite professional sport) that contains the data you want, then look for the yellow arrows that indicate the data may be imported. See practice exercise 10 at the end of the chapter.

Step 3: **Compute the Gain/Loss**

➤ You should see the information that was obtained via the Web query as shown in Figure 2.6c. Use pointing to enter the cell references to complete the formulas for the first investment.
- Click in cell **E5** (the cell that contains the cost of the investment) and enter the formula, **=C5*D5**.
- Click in cell **F5** (the cell that contains today's price), and enter the formula **=D17**, which references the cell that contains the current price of DIS.
- Click in cell **G5** (the cell that contains today's value of the investment) and enter the formula, **=C5*F5**.
- Click in cell **H5** (the cell that contains the gain or loss) and enter the formula, **=G5−E5**, corresponding to today's value minus the cost.
- Click in cell **I5** (the cell that contains the days held) and enter the formula, **=$B$1−B5**.

➤ If necessary, change the format in cell I5 to reflect a number, rather than a date. Click in cell **I5**, pull down the **Format menu**, click the **Cells command**, click the **Number tab**, choose **Number** as the category, and specify **zero decimal places**.

➤ Save the workbook.

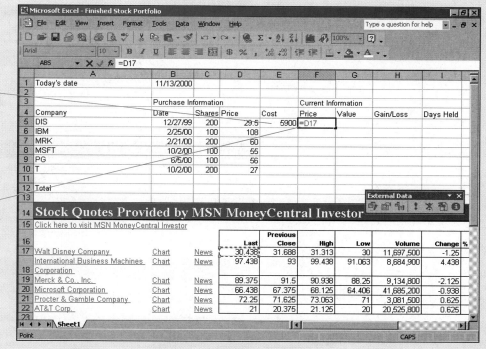

Enter =C5*D5 in cell E5

Enter =D17 in F5

(c) Compute the Gain/Loss (step 3)

FIGURE 2.6 *Hands-on Exercise 3 (continued)*

NUMBERS, DATES, AND FORMATS

Any cell that contains a numeric value may be formatted in a variety of styles such as date, number, percentage, currency, and so on. Excel does not know which format to use, and thus it is up to the user to select the cell, pull down the Format menu, click the Cells command to display the Format cells dialog box, click the Number tab, then choose the appropriate category.

Step 4: **Copy the Formulas**

➤ Click and drag to select cells **E5 through I5**, the cells containing the formulas associated with the first investment, as shown in Figure 2.6d.

➤ Point to the fill handle in the lower-right corner of cell I5, then click and drag the fill handle to copy the formulas in row 5 to rows 6 through 10. Release the mouse to complete the copy operation.

➤ Click in cell **E12**, the cell that contains the total cost of your investments. Type **=SUM(** then click and drag to select cells **E5:E10**.

➤ Type a **closing parenthesis**, then press the **enter key**. Cell E12 should contain the formula **=SUM(E5:E10)**.

➤ Copy the formula in cell **E12** to cells **G12 and H12**. The displayed value in cell E12 should be 45200. The displayed values in cells G12 and H12 depend on the current stock prices.

➤ Save the workbook.

Click and drag to select E5:I5

Click and drag the fill handle to I10

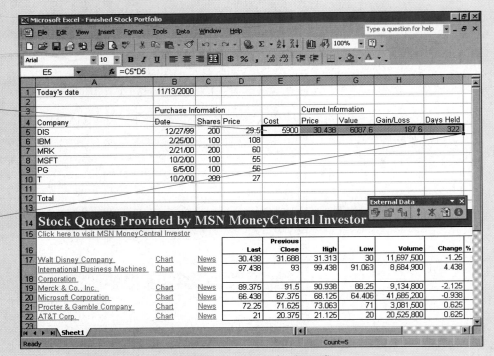

(d) Copy the Formulas (step 4)

FIGURE 2.6   *Hands-on Exercise 3 (continued)*

EDITING A CELL FORMULA

The fastest way to change the contents of a cell is to double click in the cell (or press the F2 key), then make the changes directly in the cell rather than to change the entries on the formula bar. Note, too, that if the cell contains a formula (as opposed to a literal entry), Excel will display each cell reference in the formula in a different color, which corresponds to border colors of the referenced cells elsewhere in the worksheet. This makes it easy to see which cell or cell range is referenced by the formula.

Step 5: **Format the Worksheet**

➤ Click and drag to select cells **D5 through H12**, the cells that contain dollar amounts. Pull down the **Format menu**, click the **Cells command** to display the Format Cells dialog box, then click the **Number tab**. Format these cells in **Currency format**, with **two decimal places**. Display negative values in **red** and enclosed in **parentheses**. Click **OK**.

➤ Select all of the cells that contain a label (cell **A1**, cells **A3 through I4**, **A4 through A10**, and cell **A12**). Click the **Bold button** to boldface this information.

➤ Click and drag to select cells **B3 through E3**, then click the **Merge and Center button**. Merge cells **F3 through I3** in similar fashion.

➤ Click and drag to select cells E3 through E12. Click the **down arrow** on the Borders button on the Formatting toolbar, then click the **right border icon** as shown in Figure 2.6e. Click cell A1 (to deselect these cells). You should see a vertical line separating the purchase information from the current values.

➤ Adjust the column widths if necessary. Save the workbook.

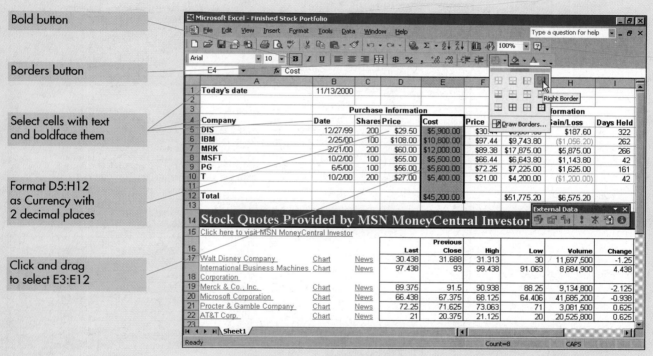

Bold button

Borders button

Select cells with text and boldface them

Format D5:H12 as Currency with 2 decimal places

Click and drag to select E3:E12

(e) Format the Worksheet (step 5)

FIGURE 2.6 *Hands-on Exercise 3 (continued)*

CAPITAL GAINS AND CONDITIONAL FORMATTING

The Internal Revenue Service offers a significant tax break on stock trans-actions that are considered a "long term" capital gain (more than one year under today's tax code). Click and drag to select cells I5 through I11, the cells that show how long a stock has been held. Pull down the Format menu, click the Conditional Formatting command, then enter the condition as cell value is > 365. Click the Format button, click the Font tab, then choose a different color (e.g., blue) to highlight those investments that qualify for this consideration.

Step 6:   **Refresh the Query**

➤ Right click anywhere within the Web query (i.e., within cells A14 to I22) to display the context-sensitive menu in Figure 2.6f. Click the **Refresh Data command** to retrieve the current prices from the Web.

➤ The numbers in your worksheet will change provided you have an Internet connection and the stock market is open. The column widths may also change since the Web query automatically adjusts the width of its columns (see boxed tip). Adjust the column widths if necessary.

➤ Save the workbook a final time. Print the workbook twice, once to show the displayed values, and once to show the cell contents.

➤ Now that you have completed this exercise, you can experiment further with the various links within the Web query. Scroll to the bottom of the query, for example, then click the link for Symbol Lookup to find the symbol for your favorite stock or index.

➤ Good luck with your stock portfolio, and congratulations on a job well done.

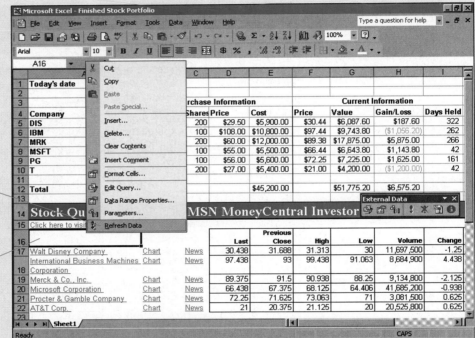

(f) Refresh the Query (step 6)

FIGURE 2.6   *Hands-on Exercise 3 (continued)*

DATA RANGE PROPERTIES

The Web query associated with MSN Stock quotes will, by default, change the column widths in the entire worksheet each time the query is refreshed. You can prevent this from happening by right clicking in the query area, then clicking the Data Range Properties command to display the associated dialog box. Clear the check box to adjust column width, then click OK to accept the settings and close the dialog box. The next time you refresh the query, the column widths will not change.

The distinction between relative, absolute, and mixed references, coupled with the importance of isolating the assumptions on which a worksheet is based, is a basic concept in spreadsheet design. A relative reference (such as A1) changes both the row and column, when the cell containing the reference is copied to other cells in the worksheet. An absolute reference (such as $A$1) remains constant throughout the copy operation. A mixed reference, either $A1 or A$1, modifies the row or column, respectively. Most spreadsheets can be built through combinations of relative and absolute addresses. Mixed references are required for more advanced spreadsheets.

The initial conditions and/or assumptions on which a spreadsheet is based should be isolated so that their values can be easily changed. The formulas in the main body of the spreadsheet typically contain absolute references to these assumptions. The placement of the assumptions and initial conditions is not a requirement of Excel per se, but is crucial to the development of accurate and flexible worksheets. The Insert Comment command creates the equivalent of a screen tip that displays information about the worksheet.

Pointing and the fill handle are two techniques that facilitate the development of a spreadsheet. Although any cell reference can be entered into a formula by typing the reference directly, it is easier and more accurate to enter the reference through pointing. In essence you click in the cell that contains the formula, type an equal sign to begin the formula, then use the mouse (or arrow keys) to enter the various cell references as you build the formula. The fill handle, a tiny black square in the lower-right corner of the selected cell(s), is the easiest way to copy a cell formula to adjacent cells. Just select the cell or cells to be copied, point to the fill handle for the selected cell(s), click and drag the fill handle over the destination range, and release the mouse.

The Internet is built into Microsoft Excel through three basic capabilities. First, a hyperlink can be inserted into any Excel worksheet, then the associated page viewed by clicking the link, without having to start the Web browser manually. Second, any worksheet or workbook can be saved as a Web page (or HTML document), which in turn can be stored on a Web server and displayed through a Web browser. And finally, information from the Web can be downloaded and inserted directly into an Excel workbook through a Web query.

Dates are entered into a worksheet by typing the date in conventional fashion such as 11/24/2000 or December 24, 2000. Either way all dates are stored as integers, beginning with January 1, 1900; that is January 1, 1900 is stored as the number 1. This simple concept enables date arithmetic, whereby calculations can be made between two dates to determine the number of days that have elapsed. The Today( ) function always returns the current date and is used in conjunction with date arithmetic.

KEY TERMS

Absolute reference (p. 66)
Conditional formatting (p. 81)
Date arithmetic (p. 87)
External Data toolbar (p. 87)
Fill handle (p. 68)
HTML document (p. 76)
Hyperlink (p. 76)

Import External Data command (p. 87)
Insert Comment command (p. 68)
Insert Hyperlink command (p. 82)
Internet (p. 76)
Pointing (p. 68)
Refresh command (p. 87)

Relative reference (p. 66)
Round trip HTML (p. 76)
Save as Web Page command (p. 76)
Template (p. 86)
Today( ) function (p. 88)
Web page (p. 76)
Web query (p. 76)

1. The formula to compute the gross pay of an employee in the payroll example that was developed in this chapter uses:
   (a) Absolute references for hourly wage, regular hours, and overtime hours
   (b) Relative references for hourly wage, regular hours, and overtime hours
   (c) Mixed references for hourly wage, regular hours, and overtime hours
   (d) Impossible to determine

2. Which of the following best describes the formula to compute the withholding tax of an employee in the payroll example that was developed in this chapter?
   (a) It contains a relative reference to the gross pay and an absolute reference to the withholding tax rate
   (b) It contains an absolute reference to the gross pay and a relative reference to the withholding tax rate
   (c) It contains absolute references to both the gross pay and withholding tax
   (d) It contains relative references to both the gross pay and withholding tax

3. Cell D12 contains the formula, =SUM (A12:C12). What will the contents of cell D13 be, if the formula in cell D12 is copied to cell D13?
   (a) =SUM (A12:C12)
   (b) =SUM (A13:C13)
   (c) =SUM (A12:C13)
   (d) =SUM (A13:C12)

4. A formula containing the entry =$B$3 is copied to a cell one column over and two rows down. How will the entry appear in its new location?
   (a) =$C$5
   (b) =$B$3
   (c) =B3
   (d) =C5

5. How do you insert a hyperlink into an Excel workbook?
   (a) Pull down the Insert menu and click the Hyperlink command
   (b) Click the Insert Hyperlink button on the Standard toolbar
   (c) Right click a cell and click the Hyperlink command
   (d) Any of the above

6. A Web browser such as Internet Explorer can display a page from:
   (a) A local drive such as drive A or drive C
   (b) A drive on a local area network
   (c) The World Wide Web
   (d) All of the above

7. What is the best way to enter the current price of a stock into an Excel worksheet?
   (a) Copy the price directly from today's copy of *The Wall Street Journal*
   (b) Save the worksheet as a Web page or HTML document
   (c) Create a Web query, then refresh the query to obtain the current price
   (d) Use Internet Explorer to locate a Web page that contains the current price

8. The estimated sales for the first year of a financial forecast are contained in cell B3. The sales for year two are assumed to be 10% higher than the first year, with the rate of increase (10%) stored in cell C23 at the bottom of the spreadsheet. Which of the following is the best way to enter the sales for year two?
   (a) =B3+B3*.10
   (b) =B3+B3*C23
   (c) =B3+B3*$C$23
   (d) All of the above are equivalent entries

9. Which of the following requires an Internet connection?
  (a) Using Internet Explorer to view a Web page that is stored locally
  (b) Updating the values that are obtained through a Web query
  (c) Clicking a hyperlink that references a document that is stored on drive C
  (d) All of the above

10. Which of the following best describes a formula to compute the sales in the second year, given that the second year is dependent on the sales of the first year, and that the rate of increase from one year to the next is a fixed percentage?
  (a) It contains a relative reference to the assumed rate of increase and an absolute reference to the sales from the previous year
  (b) It contains an absolute reference to the assumed rate of increase and a relative reference to the sales from the previous year
  (c) It contains absolute references to both the assumed rate of increase and the sales from the previous year
  (d) It contains relative references to both the assumed rate of increase and the sales from the previous year

11. What will be stored in a cell if 2/5 is entered in it?
  (a) 2/5
  (b) .4
  (c) The date value February 5 of the current year
  (d) 2/5 or .4 depending on the format in effect

12. You type 11/24/00 into a cell, press the enter key, and expect to see Nov 24, 2000. Instead you see the value 36854. Which of the following is a likely explanation?
  (a) Something is radically wrong with the date functions
  (b) The cell is formatted to display a numeric value rather than a date
  (c) You should have used an equal sign to enter the date
  (d) None of the above makes any sense at all

13. Which of the following formulas can be used to compute an individual's age, given that the individual's birth date is stored in cell A4?
  (a) =(Today( )−A4)/365
  (b) =(Today−A4)/365
  (c) =(A4−Today)/365
  (d) =(A4−Today( ))/365

14. Microsoft Excel and Internet Explorer are both open and display the "same" worksheet. You make a change in the Excel file that is not reflected in the Web page. What is the most likely explanation?
  (a) The two files are not linked to one another
  (b) The files are stored locally as opposed to a Web server
  (c) You did not refresh the Web page in Microsoft Excel
  (d) You did not refresh the Web page in Internet Explorer

15. You notice that the values in a specific column are displayed in three different colors, red for values less than zero, blue for values greater than $100,000, and black otherwise. How is this possible?
  (a) The colored formatting is automatically built into every Excel worksheet
  (b) A Web query was used to implement the red and blue formatting
  (c) Conditional formatting was applied to the column
  (d) It is not possible; that is, the question is in error

ANSWERS

1. b	**5.** d	**9.** b	**13.** a
2. a	**6.** d	**10.** b	**14.** d
3. b	**7.** c	**11.** c	**15.** c
4. b	**8.** c	**12.** b	

1. Alternate Payroll: Figure 2.7 contains an alternate version of the payroll that was created in the first hands-on exercise in the chapter. The revised spreadsheet includes the number of dependents for each employee and a fixed deduction per dependent, which combine to reduce an individual's taxable income. The revised spreadsheet also isolates the overtime rate, making it possible to change the overtime rate in a single place should that become necessary.

   a. Open the *Chapter 2 Practice 1* workbook, then complete the spreadsheet `so that it matches ours. Substitute your name for the employee named "Grauer," then sort the worksheet so that the employees appear in alphabetical order. (Click anywhere within column A and click the Sort Ascending button on the Standard toolbar. There must be a blank row above the total row, or else it will be sorted with the other rows.) Highlight the row containing your name.

   b. Print the completed worksheet twice, once with displayed values, and once to show the cell formulas. Use the Page Setup command for the cell formulas to switch to landscape printing and force the output onto one page. Print gridlines and row and column headings. Change the column headings as appropriate. Add a cover sheet, then submit all three pages (cover sheet, displayed values, and cell formulas) to your instructor as proof you did this exercise.

FIGURE 2.7 *Alternate Payroll (Exercise 1)*

2. The Sports Statistician: Figure 2.8 illustrates how Excel can be used to tabulate statistics for a hypothetical softball league. Open the worksheet in the *Chapter 2 Practice 2* workbook, then complete the worksheet as follows:

   a. An individual batting average is computed by dividing the number of hits by the number of at bats (e.g., 30/80 or .375 for Maryann Barber). The batting average should be formatted to three decimal places. (Create the Custom format .000 to eliminate the 0 before the batting average to display .375, rather than the default numerical format of 0.000.)

b. The total bases for an individual is computed by multiplying the number of singles by one, the number of doubles by two, the number of triples by three, and the number of home runs by four, then adding the results.

c. The slugging percentage is computed by dividing the total bases by the number of at bats (e.g., 48/80 or .600 for Maryann Barber). The slugging average should be formatted to three decimal places.

d. The team totals for all columns except batting average and slugging percentage are determined by summing the appropriate values. The team batting average and slugging percentage are computed by dividing the number of hits and total bases, respectively, by the number of at bats.

e. Substitute your name for Jessica Grauer (our league is coed), sort the players in alphabetical order.

f. Format the worksheet so that it matches Figure 2.8. Be sure that your name is highlighted, rather than Jessica's.

g. Add an appropriate clip art image somewhere in the worksheet using the same technique as in any other Office application. Pull down the Insert menu, click (or point to) Picture, then click Clip Art. The task pane opens and displays the Media Gallery Search pane. Click in the Search text box. Enter "baseball" to search for any clip art image that is described with this key word and click the Go button. The images are displayed in the Results box.

h. Select (click) an image to display a drop-down arrow to its right. Click the arrow to display a context menu. Click Insert to insert the image into the document. Close the task pane. Click and drag a sizing handle to make the image smaller, then click and drag to move the image as necessary.

i. Print the completed worksheet twice, once with displayed values, and once to show the cell formulas. Use the Page Setup command for the cell formulas to switch to landscape printing and force the output onto one page. Print gridlines and row and column headings.

j. Add a cover sheet, then submit all three pages (cover sheet, displayed values, and cell formulas) to your instructor.

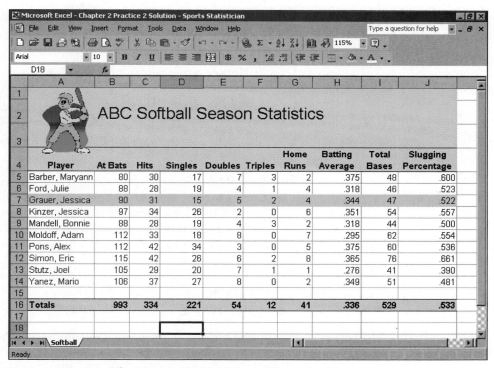

FIGURE 2.8   *The Sports Statistician (Exercise 2)*

3. Web Pages and Hyperlinks: Open the *Chapter 2 Practice 3* workbook as the basis for the Web page in Figure 2.9. Complete the worksheet as follows:

a. Compute the total points for each player by multiplying the number of free throws, 2-point field goals, and 3-point field goals by 1, 2, and 3, respectively.

b. Compute the points per game for each player by dividing the total points by the number of games. Display the result to one decimal point. Compute the rebounds per game in similar fashion.

c. Add clip art as you see fit. We used the same image twice to bracket the title of the worksheet. Format your page to match ours.

d. Add your name at the bottom of the worksheet. Instead of merely typing your name, however, add your name as a hyperlink that points to your home page if you have one. If you do not have a home page, use any Web address, such as www.nba.com for the National Basketball Association.

e. Save the workbook as a Web page, then open the workbook in Internet Explorer or Netscape Navigator. Print the Web page from your Web browser.

FIGURE 2.9 *Web Pages and Hyperlinks (Exercise 3)*

4. Wishful Thinking CD Portfolio: It must be nice to have a portfolio of CDs (Certificates of Deposit) where all you do is collect the interest as shown in Figure 2.10. Open the partially completed worksheet, which is found in the *Chapter 2 Practice 4* workbook, then complete the worksheet as follows.

a. The maturity date is computed by adding the term (converted to days) to the purchase date.

b. The days until maturity is determined by subtracting today's date from the maturity date.

c. The annual income is determined by multiplying the amount of the CD times its interest rate.

d. The estimated tax is found by multiplying the annual income by the tax rate.

e. The net income is the annual income minus the estimated tax.

f. Format the completed worksheet to match Figure 2.10.

g. Add your name in cell A19. Print the worksheet twice, once with displayed values, and once to show the cell formulas.

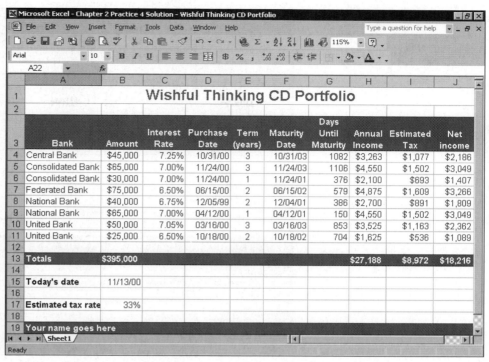

						Days			
Bank	Amount	Interest Rate	Purchase Date	Term (years)	Maturity Date	Until Maturity	Annual Income	Estimated Tax	Net income
Central Bank	$45,000	7.25%	10/31/00	3	10/31/03	1082	$3,263	$1,077	$2,186
Consolidated Bank	$65,000	7.00%	11/24/00	3	11/24/03	1106	$4,550	$1,502	$3,049
Consolidated Bank	$30,000	7.00%	11/24/00	1	11/24/01	376	$2,100	$693	$1,407
Federated Bank	$75,000	6.50%	06/15/00	2	06/15/02	579	$4,875	$1,609	$3,266
National Bank	$40,000	6.75%	12/05/99	2	12/04/01	386	$2,700	$891	$1,809
National Bank	$65,000	7.00%	04/12/00	1	04/12/01	150	$4,550	$1,502	$3,049
United Bank	$50,000	7.05%	03/16/00	3	03/16/03	853	$3,525	$1,163	$2,362
United Bank	$25,000	6.50%	10/18/00	2	10/18/02	704	$1,625	$536	$1,089
Totals	$395,000						$27,188	$8,972	$18,216
Today's date	11/13/00								
Estimated tax rate	33%								
Your name goes here									

FIGURE 2.10 *Wishful Thinking CD Portfolio (Exercise 4)*

5. Web Queries for Currency Conversion: Excel includes a Web query to determine the exchange rates for popular currencies as can be seen in Figure 2.11. The worksheet contains formulas for two parallel sets of conversions, from British pounds to dollars, and from dollars to British pounds. Open the partially completed workbook in *Chapter 2 Practice 5,* then proceed as follows:

a. Use the Import External Data command to enter the Web query (MS MoneyCentral Investor Currency Rates) into the worksheet. Click in cell B11 and enter the appropriate cell reference within the query (cell B24 in our example, which is not visible in Figure 2.11) to obtain the current value of the conversion factor. Use the value in cell B11 to convert the amounts in British pounds to the equivalent dollar amounts. Note that Microsoft is continually changing the format of its queries to include different currencies, so you may have to enter a different cell.

b. Click in cell E11 and enter the conversion factor to convert dollars to pounds. (This is the reciprocal of the value in cell B11.) Complete the entries in column E, which convert dollars to the equivalent amount in British pounds.

c. Format the worksheet to match Figure 2.11. Be sure to use the appropriate currency symbols for dollars and pounds. Add your name and today's date as shown.

d. Click the tab for the Euro (European Currency) worksheet and enter the formulas for the appropriate conversion from Euros to dollars and vice versa. You do not have to enter the query on this worksheet, because you can reference the values in the existing query. The entry in cell B11 of the Euro worksheet is Pounds!B34 on our worksheet. (Remember, the query changes continually, so you may have to adjust the cell reference.) Click in cell B11 of the Euro worksheet, type an equal sign to begin pointing, click the Pounds worksheet, and click in the cell containing the appropriate conversion, then click enter to finish the formula.

e. Format the Euro worksheet to include the European Currency Symbol as appropriate. Print both worksheets for your instructor.

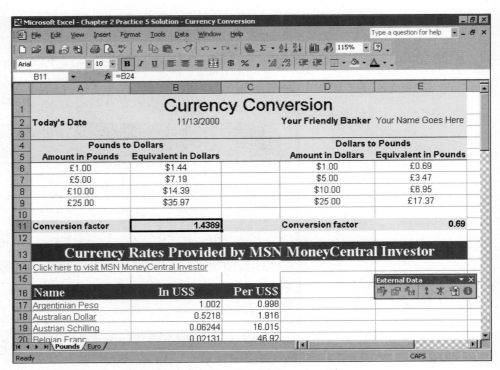

FIGURE 2.11   *Currency Conversion (Exercise 5)*

6. Accounting 101: The worksheet in Figure 2.12 computes the depreciation of an asset, an important accounting concept. You don't have to be an accounting major to create the spreadsheet, but you do have to understand the concept of depreciation. In essence, a business buys an asset, then uses that asset over a period of years. Each year the asset loses value (i.e., it depreciates) and is worth less than the year before.

   a. The amount of value that the asset loses each year is the depreciation expense for that year. The straight method assumes that the asset loses value uniformly over its projected life. To determine the depreciation amount for each year, take the cost of the asset, subtract its residual (salvage) value, then divide the result by the number of years the asset will be used.

   b. Your assignment is to open the *Chapter 2 Practice 6* workbook and enter the necessary formulas so that your worksheet matches ours. Add your name, today's date and the appropriate formatting, then print the worksheet twice, once with displayed values, and once to show the cell formulas.

7. Financial Forecast: Financial planning and budgeting is a common business application of spreadsheets. Figure 2.13 depicts one such illustration, in which the income and expenses of Get Rich Quick Enterprises are projected over a six-year period.

   a. The projected income in 2000, for example, is $225,000 based on sales of 75,000 units at a price of $3.00 per unit. The overhead (fixed costs) consists of the production facility at $50,000 and administrative expenses of $25,000. The variable costs for the same year are broken down into manufacturing and sales of $75,000 (75,000 units at $1.00 per unit) and $15,000 (75,000 units at $.20 per unit). Subtracting the total expenses from the estimated income yields a net income before taxes of $75,000. The income tax is subtracted from this amount, leaving net earnings of $38,400 in the first year. The estimated income and expenses for each succeeding year are based on an assumed percentage increase over the previous year. The projected rates of increase as well as the initial conditions are shown at the bottom of the worksheet. Specifications continue on page 104.

File Edit View Insert Format Tools Data Window Help   Type a question for help

Arial   10   B I U $ %   115%

D19   =D18-B19

	A	B	C	D	E	F	G
1		Straight Line Depreciation					
2							
3	Cost of Asset	$25,000	Prepared by	Your Name			
4	Residual Value	$5,000	Today's date	11/13/2000			
5	Useful life	8					
6							
7	Total Depreciaiton	$20,000					
8	Annual Depreciation	$2,500					
9							
10	Date	Depreciation Expense	Accumulated Depreciation	Asset Value			
11	Beginning of year 1			$25,000			
12	End of year 1	$2,500	$2,500	$22,500			
13	End of year 2	$2,500	$5,000	$20,000			
14	End of year 3	$2,500	$7,500	$17,500			
15	End of year 4	$2,500	$10,000	$15,000			
16	End of year 5	$2,500	$12,500	$12,500			
17	End of year 6	$2,500	$15,000	$10,000			
18	End of year 7	$2,500	$17,500	$7,500			
19	End of year 8	$2,500	$20,000	$5,000			
20							

Sheet1 / Sheet2 / Sheet3 /

Ready

FIGURE 2.12 *Accounting 101 (Exercise 6)*

File Edit View Insert Format Tools Data Window Help   Type a question for help

Arial   10   B I U $ %   100%

A35

	A	B	C	D	E	F	G	H	I
1		Financial Forecast - Get Rich Quick Enterprises							
2									
3		2000	2001	2002	2003	2004	2005		
4	Income								
5	Units sold	75,000	82,500	90,750	99,825	109,808	120,788		
6	Unit price	$3.00	$3.15	$3.31	$3.47	$3.65	$3.83		
7	Gross revenue	$225,000	$259,875	$300,156	$346,680	$400,415	$462,479		
8									
9	Overhead								
10	Production facility	$50,000	$54,000	$58,320	$62,986	$68,024	$73,466		
11	Administration	$25,000	$26,250	$27,563	$28,941	$30,388	$31,907		
12	Cost of Goods Sold								
13	Unit manufacturing cost	$1.00	$1.10	$1.21	$1.33	$1.46	$1.61		
14	Variable manufacturing cost	$75,000	$90,750	$109,808	$132,867	$160,769	$194,531		
15	Unit sales cost	$0.20	$0.20	$0.20	$0.20	$0.20	$0.20		
16	Variable sales cost	$15,000	$16,500	$18,150	$19,965	$21,962	$24,158		
17									
18	Earnings before taxes	$60,000	$72,375	$86,316	$101,921	$119,272	$138,418		
19	Income taxes	$21,600	$26,055	$31,074	$36,692	$42,938	$49,830		
20									
21	Net earnings	$38,400	$46,320	$55,242	$65,230	$76,334	$88,587		
22									
23	Initial conditions			Annual increase					
24	First year sales	75,000		10.0%					
25	Selling price	$3.00		5.0%					

Sheet1 / Sheet2 / Sheet3 /

Ready   CAPS

FIGURE 2.13 *Financial Forecast (Exercise 7)*

b. Your assignment is to open the partially completed worksheet in *Chapter 2 Practice 7,* then complete the spreadsheet so that it matches Figure 2.13. We suggest you use pointing throughout the exercise, as that is the most efficient way to enter cell formulas into a worksheet.

c. Develop the formulas for the first year of the forecast based on the initial conditions at the bottom of the spreadsheet.

d. Develop the formulas for the second year based on the values in year one and the assumed rates of change.

e. Copy the formulas for year two to the remaining years of the forecast.

f. Format the spreadsheet, then print the completed forecast. Add your name somewhere in the worksheet, then submit the completed assignment.

8. **Mixed References:** The majority of spreadsheets can be developed using a combination of relative and absolute references. Occasionally, however, you will need to incorporate mixed references as in the multiplication table of Figure 2.14. Creating the row and column headings is easy in that you can enter the numbers manually. (You can also use the AutoFill feature. Simply enter 1 and 2 in the first two cells for the row headings, select both of these cells, then drag the fill handle to continue the series in the remaining cells. Repeat the process to enter the column headings.)

a. The interesting part of this problem is creating the formulas in the body of the worksheet (we don't want you to enter the results manually). The trick is to use mixed references for the formula in cell B4, then copy that formula to the remainder of the table. The formula in cell B4 is a product of two numbers. To develop the proper mixed reference, you need to think about what will vary and what will remain constant. (One of the numbers in the product will always reference a value from column A, but the row will vary. The other number will always use a value from row three, but the column will vary.)

b. Add your name to the worksheet. Print the cell formulas as well so that you can see how the mixed reference changes throughout the worksheet. Submit the complete assignment to your instructor.

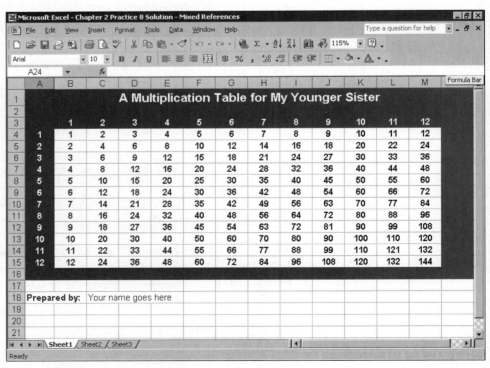

FIGURE 2.14 *Mixed References (Exercise 8)*

9. **The Birthday Problem:** How much would you bet *against* two people in your class having the same birthday? Don't be too hasty, for the odds of two class-mates sharing the same birthday (month and day) are much higher than you would expect; e.g., there is a fifty percent chance (.5063) in a class of 23 students that two people will have been born on the same day. The probability jumps to seventy percent (.7053) in a class of thirty, and to ninety percent (.9025) in a class of forty-one. Ask the question in your own class to see if the probabilities hold.

a. Your assignment is to create the worksheet in Figure 2.15 that displays the set of probabilities. Enter your name and birthdate in cells B3 and B4, respectively, then use either the Now( ) or the Today( ) function to compute your age in cell B5. Change the default alignment and number of decimal places in cell B5 so that your worksheet matches ours.

b. You need a basic knowledge of probability to create the remainder of the worksheet. In essence you calculate the probability of individuals not having the same birthday, then subtract this number from one to obtain the probability of the event coming true. In a group of two people, for example, the probability of not being born on the same day is 365/366; that is, the second person can be born on any of 365 days and still have a different birthday. The probability of two people having the same birthday becomes 1 − 365/366.

c. The probability for different birthdays in a group of three is (365/366) * (364/366). The probability of not having different birthdays—that is, of two people having the same birthday—is one minus this number. This logic continues for the remaining rows in the spreadsheet, where each row is calculated from the previous row. It's not as hard as it looks and the results are quite interesting.

d. Print the worksheet two ways, once to show displayed values and once to show cell formulas. Add a cover sheet. Submit all three pages to your instructor.

The Birthday Problem

	A	B	C
3	My name:	Jessica Grauer	
4	My birthdate:	3/16/1977	
5	My Age:	23.7	
7	Number of People	Probability of Different Birthdays	Probability of the Same Birthday
8	2	99.73%	0.27%
9	3	99.18%	0.82%
10	4	98.37%	1.63%
11	5	97.29%	2.71%
12	6	95.96%	4.04%
13	7	94.39%	5.61%
14	8	92.59%	7.41%
15	9	90.56%	9.44%
16	10	88.34%	11.66%
17	11	85.92%	14.08%
18	12	83.34%	16.66%
19	13	80.61%	19.39%
20	14	77.74%	22.26%
21	15	74.77%	25.23%

FIGURE 2.15 *The Birthday Problem (Exercise 9)*

10. **Create a New Web Query:** You can create a Web query to obtain data from virtually any site, then use that data as the basis of calculations within an Excel workbook. Start a new workbook, pull down the Data menu, click the Import External Data command, then click New Web Query to display the associated dialog box. Enter the address of any Web page as shown in Figure 2.16. We used the Microsoft Investor site (investor.msn.com), but you may want to try the home page of your favorite sport. The key is that the page contains one or more yellow arrows that indicate the data may be imported.

Click a yellow arrow to select the table, click the Import button in the New Query dialog box, then follow the regular steps to create a Web query. Continue to develop the worksheet using formulas that reference the data that was imported by the query. Save the workbook, then open it the next day. Right click in the query and click the Refresh data command to update the data. Print the workbook at two different times to show your instructor that the data is updated from the Web.

FIGURE 2.16 *Create a New Web Query (Exercise 10)*

11. **Excel Templates:** Figure 2.17a displays a worksheet that was created from the Balance Sheet template that is built into Office XP. Pull down the View menu and open the task pane. Click the General Templates command to open the Templates dialog box from where you can click the Spreadsheets Solutions tab to open the Balance Sheet template.
    a. Enter an appropriate description and initial balance, then enter data for at least three transactions of each type. Print the completed worksheet for your instructor.
    b. What is contained on the Balance over time worksheet within this workbook? Print this worksheet for your instructor as well.
    c. What happens if you attempt to add more transactions than the template provides initially? Does this limit the utility of the template? Summarize your results in a brief note to your instructor.
    d. Use the Sales Invoice template to create a worksheet similar to Figure 2.17b. Print the worksheet for your instructor.

(a) The Balance Sheet

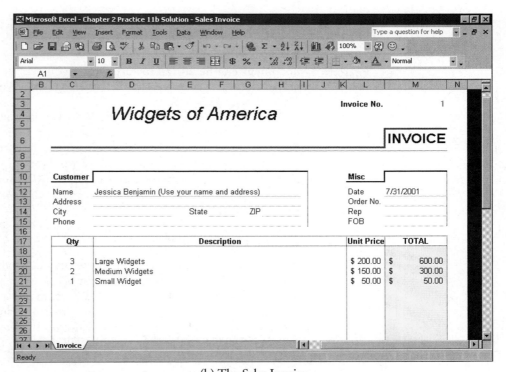

(b) The Sales Invoice

FIGURE 2.17   *Excel Templates (Exercise 11)*

The Checkbook

A spreadsheet can be created as an aid in balancing your checkbook. Each row in the spreadsheet will contain the data for a specific transaction, such as a check, deposit, or ATM withdrawal. Each row should also include the date of the transaction and the current balance. The spreadsheet is easy to create, but you need to think carefully about its design. We suggest you start with the *Checkbook* workbook that is found in the Exploring Excel folder. Open the workbook, develop the necessary formulas, then submit the completed workbook to your instructor. If you find this to be a useful exercise, then you can modify our workbook to reflect your own data.

The Spreadsheet Audit

The spreadsheet is an invaluable tool in decision making, but what if the spreadsheet contains an error? Unfortunately, it is all too easy to get caught up in the appearance of an attractively formatted spreadsheet without paying attention to its underlying accuracy. The *Erroneous Chapter 2 Practice 7* is based on problem 7, but it contains one or more errors within the body of the spreadsheet. This worksheet also contains a different set of assumptions and initial conditions, but these values are not to be considered in error; that is, the mistakes in the spreadsheet stem from formulas that are in error. Examine the spreadsheet carefully, correct the formulas that are in error (but leave the assumptions and initial conditions as is), then print the corrected worksheet. Submit the revised forecast based on the new assumptions to your instructor.

Publishing to the Web

It's easy to create a Web page (HTML document) from an Excel worksheet. The document can be stored locally, where you are the only one who can view it. It's more interesting, however, to place the page on a Web server, where it becomes part of the World Wide Web.

In order to place a page on the Web, you will need Internet access, and further, you will need storage space on a Web server. Check with your instructor to see if these resources are available to you, and if so, find out the steps necessary to upload your page to the server. Choose any worksheet that you have completed in this chapter, save the worksheet as an HTML document, then upload the document. Send a note to your instructor that contains the Web address where he or she may view your Web page.

Break-even Analysis

Widgets of America has developed the perfect product and is ready to go into production pending a review of a five-year break-even analysis. The manufacturing cost in the first year is $1.00 per unit and is estimated to increase at 5% annually. The projected selling price is $2.00 per unit and can increase at 10% annually. Overhead expenses are fixed at $100,000 per year over the life of the project. The advertising budget is $50,000 in the first year but will decrease 15% a year as the product gains acceptance. How many units have to be sold each year for the company to break even, given the current cost estimates and projected rates of increase?

Your worksheet should be completely flexible and capable of accommodating a change in any of the initial conditions or projected rates of increase. Be sure to isolate all of the assumptions (i.e., the initial conditions and rates of increase) in one area of the worksheet, and then reference these cells as absolute references when building the formulas.

CHAPTER 3

Spreadsheets in Decision Making: What If?

OBJECTIVES

AFTER READING THIS CHAPTER YOU WILL BE ABLE TO:

1. Describe the purpose of the PMT and FV functions; list the arguments associated with each function.
2. Use the PMT function to calculate the payment for a car loan or home mortgage; use the FV function to determine the future value of a retirement account.
3. Explain how the Goal Seek command can facilitate the decision-making process in conjunction with the PMT and/or FV functions.
4. Define a mixed reference; use mixed references to vary two parameters within the FV or PMT functions.
5. Use the AVERAGE, MAX, MIN, and COUNT functions in a worksheet.
6. Use the IF and VLOOKUP functions to implement decision making in a worksheet.
7. Freeze and unfreeze, hide and unhide, the rows and columns in a worksheet; explain how these commands facilitate working with large worksheets.
8. Describe the various options within the Page Setup command that are used in conjunction with printing large spreadsheets.

OVERVIEW

Excel is a truly fascinating program, but it is only a means to an end. A spreadsheet is first and foremost a tool for decision making, and the objective of this chapter is to show you just how valuable that tool can be. Decisions typically involve money, and so we begin by introducing two financial functions, PMT and FV, either of which is entered directly into a worksheet.

The PMT (Payment) function calculates the periodic payment on a loan, such as one you might incur with the purchase of an automobile. The FV (Future Value) function determines the future value of a series of periodic payments, such as annual contributions to a retirement account. Either function can be used in conjunction with the Goal Seek command that lets you enter the desired end result (such as the monthly payment on a car loan) and from that, determines the input (e.g., the price of the car) to produce that result.

The second half of the chapter presents an expanded version of the professor's grade book that uses several commands associated with large spreadsheets. We describe scrolling and explain how its effects are modified by freezing and/or hiding rows and columns in a worksheet. We describe various statistical functions such as MAX, MIN, COUNT, and COUNTA as well as the IF and VLOOKUP functions that provide decision making within a worksheet. We also review the important concepts of relative and absolute cell references, as well as the need to isolate the assumptions and initial conditions in a worksheet.

ANALYSIS OF A CAR LOAN

Figure 3.1 shows how a worksheet might be applied to the purchase of a car. In essence you need to know the monthly payment, which depends on the price of the car, the down payment, and the terms of the loan. In other words:

- Can you afford the monthly payment on the car of your choice?
- What if you settle for a less expensive car and receive a manufacturer's rebate?
- What if you work next summer to earn money for a down payment?
- What if you extend the life of the loan and receive a more favorable interest rate?

The answers to these and other questions determine whether you can afford a car, and if so, which car, and how you will pay for it. The decision is made easier by developing the worksheet in Figure 3.1, and then by changing the various parameters as indicated.

Figure 3.1a contains the *template*, or "empty" worksheet, in which the text entries and formulas have already been entered, the formatting has already been applied, but no specific data has been input. The template requires that you enter the price of the car, the manufacturer's rebate, the down payment, the interest rate, and the length of the loan. The worksheet uses these parameters to compute the monthly payment. (Implicit in this discussion is the existence of a PMT function within the worksheet program, which is explained in the next section.)

The availability of the worksheet lets you consider several alternatives, and therein lies its true value. You quickly realize that the purchase of a $14,999 car as shown in Figure 3.1b is prohibitive because the monthly payment is almost $500. Settling for a less expensive car, coming up with a substantial down payment, and obtaining a manufacturer's rebate in Figure 3.1c help considerably, but the $317 monthly payment is still too steep. Extending the loan to a fourth year at a lower interest rate in Figure 3.1d reduces the monthly payment to (a more affordable) $244.

CAR SHOPPING ON THE WEB

Why guess about the price of a car or its features if you can obtain exact information from the Web? You can go to the site of a specific manufacturer, usually by entering an address of the form www.company.com (e.g., www.ford.com). You can also go to a site that provides information about multiple vendors. Our favorite is carpoint.msn.com, which provides detailed information about specifications and current prices. See practice exercise 8 at the end of the chapter.

	A	B
1	Price of car	
2	Manufacturer's rebate	
3	Down payment	
4	Amount to finance	=B1-(B2+B3)
5	Interest rate	
6	Term (in years)	
7	Monthly payment	=PMT(B5/12,B6*12,-B4)

No specific data has been input

(a) The Template

	A	B
1	Price of car	$14,999
2	Manufacturer's rebate	
3	Down payment	
4	Amount to finance	$14,999
5	Interest rate	9%
6	Term (in years)	3
7	Monthly payment	$476.96

Data entered

(b) Initial Parameters

	A	B
1	Price of car	$13,999
2	Manufacturer's rebate	$1,000
3	Down payment	$3,000
4	Amount to finance	$9,999
5	Interest rate	9%
6	Term (in years)	3
7	Monthly payment	$317.97

Less expensive car

Rebate

Down payment made

(c) Less Expensive Car with Down Payment and Rebate

	A	B
1	Price of car	$13,999
2	Manufacturer's rebate	$1,000
3	Down payment	$3,000
4	Amount to finance	$9,999
5	Interest rate	8%
6	Term (in years)	4
7	Monthly payment	$244.10

Lower interest rate

Longer term

(d) Longer Term and Better Interest Rate

FIGURE 3.1   *Spreadsheets in Decision Making*

PMT Function

A *function* is a predefined formula that accepts one or more **arguments** as input, performs the indicated calculation, then returns another value as output. Excel has more than 100 different functions in various categories. Financial functions, such as the PMT function we are about to study, are especially important in business.

The **PMT function** requires three arguments (the interest rate per period, the number of periods, and the amount of the loan), from which it computes the associated payment on a loan. The arguments are placed in parentheses and are separated by commas. Consider the PMT function as it might apply to Figure 3.1b:

$$=PMT(.09/12,36,-14999)$$

Amount of loan (as a *negative* amount)

Number of periods (3 years × 12 months/year)

Interest rate per period (annual rate divided by 12)

Instead of using specific values, however, the arguments in the PMT function are supplied as cell references, so that the computed payment can be based on values supplied by the user elsewhere in the worksheet. Thus, the PMT function is entered as =PMT(B5/12,B6*12,-B4) to reflect the terms of a specific loan whose arguments are in cells B4, B5, and B6. (The principal is entered as a negative amount because the money is lent to you and represents an outflow of cash from the bank.)

FV Function

The **FV function** returns the future value of an investment based on constant periodic payments and a constant interest rate. It can be used to determine the future value of a retirement plan such as an IRA (Individual Retirement Account) or 401K, two plans that are very popular in today's workplace. Under either plan, an individual saves for his or her retirement by making a fixed contribution each year. The money is allowed to accumulate tax-free until retirement and it is an excellent way to save for the future.

Assume, for example, that you plan to contribute $2,000 a year to an IRA, that you expect to earn 8% annually, and that you will be contributing for 40 years (i.e., you began contributing at age 25 and will continue to contribute until age 65). The future value of that investment—that is, the amount you will have at age 65—would be $518,113! All told, you would have contributed $80,000 ($2,000 a year for 40 years). The difference, more than $400,000, results from compound interest over the life of your investment.

The FV function is entered into a worksheet in similar fashion to the PMT function. There are three arguments—the interest rate (also called the rate of return), the number of periods, and the periodic investment. The FV function corresponding to our earlier example would be:

Amount at Retirement = FV(Rate of return, Term, Periodic payment)

$2,000

40 years

8%

Computed value becomes $518,113

It's more practical, however, to enter the values into a worksheet, then use cell references within the FV function. If, for example, cells A1, A2, and A3 contained the rate of return, term, and annual contribution, respectively, the resulting FV function would be =FV(A1, A2, −A3). The periodic payment is preceded by a minus sign, just as the principal in the PMT function.

Inserting a Function

The **Insert Function command** places a function into a worksheet. You can select a function from within a category as was done in Figure 3.2a, or you can enter a brief description of the function you are searching for to see which functions are suggested. The Function Arguments dialog box in Figure 3.2b appears after you choose the function. This is where you enter the various arguments in order to compute the value of the function. (Only the first three arguments are required for the Future Value function.) Excel displays the calculated value of each argument as well as the value of the function within the dialog box.

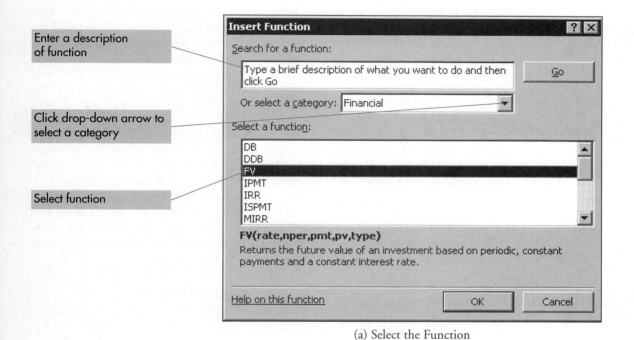

Enter a description of function

Click drop-down arrow to select a category

Select function

(a) Select the Function

Arguments

Calculated value

Computed value for function

(b) Enter the Arguments

FIGURE 3.2 *Inserting a Function*

The Goal Seek Command

The analysis in Figure 3.1 enabled us to reduce the projected monthly payment from $476 to a more affordable $244. What if, however, you can afford a payment of only $200, and you want to know the maximum you can borrow in order to keep the payment to the specified amount? The **Goal Seek command** is designed to solve this type of problem, as it enables you to set an end result (such as the monthly payment) in order to determine the input (the price of the car) to produce that result. Only one input (the price of the car, the interest rate, or the term) can be varied at a time.

Figure 3.3 extends our earlier analysis to illustrate the Goal Seek command. You create the spreadsheet as usual, then you pull down the Tools menu, and select the Goal Seek command to display the dialog box in Figure 3.3a. Enter the address of the cell containing the dependent formula (the monthly payment in cell B7) and the desired value of this cell ($200). Indicate the cell whose contents should be varied (the price of the car in cell B1), then click OK to execute the command. The Goal Seek command then varies the price of the car until the monthly payment returns the desired value of $200. (Not every problem has a solution, in which case Excel returns a message indicating that a solution cannot be found.)

In this example, the Goal Seek command is able to find a solution and returns a purchase price of $12,192 as shown in Figure 3.3b. You now have all the information you need. Find a car that sells for $12,192 (or less), hold the other parameters to the values shown in the figure, and your monthly payment will be (at most) $200.

The analysis in Figure 3.3 illustrates how a worksheet is used in the decision-making process. An individual defines a problem, then develops a worksheet that includes all of the associated parameters. He or she can then plug in specific numbers, changing one or more of the variables until a decision can be reached. Excel is invaluable in arriving at the solution.

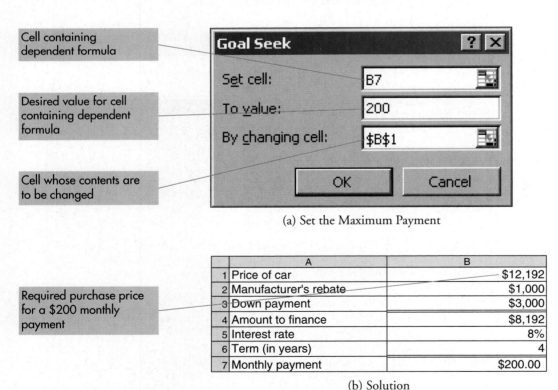

Cell containing dependent formula

Desired value for cell containing dependent formula

Cell whose contents are to be changed

(a) Set the Maximum Payment

Required purchase price for a $200 monthly payment

	A	B
1	Price of car	$12,192
2	Manufacturer's rebate	$1,000
3	Down payment	$3,000
4	Amount to finance	$8,192
5	Interest rate	8%
6	Term (in years)	4
7	Monthly payment	$200.00

(b) Solution

FIGURE 3.3 *The Goal Seek Command*

BASIC FINANCIAL FUNCTIONS

Objective   To illustrate the PMT and FV functions; to illustrate the Goal Seek command. Use Figure 3.4 as a guide in the exercise.

Step 1:   **Enter the Descriptive Labels**

➤ Start Excel. If necessary, click the **New button** on the Standard toolbar to open a new workbook or click **Blank Workbook** in the task pane.

➤ Click in cell **A1**, type the label **Basic Financial Functions**, then press the **enter key** to complete the entry. Enter the remaining labels for column A as shown in Figure 3.4a.

➤ Click and drag the column border between columns A and B to increase the column width of column A to accommodate the widest entry in column A (other than cell A3).

➤ Click in cell **B4** and type **$14,999** corresponding to the price of the automobile you hope to purchase. Be sure to include the dollar sign as you enter the data to format the cell automatically.

➤ Enter **$1,000** and **$3,000** in cells B5 and B6, respectively, corresponding to the manufacturer's rebate and down payment, respectively.

➤ Click in cell **B7**. Use pointing to enter the formula **=B4−(B5+B6)**, which calculates the amount to finance (i.e., the principal of the loan).

➤ Enter **9%** and **3** in cells **B8** and **B9**. (If necessary, click in cell **B9**, pull down the **Edit menu**, select the **Clear command**, and choose the **Format command** to remove the dollar sign.)

➤ All of the loan parameters have been entered.

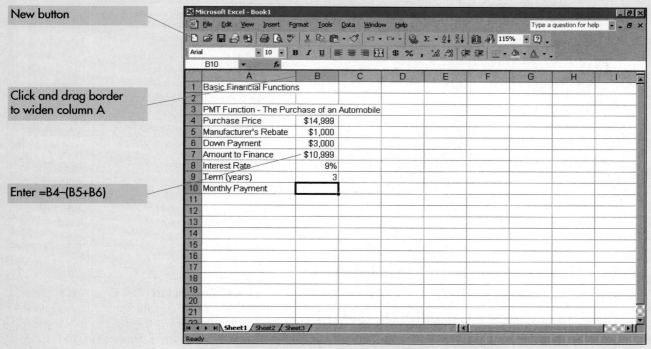

New button

Click and drag border to widen column A

Enter =B4−(B5+B6)

(a) Enter the Descriptive Labels (step 1)

FIGURE 3.4   *Hands-on Exercise 1*

Step 2: **Insert a Function**

➤ Click in cell **B10**. Pull down the **Insert menu** and click the **Function command** (or click the **Insert Function button** on the formula bar) to display the Insert Function dialog box.

➤ Click the **down arrow** in the Select a category list box and select **Financial**, select the **PMT function** and click **OK** to display the Function Arguments dialog box in Figure 3.4b.

➤ Click the **Rate text box** and use pointing to enter the rate. Click in cell **B8** of the worksheet, then type **/12**, so that the text box contains the entry B8/12.

➤ Click the **Nper text box** and use pointing to enter the number of periods. Click in cell **B9**, then type ***12**, so that the formula bar contains the entry B9*12.

➤ Click the **Pv text box**. Type a – sign, then click in cell **B7**. You should see $349.7652595 as the value for the PMT function. Click **OK** to close the Function Arguments dialog box.

➤ Pull down the **File menu** and click the **Save command** (or click the **Save button** on the Standard toolbar) to display the Save As dialog box, then save the workbook as **Basic Financial Functions** in the **Exploring Excel** folder.

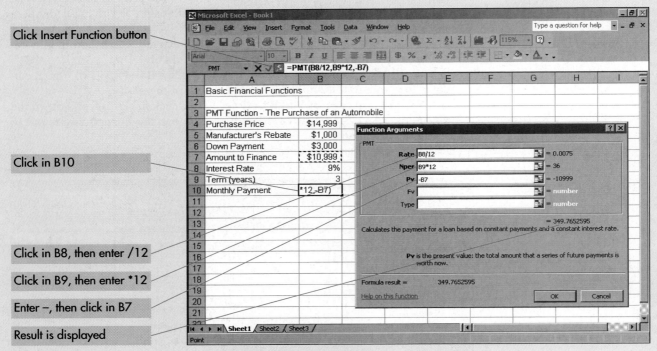

(b) Insert a Function (step 2)

FIGURE 3.4 *Hands-on Exercise 1 (continued)*

SEARCH FOR THE FUNCTION

It's easy to select a function if you know its name, but what if you are unsure of the name or don't know the category in which the function is found? Click the Insert Function button on the Standard toolbar to display the Insert Function dialog box, type a keyword such as "payment" in the search text box, then click the Go button. Excel returns four functions in this example, one of which is the PMT function that you are looking for.

Step 3: **The Goal Seek Command**

➤ You can reduce the monthly payment in various ways. Click in cell **B4** and change the price of the car to **$13,999**. The monthly payment drops to $317.97.

➤ Change the interest rate to **8%** and the term of the loan to **4** years. The payment drops to $244.10.

➤ You can reduce the payment still further by using the Goal Seek command to fix the payment at a specified level. Click in cell **B10**, the cell containing the formula for the monthly payment.

➤ Pull down the **Tools menu**. Click **Goal Seek** to display the dialog box in Figure 3.4c. Click in the **To value** text box. Type **200** (the desired payment).

➤ Click in the **By changing cell** text box. Type **B4**, the cell containing the price of the car. This is the cell whose value will be determined. Click **OK**.

➤ The Goal Seek command returns a successful solution consisting of $12,192 and $200 in cells B4 and B10, respectively. Click **OK** to accept the solution and close the Goal Seek dialog box.

➤ Save the workbook.

Enter $13,999

Enter 8%

Enter 4

Click in B10

Enter 200

Enter B4

(c) The Goal Seek Command (step 3)

FIGURE 3.4 *Hands-on Exercise 1 (continued)*

THE FORMATTING IS IN THE CELL

Once a number format has been assigned to a cell, either by including the format as you entered a number, or through execution of a formatting command, the formatting remains in the cell. Thus, to change the contents in a formatted cell, all you need to do is enter the new number without the formatting. Entering 5000, for example, in a cell that was previously formatted as currency will display the number as $5,000. To remove the formatting, pull down the Edit menu, select the Clear command, then choose Format.

Step 4:   **The Future Value Function**

➤ Check your work to be sure that your worksheet matches the top half of Figure 3.4d. Make corrections as necessary.

➤ Enter the labels in cells **A13 through A17** as shown in the figure. Click in cell **B14** and type **$2,000** corresponding to the annual contribution. Be sure to include the dollar sign.

➤ Enter **8%** (type the percent sign) and **40**, in cells **B15 and B16**, respectively.

➤ Click in cell **B17**, type **=FV(** . You will see a ScreenTip that shows the arguments in the FV function. There are five arguments, but only the first three (rate, nper, and pv) are required. (The last two arguments are enclosed in square brackets to indicate they are optional.)

➤ Use pointing to complete the function, which is **=FV(B15,B16,B14)**. Press **enter** when you have finished.

➤ You should see $518,113.04 in cell B17. This is the amount you will have at retirement, given that you save $2,000 a year for 40 years and earn 8% interest over the life of your investment.

➤ Save the workbook.

ScreenTip shows arguments for FV function

Enter labels in A13:A17

Use pointing to enter FV function

(d) The Future Value (FV) Function (step 4)

FIGURE 3.4   *Hands-on Exercise 1 (continued)*

IT'S COLOR CODED

Double click in the cell that contains the FV function, then look closely at the arguments within the function to see that each argument is a different color. Each color corresponds to the border color of the referenced cell. You can change any reference in the function (e.g., from B15 to C15) by dragging the color-coded border surrounding cell B15 (the reference you want to change) to cell C15 (the new reference).

Step 5:   **Format the Worksheet**

➤ Your workbook should match Figure 3.4e except for the formatting. Click and drag cells **A1 and B1**, then click the **Merge and Center button**.

➤ Click the **down arrow** on the Font Size list box to change the font size to **12**. Click the **Bold button** to boldface the title.

➤ Click cell **A3**. Press and hold the **Ctrl key** as you click cells **A10:B10, A13**, and **A17:B17** to select all of these cells. Click the **Bold button** to boldface the contents of these cells.

➤ Click and drag to select cells **A4 through A9**. Press and hold the **Ctrl key** as you click and drag to select cells **A14 through A16** (in addition to cells A4 through A9).

➤ Click the **Increase Indent button** on the Formatting toolbar to indent the labels as shown in Figure 3.4e.

➤ Click in cell **A19** and enter your name, then click the **Bold button** to boldface the type.

➤ Save the workbook.

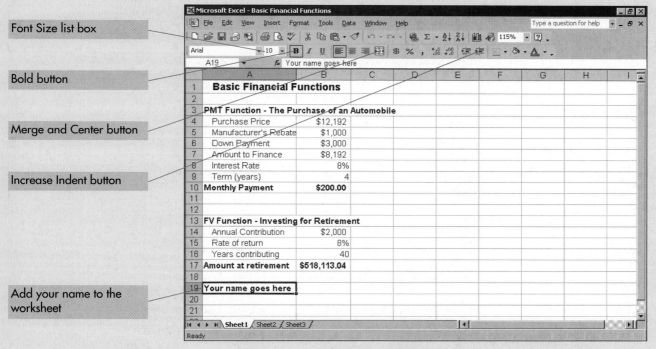

(e) Format the Worksheet (step 5)

FIGURE 3.4   *Hands-on Exercise 1 (continued)*

SELECTING NONCONTIGUOUS RANGES

You can apply the same formatting to noncontiguous (nonadjacent) cells within a worksheet by using the Ctrl key to select the cells. Click and drag to select the first cell range, then press and hold the Ctrl key as you select a second range. Continue to press the Ctrl key to select additional ranges, then format all of the selected cells with a single command. Click anywhere in the worksheet to deselect the cells.

Step 6: Print the Cell Formulas

➤ Pull down the **File menu** and click the **Page Setup command** to display the Page Setup dialog box. Click the **Sheet tab**, then check the boxes to print gridlines and row and column headings.

➤ Click the **Margins tab** and check the box to center the worksheet horizontally. Click **OK** to accept the settings and close the dialog box.

➤ Save the workbook. Click the **Print Preview button** on the Standard toolbar to be sure you are satisfied with the appearance of the workbook. Click the **Print button**, then click **OK** to print the worksheet.

➤ Press **Ctrl+~** to display the cell contents as opposed to the displayed values. Preview the worksheet in this format, then print it when you are satisfied with its appearance. Press **Ctrl+~** to return the worksheet to displayed values.

➤ Submit printouts—the displayed values and the cell formulas—to your instructor as proof that you did this exercise.

➤ Exit Excel if you do not want to continue with the next exercise at this time.

(f) Print the Cell Formulas (step 6)

FIGURE 3.4 *Hands-on Exercise 1 (continued)*

ARE THE PAYMENTS MONTHLY OR ANNUAL?

The FV function in this example computes the future value of a series of annual payments, with the term and interest rate specified as annual values, and thus there is no need to multiply or divide these values by 12. The car payment in the previous example, however, was on a monthly basis. Thus the annual interest rate was divided by 12 (to obtain the monthly rate), while the term of the loan was multiplied by 12, in order to put the numbers on a monthly basis.

The PMT function is used in our next example in conjunction with the purchase of a home. The example also reviews the concept of relative and absolute addresses from Chapter 2. In addition, it introduces several other techniques to make you more proficient in Excel.

The spreadsheets in Figure 3.5 illustrate a variable rate mortgage, which will be developed over the next several pages. The user enters the amount he or she wishes to borrow and a starting interest rate, and the spreadsheet displays the associated monthly payment. The spreadsheet in Figure 3.5a enables the user to see the monthly payment at varying interest rates, and to contrast the amount of the payment for a 15- and a 30-year mortgage.

Most first-time buyers opt for the longer term, but they would do well to consider a 15-year mortgage. Note, for example, that the difference in monthly payments for a $100,000 mortgage at 7.5% is only $227.80 (the difference between $927.01 for a 15-year mortgage versus $699.21 for the 30-year mortgage). This is a significant amount of money, but when viewed as a percentage of the total cost of a home (property taxes and maintenance), it becomes less important, especially when you consider the substantial saving in interest over the life of the mortgage.

Figure 3.5b expands the spreadsheet to show the total interest over the life of the loan for both the 15- and the 30-year mortgage. The total interest on a $100,000 loan at 7.5% is $151,717 for a 30-year mortgage, but only $66,862 for a 15-year mortgage. In other words, you will pay back the $100,000 in principal plus another $151,717 in interest if you select the longer term.

Difference in monthly payment between a 30-year and a 15-year mortgage at 7.5%

	A	B	C	D
1	Amount Borrowed		$100,000	
2	Starting Interest		7.50%	
3				
4		Monthly Payment		
5	Interest	30 Years	15 Years	Difference
6	7.50%	$699.21	$927.01	$227.80
7	8.50%	$768.91	$984.74	$215.83
8	9.50%	$840.85	$1,044.22	$203.37
9	10.50%	$914.74	$1,105.40	$190.66
10	11.50%	$990.29	$1,168.19	$177.90
11	12.50%	$1,067.26	$1,232.52	$165.26

(a) Difference in Monthly Payment

Less interest is paid on a 15-year loan ($66,862 vs $151,717 on a 30-year loan)

	A	B	C	D	E
1	Amount Borrowed			$100,000	
2	Starting Interest			7.50%	
3					
4		30 Years		15 Years	
5	Interest	Monthly Payment	Total Interest	Monthly Payment	Total Interest
6	7.50%	$699.21	$151,717	$927.01	$66,862
7	8.50%	$768.91	$176,809	$984.74	$77,253
8	9.50%	$840.85	$202,708	$1,044.22	$87,960
9	10.50%	$914.74	$229,306	$1,105.40	$98,972
10	11.50%	$990.29	$256,505	$1,168.19	$110,274
11	12.50%	$1,067.26	$284,213	$1,232.52	$121,854

(b) Total Interest

FIGURE 3.5 *15- versus 30-Year Mortgage*

Relative versus Absolute Addresses

Figure 3.6 displays the cell formulas for the mortgage analysis. All of the formulas are based on the amount borrowed and the starting interest, in cells C1 and C2, respectively. You can vary either or both of these parameters, and the worksheet will automatically recalculate the monthly payments.

The similarity in the formulas from one row to the next implies that the copy operation will be essential to the development of the worksheet. You must, however, remember the distinction between a **relative** and an **absolute reference**—that is, a cell reference that changes during a copy operation (relative) versus one that does not (absolute). Consider the PMT function as it appears in cell B6:

$$=PMT(A6/12,30*12,-\$C\$1)$$

> └── The amount of the loan, −$C$1, is an absolute reference that remains constant
>
> └── Number of periods (30 years*12 months/year)
>
> └── The interest rate, A6/12, is a relative reference that changes

The entry A6/12 (which is the first argument in the formula in cell B6) is interpreted to mean "divide the contents of the cell one column to the left by 12." Thus, when the PMT function in cell B6 is copied to cell B7, it (the copied formula) is adjusted to maintain this relationship and will contain the entry A7/12. The Copy command does not duplicate a relative address exactly, but adjusts it from row to row (or column to column) to maintain the relative relationship. The cell reference for the amount of the loan should not change when the formula is copied, and hence it is specified as an absolute address.

Relative reference (adjusts during copy operation)

Absolute reference (doesn't adjust during copy operation)

	A	B	C	D
1	Amount Borrowed		$100,000	
2	Starting Interest		7.50%	
3				
4		Monthly Payment		
5	Interest	30 Years	15 Years	Difference
6	=C2	=PMT(A6/12,30*12,-$C$1)	=PMT(A6/12,15*12,-$C$1)	=C6-B6
7	=A6+0.01	=PMT(A7/12,30*12,-$C$1)	=PMT(A7/12,15*12,-$C$1)	=C7-B7
8	=A7+0.01	=PMT(A8/12,30*12,-$C$1)	=PMT(A8/12,15*12,-$C$1)	=C8-B8
9	=A8+0.01	=PMT(A9/12,30*12,-$C$1)	=PMT(A9/12,15*12,-$C$1)	=C9-B9
10	=A9+0.01	=PMT(A10/12,30*12,-$C$1)	=PMT(A10/12,15*12,-$C$1)	=C10-B10
11	=A10+0.01	=PMT(A11/12,30*12,-$C$1)	=PMT(A11/12,15*12,-$C$1)	=C11-B11

FIGURE 3.6   *Cell Formulas*

ISOLATE ASSUMPTIONS

The formulas in a worksheet should be based on cell references rather than specific values—for example, C1 or $C$1 rather than $100,000. The cells containing these values should be clearly labeled and set apart from the rest of the worksheet. You can then vary the inputs (**assumptions**) to the worksheet and immediately see the effect. The chance for error is also minimized because you are changing the contents of a single cell, rather than changing multiple formulas.

Mixed References

Figure 3.7 displays a new worksheet that uses the FV function to calculate the value of an *IRA (Individual Retirement Account)* under various combinations of interest rates and years for investing. The annual contribution is $2,000 in all instances (the maximum that is allowed under current law). The interest rates appear in row 5, while the years for investing are shown in column B. The intersection of a row and column contains the future value of a series of $2,000 investments for the specific interest rate and year combination. Cell F21, for example, shows that $2,000 a year, invested over 40 years at 8%, will compound to $518,113.

The key to the worksheet is to realize that the Future Value function requires *mixed references* for both the interest rate and number of years. The interest rate will always come from row 5, but the column will vary. In similar fashion, the number of years will always come from column B, but the row will vary. Using this information we can enter the appropriate formula in cell C6, then copy that formula to the remaining cells in row 6, and finally copy row 6 to the remaining rows in the worksheet. The key to the worksheet is the formula in cell C6. Consider:

Future Value = FV(C$5, $B6, –$D$3)

Absolute reference to cell D3, the cell containing the periodic investment

Mixed reference to cell $B6, the cell containing the the term; the column stays constant, but the row changes

Mixed reference to cell C$5; the column changes, but the row stays constant.

The majority of spreadsheets can be developed using a combination of relative and absolute references. Occasionally, however, you will need to incorporate mixed references as you will see in our next exercise.

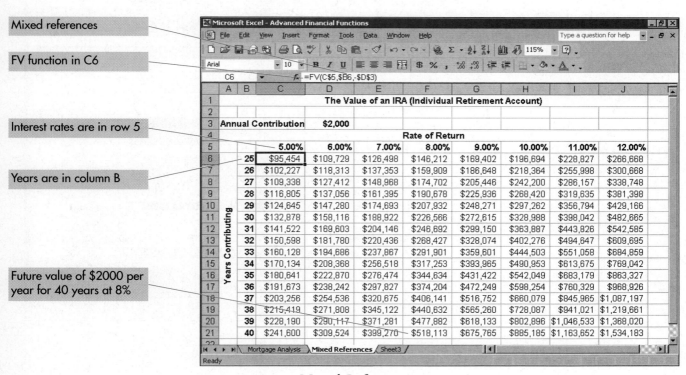

FIGURE 3.7   *Mixed References*

ADVANCED FINANCIAL FUNCTIONS

Objective   To use relative, absolute, and mixed references in conjunction with the PMT and FV functions; to practice various formatting commands. Use Figure 3.8 as a guide in the exercise.

Step 1:   **The Spell Check**

> ➤ Start Excel. Close the task pane if it is open. Click in cell **A1**. Type **Amount Borrowed**. Do not be concerned that the text is longer than the cell width, as cell B1 is empty and thus the text will be displayed in its entirety. Press the **enter key** or **down arrow** to complete the entry.
> ➤ Type **Starting Interest** in cell **A2**. Click in cell **A4**. Type **Monthly Payment**. Enter the remaining labels in cells **A5 through D5**, as shown in Figure 3.8a without concern for the column width.
> ➤ We suggest that you deliberately misspell one or more words in order to try the spell check. Click in cell **A1** to begin the spell check at the beginning of the worksheet.
> ➤ Click the **Spelling button** on the Standard toolbar to initiate the spell check as shown in Figure 3.8a. Make corrections, as necessary, just as you would in Microsoft Word.
> ➤ Click in cell **C1**. Type **$100,000** (include the dollar sign). Press the **enter key** or **down arrow** to complete the entry and move to cell **C2**. Type **7.5%** (include the percent sign). Press **enter**.
> ➤ Save the workbook as **Advanced Financial Functions** in the **Exploring Excel** folder on the appropriate drive.

Spelling button

Click in A1

Dfference is misspelled word

Click correct spelling

Click Change

(a) The Spell Check (step 1)

FIGURE 3.8   *Hands-on Exercise 2*

Step 2: **The Fill Handle**

➤ Click in cell **A6**. Use pointing to enter the formula **=C2** to reference the starting interest rate in cell C2.

➤ Click in cell **A7**. Use pointing to enter the formula **=A6+.01** to compute the interest rate in this cell, which is one percent more than the interest rate in row six. Press **enter**.

➤ Click in cell **A7**. Point to the **fill handle** in the lower corner of cell A7. The mouse pointer changes to a thin crosshair.

➤ Drag the **fill handle** over cells **A8 through A11**. A border appears to indicate the destination range as in Figure 3.8b. Release the mouse to complete the copy operation. The formula and associated percentage format in cell A7 have been copied to cells A8 through A11.

➤ Click in Cell **C2**. Type **5%**. The entries in cells A6 through A11 change automatically. Click the **Undo button** on the Standard toolbar to return to the 7.5% interest rate.

➤ Save the workbook.

Undo button

Enter =C2

Enter =A6+.01

Click and drag
fill handle to A11

(b) The Fill Handle (step 2)

FIGURE 3.8   *Hands-on Exercise 2 (continued)*

FIND AND REPLACE

Anyone familiar with a word processor takes the Find and Replace commands for granted, but did you know the same capabilities exist in Excel? Pull down the Edit menu and choose either command. You have the same options as in the parallel command in Word, such as a case-sensitive (or insensitive) search. Use the command in the current worksheet to change "Interest" to "Interest Rate".

Step 3: **Determine the 30-year Payments**

> ➤ Click in cell **B6** and enter the formula **=PMT(A6/12,30*12,−$C$1)** as shown in Figure 3.8c. Note the ScreenTip that appears as you enter the function to indicate the order of the arguments. Note, too, that you can enter the references directly or you can use pointing (click the **F4 key** as necessary to change from relative to absolute addresses).
>
> ➤ Click in cell **B6**, which should display the value $699.21, as shown in Figure 3.8c. Click and drag the **fill handle** in the bottom right corner of cell B6 over cells B7 through B11. Release the mouse to complete the copy operation.
>
> ➤ The PMT function in cell B6 has been copied to cells B7 through B11. The payment amounts are visible in cells B7 through B10, but cell B11 displays a series of number signs, meaning that the cell (column) is too narrow to display the computed results in the selected format.
>
> ➤ Check that cells B6:B11 are still selected. Pull down the **Format menu**, click **Column**, then click **AutoFit Selection** from the cascaded menu. Cell B11 should display $1,067.26.
>
> ➤ Save the workbook.

Click in B6 and enter PMT function

ScreenTip shows arguments for the PMT function

(c) Determine the 30-year Payments (step 3)

FIGURE 3.8   *Hands-on Exercise 2 (continued)*

POUND SIGNS AND COLUMN WIDTH

The appearance of pound signs within a cell indicates that the cell width (column width) is insufficient to display the computed results in the selected format. Double click the right border of the column heading to change the column width to accommodate the widest entry in that column. For example, to increase the width of column B, double click the border between the column headings for columns B and C.

Step 4: **Determine the 15-year Payments**

➤ Click in cell **C6** and enter the formula **=PMT(A6/12,15*12,−$C$1)** as shown in Figure 3.8d. Note the ScreenTip that appears as you enter the function to indicate the order of the arguments. You can enter the references directly, or you can use pointing (click the **F4 key** as necessary to change from relative to absolute addresses).

➤ Press **enter** to complete the formula. Check that cell C6 displays the value $927.01. Make corrections as necessary.

➤ Use the **fill handle** to copy the contents of cell **C6** to cells **C7 through C11**. If necessary, increase the width of column C. Cell C11 should display $1,232.52 if you have done this step correctly.

➤ Click in cell **D6** and enter the formula **=C6−B6**, then copy this formula to the remaining cells in this column. Cell D11 should display $165.26.

➤ Save the workbook.

Click in C6 and enter PMT function

ScreenTip shows arguments for the PMT function

(d) Determine the 15-year Payments (step 4)

FIGURE 3.8   *Hands-on Exercise 2 (continued)*

KEYBOARD SHORTCUTS—CUT, COPY, AND PASTE

Ctrl+X (the X is supposed to remind you of a pair of scissors), Ctrl+C, and Ctrl+V are keyboard shortcuts to cut, copy, and paste, respectively, and apply to Excel as well as to Windows applications in general. The keystrokes are easier to remember when you realize that the operative letters X, C, and V are next to each other at the bottom left side of the keyboard. There is no need to memorize the keyboard shortcuts, but as you gain proficiency they will become second nature.

Step 5: **Format the Worksheet**

➤ Click in cell **A13** and enter the label **Financial Consultant**. Enter **your name** in cell A14. Add formatting as necessary using Figure 3.8e as a guide.

➤ Click cell **A4**. Drag the mouse over cells **A4 through D4**. Click the **Merge and Center button** on the Formatting toolbar to center the entry.

➤ Center the column headings in row 5. Add boldface and/or italics to the text and/or numbers as you see fit. Widen columns as necessary.

➤ Pull down the **File menu** and click the **Page Setup command** to display the Page Setup dialog box.

➤ Click the **Margins tab**. Check the box to center the worksheet horizontally. Click the **Sheet tab**. Check the boxes to include row and column headings and gridlines. Click **OK** to exit the Page Setup dialog box.

➤ Save the workbook. Pull down the **File menu**, click the **Print command** to display the Print dialog box, then click **OK** to print the worksheet. Press **Ctrl+~** to display the cell formulas. Widen the columns as necessary, then print.

➤ Press **Ctrl+~** to return to displayed values.

Merge and Center button

Click and drag to select A4:D4

Enter text in A13 and your name in A14

(e) Format the Worksheet (step 5)

FIGURE 3.8 *Hands-on Exercise 2 (continued)*

THE PPMT AND IPMT FUNCTIONS

The PMT function determines the periodic payment for a loan, which in turn is comprised of two components, interest and principal. The amount of the payment that goes toward interest decreases each period, and conversely, the amount for the principle increases. These values can be computed through the IPMT and PPMT functions, respectively, which are used to compute the amortization schedule (payoff) for the loan. See practice exercise 7 at the end of the chapter.

Step 6: **Merge and Center Text**

> Click the **Sheet2 tab** to change to this worksheet. Click in cell **A1** and enter the title of the worksheet, **The Value of an IRA (Individual Retirement Account)**.

> Enter the indicated labels in cells **A3 and C4** as shown in Figure 3.8f. Click in cell **A6** and type the label **Years Contributing**.

> Click and drag to select cells **A6 through A21**, then click the **Merge and Center button** on the Standard toolbar to merge the cells. Right click within the merged cell, then click the **Format Cells command** to display the Format cells dialog box. Click the **Alignment tab**.

> Enter **90** in the **Degrees list box** to change to 90 degrees. Click the **down arrow** on the Vertical list box and choose **Center**. Click **OK**. Click the **Undo button** if the results are different from what you intended.

> Click and drag to select cells **A1 through J1**, then click the **Merge and Center button** to center the title. Merge and center cells **C4 through J4** in similar fashion.

> Click and drag the border between columns A and B to make the column narrower, as appropriate. Save the workbook.

Undo button

Merge and Center button

Enter labels

Click and drag to select A6:A21

Click the Alignment tab

Click drop-down arrow and select Center

Enter 90 degrees

(f) Merge and Center Text (step 6)

FIGURE 3.8 *Hands-on Exercise 2 (continued)*

THE MERGE AND CENTER COMMAND

The Merge and Center command combines multiple cells into a single cell and is best used in conjunction with the headings in a worksheet. Cells can be merged horizontally or vertically, then the text in the merged cells can be aligned in a variety of styles. Text can also be rotated to provide interest in the worksheet. If necessary, you can restore the individual cells and remove the associated formatting using the Edit Clear command. Click in the merged cell, pull down the Edit menu, and click the Clear command. Click Formats to restore the individual cells to the default format.

Step 7:   **Enter the Row and Column Headings**

➤ Check that the labels in your worksheet match those in Figure 3.8g. Click in cell **D3** and enter **$2,000**. Click in cell **C5** and type **5.00%**. Be sure to include the decimal point, zeros, and percent sign.

➤ Click in cell **D5** and enter the formula **=C5+.01**, then click and drag the **fill handle** to copy this formula to cells **E5 through J5**.

➤ Click in cell **B6** and type the number **25**. Click in cell **B7** and enter the formula **=B6+1**, then click and drag the **fill handle** to copy this formula to cells **B8 through B21**.

➤ Double click the **Sheet2 tab** to select the worksheet name, then type **Mixed References** as the name of this worksheet. Double click the **Sheet1 tab** to select the worksheet name, then type **Mortgage Analysis** as the name of this worksheet.

➤ Click the newly named **Mixed References worksheet** tab to return to this worksheet and continue working.

➤ Save the workbook.

Enter $2,000

Enter 5.00%

Enter =C5+.01

Fill handle

Double click Sheet2 tab to rename it

(g) Enter the Row and Column Headings (step 7)

FIGURE 3.8   *Hands-on Exercise 2 (continued)*

AUTOMATIC FORMATTING

Excel converts any number entered with a beginning dollar sign to currency format, and any number entered with an ending percent sign to percentage format. The automatic formatting enables you to save a step by typing $100,000 or 7.5% directly into a cell, rather than entering 100000 or .075 and having to format the number. The formatting is applied to the cell and affects any subsequent numbers in that cell. (Use the Clear command in the Edit menu to remove the formatting.)

Step 8: **Create the Mixed References**

➤ Click in cell **C6**. Pull down the **Insert menu** and click **Function** (or click the **Insert Function button** on the formula bar) to display the Insert Function dialog box.

➤ Click the **drop-down arrow**, then click **Financial** in the Function Category list box. Click **FV** in the Function Name list box. Click **OK**.

➤ Click and drag the **Formula Palette** so that you can see the underlying cells as shown in Figure 3.8h.

➤ Click the text box for rate, click in cell **C5**, then press the **F4 key** until you see **C$5** within the dialog box.

➤ Press **Tab** to move to (or click in) the **Nper text box**, click in cell **B6**, then press the **F4 key** until you see $B6 within the dialog box.

➤ Press **Tab** to move to (or click in) the **Pmt text box**, type a **minus sign**, click in cell **D3**, then press the **F4 key** until you see −**$D$3** in the dialog box.

➤ Check that the entries on your screen match those in Figure 3.8h, then click **OK**. Cell C6 should display the value $95,454.20.

➤ Save the workbook.

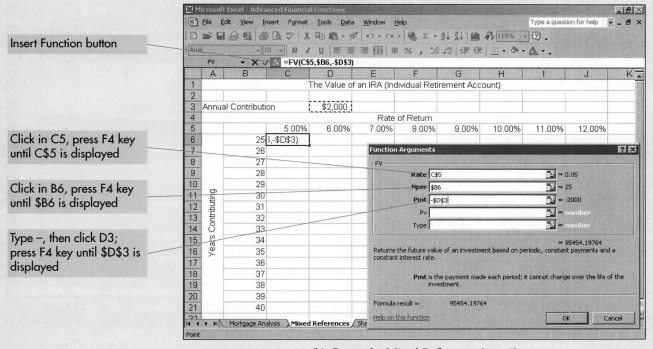

(h) Create the Mixed References (step 8)

FIGURE 3.8   *Hands-on Exercise 2 (continued)*

MIXED REFERENCES ARE NOT DIFFICULT

Mixed references are not difficult, provided you think clearly about what is required. In our example, the interest rate will always come from row 5, but the column will change. Hence you enter C$5 for this parameter within the FV function. In similar fashion, the term of the investment will always come from column B, but the row will change. Thus you enter $B6 for this parameter. It's easy and it's powerful.

Step 9: **Copy the Formula**

➤ If necessary, click in cell **C6**, the cell that contains the formula you just created. Click and drag the **fill handle** in cell **C6** to cells **D6 through J6**.

➤ Change the formatting to **zero decimal places**, then change column widths as necessary. Cell J6 should display the value $266,668.

➤ If necessary, select cells **C6 through D6** as shown in Figure 3.8i. Click and drag the fill handle in cell **J6** to **cell J21** to copy the entire row to the remaining rows in the worksheet.

➤ Release the mouse. Cell J21 should display the value $1,534,183, corresponding to the future value of a $2,000 investment for 40 years at 12 percent. Change column widths as necessary.

➤ Click in cell **C6**, then press the **right arrow** to move from one cell to the next in this row to see how the cell formulas change to reflect the mixed references. Return to cell C6, then press the **down arrow** to view the cell formulas for the other cells in this column.

➤ Save the workbook.

(i) Copy the Formula (step 9)

FIGURE 3.8 *Hands-on Exercise 2 (continued)*

THE ROTH IRA

Anyone can start a Roth IRA provided his or her annual earnings are less than $95,000 (under current law). The Roth IRA is different from a traditional IRA in that the annual contribution is not tax-deductible, but all future earnings are. If, for example, you contribute $2,000 a year for 40 years and earn 8%, you will accumulate more than $500,000 at retirement. Once you retire, you can withdraw as much as you like each year, and any money that you withdraw is tax-free. The remaining funds continue to compound on a tax-free basis.

Step 10:   **The Finishing Touches**

➤ Check that the numbers in your worksheet match those in Figure 3.8j. Make corrections as necessary, then format the worksheet as shown.

➤ Print the worksheet two ways, once with the displayed values and once with the cell contents.

➤ Use the **Page Setup command** to include gridlines and row and column headings. Use landscape formatting if necessary.

➤ Add a cover sheet, then submit all five pages (the cover sheet, the displayed values and cell formulas for the mortgage analysis from step 5, and the displayed values and cell formulas from this step) to your instructor as proof that you completed this exercise.

➤ Exit Excel if you do not want to continue with the next exercise at this time.

Formula bar shows mixed references

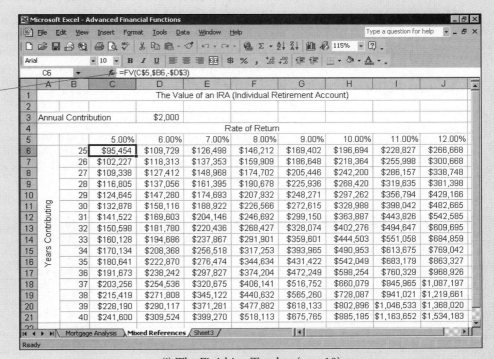

(j) The Finishing Touches (step 10)

FIGURE 3.8   *Hands-on Exercise 2 (continued)*

START SAVING EARLY

The longer you invest, the more time that compound interest has to work its magic. Investing $2,000 for 40 years at 8%, for example, yields a future value of $518,113. Delay for five years, that is invest for 35 years rather than 40, and the amount goes down to $344,634. Put another way—Start your IRA at age 25 and 40 years later you will have accumulated more than half a million dollars. Wait until age 30 and you wind up with significantly less. The out of pocket difference is only $10,000 ($2,000 a year for five years), but the end result at retirement is more than $170,000. Too many people try to time the stock market, which is impossible. It is the time *in* the market that matters.

Financial functions are only one of several categories of functions that are included in Excel. Our next example presents an expanded version of the professor's grade book. It introduces several new functions and shows how those functions can aid in the professor's determination of a student's grade. The expanded grade book is shown in Figure 3.9. Consider:

Statistical functions: The AVERAGE, MAX, and MIN functions are used to compute the statistics on each test for the class as a whole. The range on each test is computed by subtracting the minimum value from the maximum value.

IF function: The IF function conditionally adds a homework bonus of three points to the semester average, prior to determining the letter grade. The bonus is awarded to those students whose homework is "OK." Students whose homework is not "OK" do not receive the bonus.

VLOOKUP function: The expanded grade book converts a student's semester average to a letter grade, in accordance with the table shown in the lower-right portion of the worksheet. A student with an average of 60 to 69 will receive a D, 70 to 79 a C, 80 to 89 a B, and 90 or higher an A. Any student with an average less than 60 receives an F.

The Sort command: The rows within a spreadsheet can be displayed in any sequence by clicking on the appropriate column within the list of students, then clicking the Ascending or Descending sort button on the Standard toolbar. The students in Figure 3.9 are listed alphabetically, but could just as easily have been listed by social security number.

	Name	Soc Sec Num	Test 1	Test 2	Test 3	Test 4	Test Average	Homework	Semester Average	Grade
1	Professor's Grade Book - Final Semester Averages									
2										
3	Name	Soc Sec Num	Test 1	Test 2	Test 3	Test 4	Test Average	Homework	Semester Average	Grade
4	Adams, John	111-22-3333	80	71	70	84	77.8	Poor	77.8	C
5	Barber, Maryann	444-55-6666	96	98	97	90	94.2	OK	97.2	A
6	Boone, Dan	777-88-9999	78	81	70	78	77.0	OK	80.0	B
7	Borow, Jeff	123-45-6789	65	65	65	60	63.0	OK	66.0	D
8	Brown, James	999-99-9999	92	95	79	80	85.2	OK	88.2	B
9	Carson, Kit	888-88-8888	90	90	90	70	82.0	OK	85.0	B
10	Coulter, Sara	100-00-0000	60	50	40	79	61.6	OK	64.6	D
11	Fegin, Richard	222-22-2222	75	70	65	95	80.0	OK	83.0	B
12	Ford, Judd	200-00-0000	90	90	80	90	88.0	Poor	88.0	B
13	Glassman, Kris	444-44-4444	82	78	62	77	75.2	OK	78.2	C
14	Goodman, Neil	555-55-5555	92	88	65	78	80.2	OK	83.2	B
15	Milgrom, Marion	666-66-6666	94	92	86	84	88.0	OK	91.0	A
16	Moldof, Adam	300-00-0000	92	78	65	84	80.6	OK	83.6	B
17	Smith, Adam	777-77-7777	60	50	65	80	67.0	Poor	67.0	D
18										
19	Average		81.9	78.3	71.4	80.6	HW Bonus	3	Grading Criteria	
20	Highest Grade		96.0	98.0	97.0	95.0			0	F
21	Lowest Grade		60.0	50.0	40.0	60.0			60	D
22	Range		36.0	48.0	57.0	35.0			70	C
23									80	B
24	Exam Weights		20%	20%	20%	40%			90	A

Statistical functions   IF Function   VLOOKUP Function

FIGURE 3.9 *The Expanded Grade Book*

Statistical Functions

The *MAX*, *MIN*, and *AVERAGE functions* return the highest, lowest, and average values, respectively, from an argument list. The list may include individual cell references, ranges, numeric values, functions, or mathematical expressions (formulas). The *statistical functions* are illustrated in the worksheet of Figure 3.10.

The first example, =AVERAGE(A1:A3), computes the average for cells A1 through A3 by adding the values in the indicated range (70, 80, and 90), then dividing the result by three, to obtain an average of 80. Additional arguments in the form of values and/or cell addresses can be specified within the parentheses; for example, the function =AVERAGE(A1:A3,200), computes the average of cells A1, A2, and A3, and the number 200.

Cells that are empty or cells that contain text values are *not* included in the computation. Thus, since cell A4 is empty, the function =AVERAGE(A1:A4) also returns an average of 80 (240/3). In similar fashion, the function =AVERAGE(A1:A3,A5) includes only three values in its computation (cells A1, A2, and A3), because the text entry in cell A5 is excluded. The results of the MIN and MAX functions are obtained in a comparable way, as indicated in Figure 3.10. Empty cells and text entries are not included in the computation.

The COUNT and COUNTA functions each tally the number of entries in the argument list and are subtly different. The *COUNT function* returns the number of cells containing a numeric entry, including formulas that evaluate to numeric results. The *COUNTA function* includes cells with text as well as numeric values. The functions =COUNT(A1:A3) and =COUNTA(A1:A3) both return a value of 3 as do the two functions =COUNT(A1:A4) and =COUNTA(A1:A4). (Cell A4 is empty and is excluded from the latter computations.) The function =COUNT(A1:A3,A5) also returns a value of 3 because it does not include the text entry in cell A5. However, the function =COUNTA(A1:A3,A5) returns a value of 4 because it includes the text entry in cell A5.

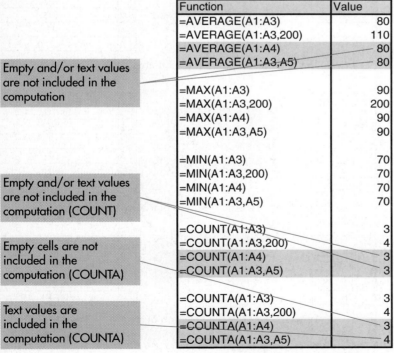

Empty and/or text values are not included in the computation

Empty and/or text values are not included in the computation (COUNT)

Empty cells are not included in the computation (COUNTA)

Text values are included in the computation (COUNTA)

Function	Value
=AVERAGE(A1:A3)	80
=AVERAGE(A1:A3,200)	110
=AVERAGE(A1:A4)	80
=AVERAGE(A1:A3,A5)	80
=MAX(A1:A3)	90
=MAX(A1:A3,200)	200
=MAX(A1:A4)	90
=MAX(A1:A3,A5)	90
=MIN(A1:A3)	70
=MIN(A1:A3,200)	70
=MIN(A1:A4)	70
=MIN(A1:A3,A5)	70
=COUNT(A1:A3)	3
=COUNT(A1:A3,200)	4
=COUNT(A1:A4)	3
=COUNT(A1:A3,A5)	3
=COUNTA(A1:A3)	3
=COUNTA(A1:A3,200)	4
=COUNTA(A1:A4)	3
=COUNTA(A1:A3,A5)	4

Empty cell

Text value

	A
1	70
2	80
3	90
4	
5	Study hard

(b) The Spreadsheet

(a) Illustrative Functions

FIGURE 3.10 *Statistical Functions with a Text Entry*

Arithmetic Expressions versus Functions

Many worksheet calculations, such as an average or a sum, can be performed in two ways. You can enter a formula such as =(A1+A2+A3)/3, or you can use the equivalent function =AVERAGE(A1:A3). *The use of functions is generally preferable* as shown in Figure 3.11.

The two worksheets in Figure 3.11a may appear equivalent, but the SUM function is superior to the arithmetic expression. This is true despite the fact that the entries in cell A5 of both worksheets return a value of 100.

Consider what happens if a new row is inserted between existing rows 2 and 3, with the entry in the new cell equal to 25 as shown in Figure 3.11b. The SUM function adjusts automatically to include the new value (returning a sum of 125) because the SUM function was defined originally for the cell range *A1 through A4*. The new row is inserted within these cells, moving the entry in cell A4 to cell A5, and changing the range to include cell A5.

No such accommodation is made in the arithmetic expression, which was defined to include four *specific* cells rather than a range of cells. The addition of the new row modifies the cell references (since the values in cells A3 and A4 have been moved to cells A4 and A5), and does not include the new row in the adjusted expression.

Similar reasoning holds for deleting a row. Figure 3.11c deletes row two from the *original* worksheets, which moves the entry in cell A4 to cell A3. The SUM function adjusts automatically to =SUM(A1:A3) and returns the value 80. The formula, however, returns an error (to indicate an illegal cell reference) because it is still attempting to add the entries in four cells, one of which no longer exists. In summary, a function expands and contracts to adjust for insertions or deletions, and should be used wherever possible.

(a) Spreadsheets as Initially Entered

(b) Spreadsheets after the Addition of a New Row

(c) Spreadsheets after the Deletion of a Row

FIGURE 3.11 *Arithmetic Expressions versus Functions*

IF Function

The *IF function* enables decision making to be implemented within a worksheet. It has three arguments: a condition that is either true or false, the value if the condition is true, and the value if the condition is false. Consider:

=IF(condition,value-if-true,value-if-false)
— Value returned for a false condition
— Value returned for a true condition
— Condition is either true or false

The IF function returns either the second or third argument, depending on the result of the condition; that is, if the condition is true, the function returns the second argument. If the condition is false, the function returns the third argument.

The condition includes one of the six *relational operators* in Figure 3.12a. The IF function is illustrated in the worksheet in Figure 3.12b, which is used to create the examples in Figure 3.12c. The arguments may be numeric (1000 or 2000), a cell reference to display the contents of the specific cell (B1 or B2), a formula (=B1+10 or =B1−10), a function (MAX(B1:B2) or MIN(B1:B2)), or a text entry enclosed in quotation marks ("Go" or "Hold").

Operator	Description
=	Equal to
<>	Not equal to
<	Less than
>	Greater than
<=	Less than or equal to
>=	Greater than or equal to

(a) Relational Operators

	A	B	C
1	10	15	April
2	10	30	May

(b) The Spreadsheet

IF Function	Evaluation	Result
=IF(A1=A2,1000,2000)	10 is equal to 10: TRUE	1000
=IF(A1<>A2,1000,2000)	10 is not equal to 10: FALSE	2000
=IF(A1<>A2,B1,B2)	10 is not equal to 10:FALSE	30
=IF(A1<B2,MAX(B1:B2),MIN(B1:B2))	10 is less than 30: TRUE	30
=IF(A1<A2,B1+10,B1-10)	10 is less than 10:FALSE	5
=IF(A1=A2,C1,C2)	10 is equal to 10: TRUE	April
=IF(SUM(A1:A2)>20,"Go","Hold")	10+10 is greater than 20:FALSE	Hold

(c) Examples

FIGURE 3.12   *The IF Function*

The IF function is used in the grade book of Figure 3.9 to award a bonus for homework. Students whose homework is "OK" receive the bonus, whereas other students do not. The IF function to implement this logic for the first student is entered in cell H4 as follows:

=IF(H4="OK",G4+$H$19,G4)
— Average is unchanged if homework *not* "OK"
— Average is incremented by the bonus in cell H19 if homework is "OK"
— Condition determines if homework is "OK"

The IF function compares the value in cell H4 (the homework grade) to the literal "OK." If the condition is true (the homework is "OK"), the bonus in cell H19 is added to the student's test average in cell G4. If, however, the condition is false (the homework is not "OK"), the average is unchanged.

VLOOKUP Function

Consider, for a moment, how the professor assigns letter grades to students at the end of the semester. He or she computes a test average for each student and conditionally awards the bonus for homework. The professor then determines a letter grade according to a predetermined scale; for example, 90 or above is an A, 80 to 89 is a B, and so on.

The **VLOOKUP** (vertical lookup) **function** duplicates this process within a worksheet by assigning an entry to a cell based on a numeric value contained in another cell. The **HLOOKUP** (horizontal lookup) **function** is similar in concept except that the table is arranged horizontally. In other words, just as the professor knows where on the grading scale a student's numerical average will fall, the VLOOKUP function determines where within a specified table (the grading criteria) a numeric value (a student's average) is found, and retrieves the corresponding entry (the letter grade).

The VLOOKUP function requires three arguments: the numeric value to look up, the range of cells containing the table in which the value is to be looked up, and the column-number within the table that contains the result. These concepts are illustrated in Figure 3.13, which was taken from the expanded grade book in Figure 3.9. The table in Figure 3.13 extends over two columns (I and J), and five rows (20 through 24); that is, the table is located in the range I20:J24. The **breakpoints** or matching values (the lowest numeric value for each grade) are contained in column I (the first column in the table) and are in ascending order. The corresponding letter grades are found in column J.

The VLOOKUP function in cell J4 determines the letter grade (for John Adams) based on the computed average in cell I4. Consider:

=VLOOKUP(I4,$I$20:$J$24,2)

└─ The column number containing the grade

└─ The range of the table

└─ Numeric value to look up (the student's average)

The first argument is the value to look up, which in this example is Adams's computed average, found in cell I4. A relative reference is used so that the address will adjust when the formula is copied to the other rows in the worksheet.

	A	. . .	G	H	I	J
1	Professor's Grade Book - Final Semester Averages					
2						
3	Name		Test Average	Homework	Semester Average	Grade
4	Adams, John		77.8	Poor		
	.	.	.	.	.	.
	.	.	.	.	.	.
	.	.	.	.	.	.
19	Average		HW Bonus	3	Grading Criteria	
20	Highest Grade				0	F
21	Lowest Grade				60	D
22	Range				70	C
23					80	B
24	Exam Weights				90	A

=VLOOKUP(I4,$I$20:$J$24,2) Breakpoints (in ascending order) Grades are in column 2 of table

FIGURE 3.13 *Table Lookup Function*

A large worksheet, such as the extended grade book, can seldom be seen on the monitor in its entirety. It's necessary, therefore, to learn how to view the distant parts of a worksheet, to keep certain parts of the worksheet in constant view, and/or to hide selected rows and columns. These concepts are illustrated in Figure 3.14. Figure 3.14a displays the initial worksheet, with cell A1 selected as the active cell, so that you see the upper-left portion of the worksheet, rows 1 through 20 inclusive, and columns A through I inclusive. You cannot see the semester grades in column J, nor can you see the class averages and other statistics that begin in row 21.

Clicking the right arrow on the horizontal scroll bar (or pressing the right arrow key when the active cell is already in the rightmost column of the screen) causes the entire screen to move one column to the right. In similar fashion, clicking the down arrow in the vertical scroll bar (or pressing the down arrow key when the active cell is in the bottom row of the screen) causes the entire screen to move down one row. This is known as *scrolling* and it comes about automatically as the active cell is changed as you work with the worksheet.

Freezing Panes

Scrolling brings the distant portions of a worksheet into view, but it also moves the headings for existing rows and/or columns off the screen. You can, however, retain the headings by freezing panes as shown in Figure 3.14b. The letter grades and the grading criteria are visible as in the previous figure, but so too are the names at the left of the worksheet and the column headings at the top of the worksheet.

Look closely at Figure 3.14b and you will see column B (containing the Social Security numbers) is missing, as are rows 4 through 7 (the first four students). You will also notice a horizontal line under row three and a vertical line after column A, to indicate that these rows and columns have been frozen. This is accomplished through the *Freeze Panes command* that always displays the desired row or column headings (column A and rows 1, 2 and 3 in this example) regardless of the scrolling in effect. The rows and/or columns that are frozen are the ones above and to the left of the active cell when the command is issued. The *Unfreeze Panes command* returns to normal scrolling.

Hiding Rows and Columns

Figure 3.14c illustrates the ability to hide rows and/or columns in a worksheet. We have hidden columns C through F (inclusive) that contain the results of the individual tests, and rows 19 through 24 that contain the summary statistics. The "missing" rows and columns remain in the workbook but are hidden from view. The cells are not visible in the monitor, nor do they appear when the worksheet is printed. To hide a row or column, click the row or column heading to select the entire row or column, then execute the Hide command from within the Format menu. *Unhiding cells* is trickier because you need to select the adjacent rows or columns prior to executing the Unhide command.

Printing a Large Worksheet

The *Page Break Preview command* (in the View menu) lets you see and/or modify the page breaks that will occur when the worksheet is printed as shown in Figure 3.14d. The dashed blue line between columns H and I indicate that the worksheet will print on two pages, with columns A to H on page 1 and columns I and J on page 2. The dialog box shows that you adjust (eliminate) the page break by dragging the dashed line to the right.

The **Page Setup command** also contains various options that are used in conjunction with printing a large worksheet. You might, for example change from Portrait (8½ × 11) orientation to Landscape (11 × 8½), use scaling to force the entire worksheet on one page, and/or reduce the margins. You can also select an option to repeat the row and/or column headings on every page of a multiple-page printout.

(a) The Grade Book

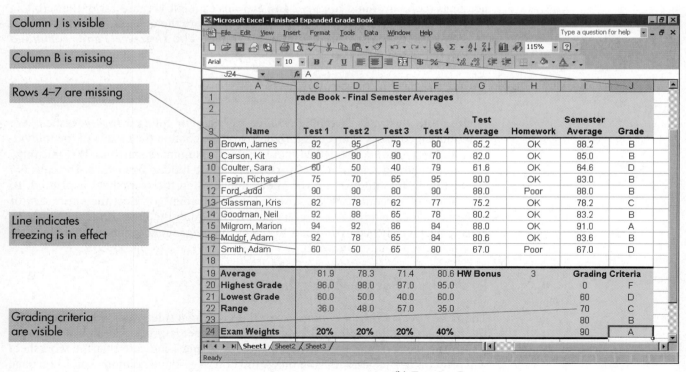

(b) Freezing Panes

FIGURE 3.14 *Working with Large Spreadsheets*

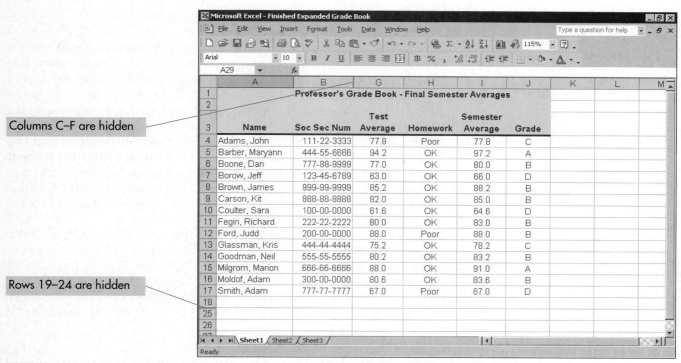

Columns C–F are hidden

Rows 19–24 are hidden

(c) Hiding Rows and Columns

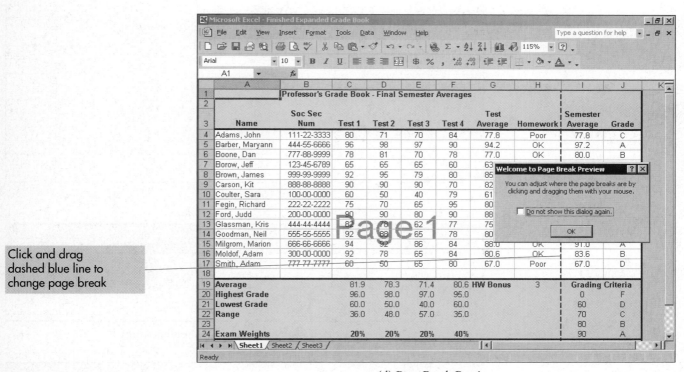

Click and drag
dashed blue line to
change page break

(d) Page Break Preview

FIGURE 3.14 *Working with Large Spreadsheets (continued)*

AutoFilter Command

The **AutoFilter command** lets you display a selected set of students (rows) within a worksheet as shown in Figure 3.15. The hidden rows are *not* deleted, but are simply not displayed. We begin with Figure 3.15a, which shows the list of all students (with selected columns hidden from view). Look closely at the column headings in row three and note the presence of drop-down arrows that appear in response to the AutoFilter command.

Clicking a drop-down arrow produces a list of the unique values for that column, enabling you to establish the criteria-selected records. To display the students with poor homework, for example, click the drop-down arrow for Homework, then click Poor from the resulting list. Figure 3.15b shows three students in rows 4, 12, and 17 that satisfy the filter. The remaining students are still in the worksheet but are not shown because of the selection criterion.

A filter condition can be imposed on multiple columns as shown in Figure 3.15c. As indicated, the worksheet in Figure 3.15b displays the only students with poor homework. Clicking the arrow next to Grade, then clicking "B", will filter the list further to display the students who received a "B" *and* who have poor homework. Only one student meets both conditions, as shown in Figure 3.15c. The drop-down arrows next to Homework and Grade are displayed in blue to indicate that a filter is in effect for these columns.

Drop-down arrows appear next to each field name

Only students with poor homework will be displayed

3	A — Name	G — Test Avg	H — Homework	I — Semester Avg	J — Grade
4	Adams, John	77.8	(All) (Top 10...) (Custom...) OK Poor	77.8	C
5	Barber, Maryann	94.2		97.2	A
6	Boone, Dan	77.0		80.0	B
7	Borow, Jeff	63.0		66.0	D
8	Brown, James	85.2	OK	88.2	B
9	Carson, Kit	82.0	OK	85.0	B
10	Coulter, Sara	61.6	OK	64.6	D
11	Fegin, Richard	80.0	OK	83.0	B
12	Ford, Judd	88.0	Poor	88.0	B
13	Glassman, Kris	75.2	OK	78.2	C
14	Goodman, Neil	80.2	OK	83.2	B
15	Milgrom, Marion	88.0	OK	91.0	A
16	Moldof, Adam	80.6	OK	83.6	B
17	Smith, Adam	67.0	Poor	67.0	D

(a) Unfiltered List

Blue arrow indicates filter is in effect

3	A — Name	G — Test Avg	H — Homework	I — Semester Avg	J — Grade
4	Adams, John	77.8	Poor	77.8	(All) (Top 10...) (Custom...) B C D
12	Ford, Judd	88.0	Poor	88.0	
17	Smith, Adam	67.0	Poor	67.0	
18					
19					

(b) Filtered List (students with poor homework)

Intermediate rows are hidden from view

3	A — Name	G — Test Avg	H — Homework	I — Semester Avg	J — Grade
12	Ford, Judd	88.0	Poor	88.0	B

(c) Imposing a Second Condition

FIGURE 3.15 *The AutoFilter Command*

THE EXPANDED GRADE BOOK

Objective To develop the expanded grade book; to use statistical (AVERAGE, MAX, and MIN) and logical (IF and VLOOKUP) functions; to demonstrate scrolling and the Freeze Panes command. Use Figure 3.16 as a guide.

Step 1: **The Fill Handle**

➤ Open the **Expanded Grade Book** in the Exploring Excel folder. Click in cell **C3**, the cell containing the label Test 1 as shown in Figure 3.16a.

➤ Click and drag the **fill handle** over cells **D3, E3, and F3** (a ScreenTip shows the projected result in cell F3), then release the mouse. Cells D3, E3, and F3 contain the labels Test 2, Test 3, and Test 4, respectively.

➤ Save the workbook as **Finished Expanded Grade Book** so that you can always return to the original workbook if necessary.

Click and drag fill handle to F3

(a) The Fill Handle (step 1)

FIGURE 3.16 *Hands-on Exercise 3*

THE AUTOFILL CAPABILITY

The AutoFill capability is the fastest way to enter certain series into contiguous cells. Enter the starting value(s) in a series, then drag the fill handle to the adjacent cells. Excel completes the series based on the initial value. Type January (or Jan), Monday (or Mon), then drag the fill handle in the direction you want to fill. Excel will enter the appropriate months or days of the week, respectively. You can also type text followed by a number, such as Product 1 or Quarter 1, then use the fill handle to extend the series.

Step 2: **Format the Social Security Numbers**

➤ Click and drag to select cells **B4 through B17**, the cells containing the unformatted Social Security numbers.

➤ Point to the selected cells and click the **right mouse button** to display a shortcut (context-sensitive) menu.

➤ Click the **Format Cells command**, click the **Number tab**, then click **Special** in the Category list box as shown in Figure 3.16b.

➤ Click **Social Security Number** in the Type box, then click **OK** to accept the formatting and close the Format Cells dialog box. The Social Security numbers are displayed with hyphens.

➤ Save the workbook.

(b) Format the Social Security Numbers (step 2)

FIGURE 3.16 *Hands-on Exercise 3 (continued)*

THE LEFT AND RIGHT FUNCTIONS

A professor may want to post grades, but cannot do so by student name or Social Security Number. One can, however, create an "ID number" consisting of the left- or rightmost digits in the Social Security number. Insert a new column into the worksheet, then go to the cell for the first student in this column (e.g., cell C4 if you insert a new column C). Enter the function =LEFT(B4,4) to display the first four digits from cell B4, corresponding to the first four (leftmost) digits in Adams's Social Security Number. You could also enter the function =RIGHT(B4,4) to display the last four (rightmost) digits. Hide the columns containing the names and Social Security numbers, then post the grades. See practice exercise 9 at the end of the chapter.

Step 3: **The Freeze Panes Command**

➤ Press **Ctrl+Home** to move to cell A1. Click the **right arrow** on the horizontal scroll bar until column A scrolls off the screen. Cell A1 is still the active cell, because scrolling with the mouse does not change the active cell.

➤ Press **Ctrl+Home**. Press the **right arrow key** until column A scrolls off the screen. The active cell changes as you scroll with the keyboard.

➤ Press **Ctrl+Home** again, then click in cell **B4**. Pull down the **Window menu**. Click **Freeze Panes** as shown in Figure 3.16c. You will see a line to the right of column A and below row 3.

➤ Click the **right arrow** on the horizontal scroll bar (or press the **right arrow key**) repeatedly until column J is visible. Note that column A is visible (frozen), but that one or more columns are not shown.

➤ Click the **down arrow** on the vertical scroll bar (or press the **down arrow key**) repeatedly until row 25 is visible. Note that rows one through three are visible (frozen), but that one or more rows are not shown.

(c) The Freeze Panes Command (step 3)

FIGURE 3.16 *Hands-on Exercise 3 (continued)*

GO TO A SPECIFIC CELL

Ctrl+Home and Ctrl+End will take you to the upper-left and bottom-right cells within a worksheet, but how do you get to a specific cell? One way is to click in the Name box (to the left of the formula bar), enter the cell reference (e.g., K250), and press the enter key. You can also pull down the Edit menu and click the Go To command (or press the F5 key) to display the Go To dialog box, enter the name of the cell in the Reference text box, then press enter to go directly to the cell.

Step 4: **The IF Function**

➤ Scroll until Column I is visible on the screen. Click in cell **I4**.
➤ Click the **Insert Function button** on the formula bar. Click the **down arrow** and click **Logical** in the category list box. Click **IF** in the Function name list box, then click **OK** to display the Function Arguments dialog box in Figure 3.16d.
➤ You can enter the arguments directly, or you can use pointing as follows:
  • Click the **Logical_test** text box. Click cell **H4** in the worksheet. (You may need to click and drag the top border of the Formula Palette of the dialog box to move it out of the way.) Type =**"OK"** to complete the logical test.
  • Click the **Value_if_true** text box. Click cell **G4** in the worksheet, type a **plus sign**, click cell **H19** in the worksheet (scrolling if necessary), and finally press the **F4 key** (see boxed tip) to convert the reference to cell H19 to an absolute reference ($H$19).
  • Click the **Value_if_false** text box. Click cell **G4** in the worksheet.
➤ Check that the dialog box on your worksheet matches the one in Figure 3.16d. Click **OK** to insert the function into your worksheet.
➤ Save the workbook.

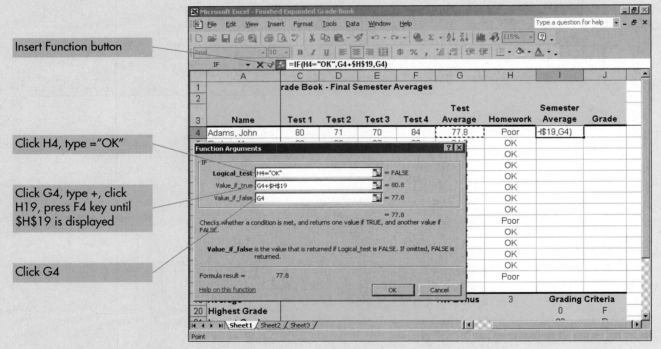

(d) The IF Function (step 4)

FIGURE 3.16 *Hands-on Exercise 3 (continued)*

THE F4 KEY

The F4 key cycles through relative, absolute, and mixed addresses. Click on any reference within the formula bar; for example, click on A1 in the formula =A1+A2. Press the F4 key once, and it changes to an absolute reference. Press the F4 key a second time, and it becomes a mixed reference, A$1; press it again, and it is a different mixed reference, $A1. Press the F4 key a fourth time, and return to the original relative address, A1.

Step 5: **The VLOOKUP Function**

➤ Click in cell **J4**. Click the **Insert Function button** on the formula bar. Click **Lookup & Reference** in the category list box. Scroll in the Function name list box until you can select **VLOOKUP**. Click **OK** to display the Function Arguments dialog box in Figure 3.16e.

➤ Enter the arguments for the VLOOKUP function as shown in the figure. You can enter the arguments directly, or you can use pointing as follows:
   • Click the **Lookup_value** text box. Click cell **I4** in the worksheet.
   • Click the **Table_array** text box. Click cell **I20** and drag to cell **J24** (scrolling if necessary). Press the **F4 key** to convert to an absolute reference.
   • Click the **Col_index_num** text box. Type **2**.

➤ Check that the dialog box on your worksheet matches the one in Figure 3.16e. Make corrections as necessary. Click **OK** to insert the completed function into your worksheet.

➤ Save the workbook.

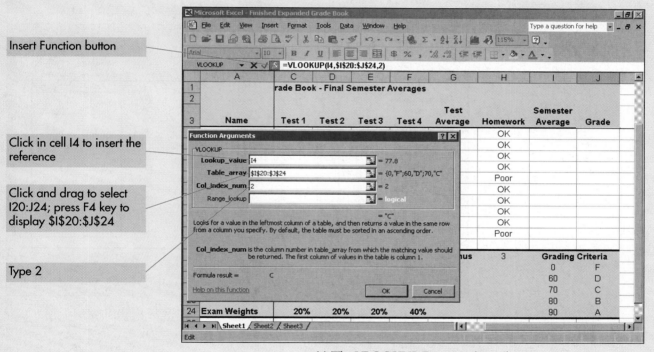

(e) The VLOOKUP Function (step 5)

FIGURE 3.16 *Hands-on Exercise 3 (continued)*

THE COLLAPSE DIALOG BUTTON

You can enter a cell reference in one of two ways: you can type it directly in the Function Arguments dialog box, or click the cell in the worksheet. The Function Arguments dialog box typically hides the necessary cell, however, in which case you can click the Collapse Dialog button (which appears to the right of any parameter within the dialog box). This collapses (hides) the Function Arguments dialog box so that you can click the underlying cell, which is now visible. Click the Collapse Dialog button a second time to display the entire dialog box.

Step 6: **Copy the IF and VLOOKUP Functions**

➤ If necessary, scroll to the top of the worksheet. Select cells **I4** and **J4** as in Figure 3.16f.

➤ Point to the **fill handle** in the lower-right corner of the selected range. The mouse pointer changes to a thin crosshair.

➤ Drag the **fill handle** over cells **I5 through J17**. A border appears, indicating the destination range as shown in Figure 3.16f. Release the mouse to complete the copy operation.

➤ If you have done everything correctly, Adam Smith should have a grade of D based on a semester average of 67.

➤ Format the semester averages in column I to one decimal place.

➤ Save the workbook.

(f) Copy the IF and VLOOKUP Functions (step 6)

FIGURE 3.16 *Hands-on Exercise 3 (continued)*

USE NESTED IFS FOR MORE COMPLEX DECISION MAKING

A "nested IF" (or "IF within an IF") is a common logic structure in every programming language. It could be used in the expanded grade book to implement more complicated logic such as a variable homework bonus (of −2, 3, and 5), depending on the grade (for "poor", OK, and good, respectively). The IF function in Excel has three arguments—a condition, a value if the condition is true, and a value if the condition is false. A nested IF simply replaces the true and/or false value with another IF statement. See practice exercise 9 at the end of the chapter.

Step 7: **Create the Summary Statistics**

➤ Scroll until you can click in cell **C19**. Type **=AVERAGE(C4:C17)**. Press **enter**. Cell C19 should display 81.9 as shown in Figure 3.16g.

➤ Click in cell **C20** and enter the formula **=MAX(C4:C17)**. Click in cell **C21** and enter the formula **=MIN(C4:C17)**.

➤ Click in cell **C22** and enter the formula **=C20−C21**. Check that the displayed values match those in Figure 3.16g.

➤ Click and drag to select cells C19 through C22, then click and drag the **fill handle** to cell F22. Release the mouse. Click outside the selection to deselect the cells.

➤ Save the workbook.

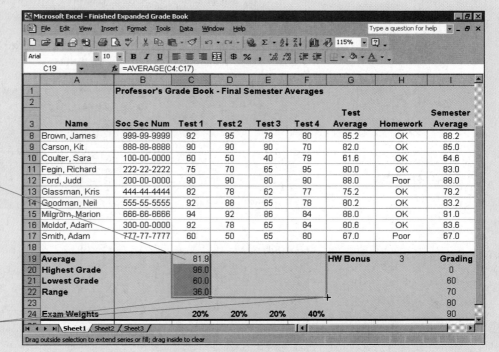

(g) Create the Summary Statistics (step 7)

FIGURE 3.16   *Hands-on Exercise 3 (continued)*

RANK IN CLASS

Use the Rank function to determine a student's rank in class. (Excel also has functions for quartiles and percentiles.) Add a new column to the worksheet, column K in this example, then click in the cell for the first student in the list (cell K4). Enter the function =RANK(I4,$I$4:$I$17), where I4 contains the value you want to look up (the individual student's semester average) and $I$4:$I$17 references the set of numbers on which to base the rank. The latter is entered as an absolute reference so that the cell formula may be copied to the remaining cells in column K. See practice exercise 9 at the end of the chapter.

Step 8: **The Page Break Preview Command**

➤ Pull down the **View menu** and click the **Page Break Preview command** to see the potential page breaks as shown in Figure 3.16h. Click **OK** if you see the welcome message.

➤ Click and drag the dashed blue line to the right to eliminate the page break. (You can also drag the solid blue line that appears on the right border to the left to create a page break.)

➤ Pull down the **View menu** and click **Normal** to return to the Normal view.

➤ Pull down the **File menu**. Click **Page Setup** to display the Page Setup dialog box. Click the **Margins tab**. Check the box to center the worksheet horizontally on the page.

➤ Click the **Sheet tab**. Check the boxes for **Row and Column Headings** and for **Gridlines**.

➤ Click the **Print Preview button** to display the completed spreadsheet. Click the **Print button** and click **OK** to print the workbook.

➤ Print the worksheet with the cell formulas.

Print Preview button

Blue dashed line indicates page break

Click and drag dashed line to right

(h) The Page Break Preview Command (step 8)

FIGURE 3.16   *Hands-on Exercise 3 (continued)*

SET PRINT AREA(S)

Press and hold the Ctrl key as you click and drag to select one or more areas in the worksheet, then pull down the File menu, select the Print Area command and click Set Print Area. The print area is enclosed in dashed lines. The next time you execute the Print command, you will print just the print area(s), with each print area appearing on a separate page. Use the Print Area command in the File menu to clear the print area.

Step 9:   **Hide the Rows and Columns**

➤ Click and drag the column headings for columns **C through F** to select these columns, point to the selected columns then click the **right mouse button** to display the context-sensitive menu in Figure 3.16h. Click **Hide** to hide these columns.

➤ Click and drag the row headings for rows **19 through 24** to select these rows, point to the selected rows, click the **right mouse button**, and click the **Hide command**. Print the worksheet.

➤ Now reverse the process and unhide the rows, but leave the columns hidden. Click and drag to select the row headings for rows **18 and 25** (which are contiguous), right click to display a context-sensitive menu, then click the **Unhide command**.

➤ You should see all of the rows in the entire worksheet (within the limitations of scrolling). Save the workbook.

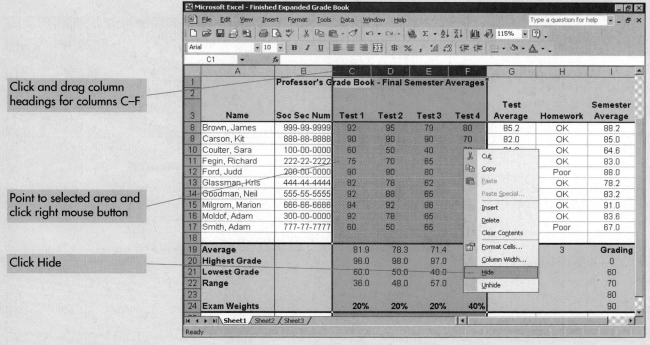

(i) Hide the Rows and Columns (step 9)

FIGURE 3.16   *Hands-on Exercise 3 (continued)*

UNHIDING ROWS AND COLUMNS

Hiding a row or column is easy; you just select the row or column(s) you want to hide, click the right mouse button, then select the Hide command from the shortcut menu. Unhiding a row or column is trickier, because you cannot see the target cells. To unhide a column, for example, you need to select the columns on either side; for example, select columns A and C if you are trying to unhide column B. To unhide column A, however, click in the Name box and enter A1. Pull down the Format menu, click Column, then click the Unhide command.

Step 10: **The AutoFilter Command**

> ➤ Click anywhere within the list of students. Pull down the **Data menu**, click the **Filter command**, then click **AutoFilter**. The worksheet is essentially unchanged except that each column heading is followed by a drop-down arrow.
> ➤ Click the **drop-down arrow** in cell H3 (the column containing the students' homework grades). Click **Poor**. The list of students changes to show only those students who received this grade on their homework as shown in Figure 3.16j.
> ➤ Click the **drop-down arrow** in cell J3, then select **B** from the drop-down list of grade values. The list changes to show the one student who managed to receive a "B" despite having poor homework.
> ➤ Add your name and title (**Grading Assistant**) in cells G26 and G27. Save the workbook, then print it for your instructor.
> ➤ Pull down the **Data menu** and click the **AutoFilter command** to remove the filter and display all of the students.
> ➤ Exit Excel.

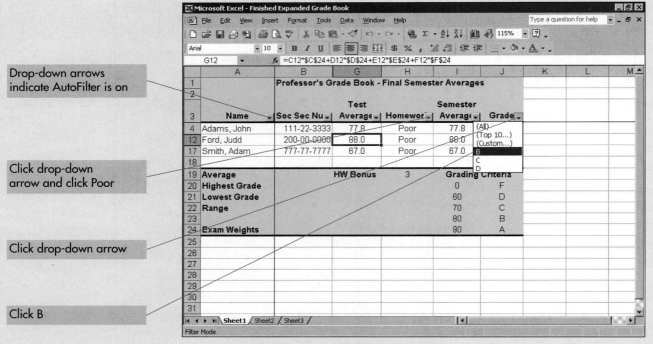

(j) The AutoFilter Command (step 10)

FIGURE 3.16   *Hands-on Exercise 3 (continued)*

USE COMMENTS WITH COLLEAGUES

It's helpful to insert comments into a workbook to send suggestions to colleagues who will be using the same workbook. Click in the cell where you want the comment to go, pull down the Insert menu to enter the comment, then click elsewhere in the worksheet when you are finished. Point to the cell (which should have a tiny red triangle) and you will see the comment you just entered. Right click in the cell after the comment has been entered to edit and/or delete the comment if necessary. See practice exercise 2 at the end of the chapter.

Excel contains several categories of built-in functions. The PMT function computes the periodic payment for a loan based on three arguments (the interest rate per period, the number of periods, and the amount of the loan). The IPMT and PPMT functions determine the amount of each payment that goes toward interest and principal, respectively. The FV function returns the future value of an investment based on constant periodic payments and a constant interest rate.

Statistical functions were also discussed. The AVERAGE, MAX, and MIN functions return the average, highest, and lowest values in the argument list. The COUNT function returns the number of cells with numeric entries. The COUNTA function displays the number of cells with numeric and/or text entries.

The IF, VLOOKUP, and HLOOKUP functions implement decision making within a worksheet. The IF function has three arguments: a condition, which is evaluated as true or false; a value if the test is true; and a value if the test is false. The VLOOKUP and HLOOKUP functions also have three arguments: the numeric value to look up, the range of cells containing the table, and the column or row number within the table that contains the result.

The hands-on exercises introduced several techniques to make you more proficient. The fill handle is used to copy a cell or group of cells to a range of adjacent cells. Pointing is a more accurate way to enter a cell reference into a formula as it uses the mouse or arrow keys to select the cell as you build the formula. The AutoFill capability creates a series based on the initial value(s) you supply.

Scrolling enables you to view any portion of a large worksheet but moves the labels for existing rows and/or columns off the screen. The Freeze Panes command keeps the row and/or column headings on the screen while scrolling within a large worksheet.

A spreadsheet is first and foremost a tool for decision making, and thus Excel includes several commands to aid in that process. The Goal Seek command lets you enter the desired end result of a spreadsheet model (such as the monthly payment on a car loan) and determines the input (the price of the car) necessary to produce that result.

The assumptions and initial conditions in a spreadsheet should be clearly labeled and set apart from the rest of the worksheet. This facilitates change and reduces the chance for error.

Absolute reference (p. 122)
Arguments (p. 112)
Assumptions (p. 122)
AutoFill capability (p. 143)
AutoFilter command (p. 142)
AVERAGE function (p. 135)
Breakpoint (p. 138)
COUNT function (p. 135)
COUNTA function (p. 135)
Freeze Panes command (p. 139)
Function (p. 112)
FV function (p. 112)
Goal Seek command (p. 114)

HLOOKUP function (p. 138)
IF function (p. 137)
Insert Function command (p. 113)
IRA (Individual Retirement
    Account) (p. 123)
MAX function (p. 135)
MIN function (p. 135)
Mixed reference (p. 123)
Nested IF (p. 148)
Page Break Preview command
    (p. 139)
Page Setup command (p. 140)
PMT function (p. 112)

Relational operator (p. 137)
Relative reference (p. 122)
Scrolling (p. 139)
Sort command (p. 134)
Spell check (p. 124)
Statistical functions (p. 135)
SUM function (p. 136)
Template (p. 110)
Unfreeze Panes command (p. 139)
Unhiding cells (p. 139)
VLOOKUP function (p. 138)

1. Which of the following options may be used to print a large worksheet?
   (a) Landscape orientation
   (b) Scaling
   (c) Reduced margins
   (d) All of the above

2. If the results of a formula contain more characters than can be displayed according to the present format and cell width,
   (a) The extra characters will be truncated under all circumstances
   (b) All of the characters will be displayed if the cell to the right is empty
   (c) A series of asterisks will be displayed
   (d) A series of pound signs will be displayed

3. Which cell—A1, A2, or A3—will contain the amount of the loan, given the function =PMT(A1,A2,A3)?
   (a) A1
   (b) A2
   (c) A3
   (d) Impossible to determine

4. Which of the following will compute the average of the values in cells D2, D3, and D4?
   (a) The function =AVERAGE(D2:D4)
   (b) The function =AVERAGE(D2,D4)
   (c) Both (a) and (b)
   (d) Neither (a) nor (b)

5. The function =IF(A1>A2,A1+A2,A1*A2) returns
   (a) The product of cells A1 and A2 if cell A1 is greater than A2
   (b) The sum of cells A1 and A2 if cell A1 is less than A2
   (c) Both (a) and (b)
   (d) Neither (a) nor (b)

6. Which of the following is the preferred way to sum the values contained in cells A1 to A4?
   (a) =SUM(A1:A4)
   (b) =A1+A2+A3+A4
   (c) Either (a) or (b) is equally good
   (d) Neither (a) nor (b) is correct

7. Which of the following will return the highest and lowest arguments from a list of arguments?
   (a) HIGH/LOW
   (b) LARGEST/SMALLEST
   (c) MAX/MIN
   (d) All of the above

8. Which of the following is a *required* technique to develop the worksheet for the mortgage analysis?
   (a) Pointing
   (b) Copying with the fill handle
   (c) Both (a) and (b)
   (d) Neither (a) nor (b)

9. Given that cells B6, C6, and D6 contain the numbers 10, 20, and 30, respectively, what value will be returned by the function =IF(B6>10,C6*2,D6*3)?
   (a) 10
   (b) 40
   (c) 60
   (d) 90

10. Which of the following is not an input to the Goal Seek command?
   (a) The cell containing the end result
   (b) The desired value of the end result
   (c) The cell whose value will change to reach the end result
   (d) The value of the input cell that is required to reach the end result

11. What is the correct order of the arguments for the FV function?
   (a) Interest Rate, Term, Principal
   (b) Term, Interest Rate, Principal
   (c) Interest Rate, Term, Annual Amount
   (d) Term, Interest Rate, Annual Amount

12. Which function will return the number of nonempty cells in the range A2 through A6, including in the result cells that contain text as well as numeric entries?
   (a) =COUNT(A2:A6)
   (b) =COUNTA(A2:A6)
   (c) =COUNT(A2,A6)
   (d) =COUNTA(A2,A6)

13. The annual interest rate, term in years, and principal of a loan are stored in cells A1, A2, and A3, respectively. Which of the following is the correct PMT function given monthly payments?
   (a) =PMT(A1, A2, −A3)
   (b) =PMT(A1/12, A2*12, −A3)
   (c) =PMT(A1*12, A2/12, −A3)
   (d) =PMT(A1, A2, A3)

14. The worksheet displayed in the monitor shows columns A and B, skips columns D, E, and F, then displays columns G, H, I, J, and K. What is the most likely explanation for the missing columns?
   (a) The columns were previously deleted
   (b) The columns are empty and thus are automatically hidden from view
   (c) Either (a) or (b) is a satisfactory explanation
   (d) Neither (a) nor (b) is a likely reason

15. Given the function =VLOOKUP(C6,D12:F18,3)
   (a) The entries in cells D12 through D18 are in ascending order
   (b) The entries in cells D12 through D18 are in descending order
   (c) The entries in cells F12 through F18 are in ascending order
   (d) The entries in cells F12 through F18 are in descending order

ANSWERS

1. d	**6.** a	**11.** c
2. d	**7.** c	**12.** b
3. c	**8.** d	**13.** b
4. a	**9.** d	**14.** d
5. d	**10.** d	**15.** a

1. **Calculating Your Retirement:** Retirement is years away, but it is never too soon to start planning. Most corporations include some type of retirement contribution in their benefits package, and/or you can supplement that money through an individual retirement account (IRA). In any event, the Future Value function enables you to calculate the amount of money you will have at retirement, based on a series of uniform contributions during your working years. Once you reach retirement, however, you do not withdraw all of the money immediately, but withdraw it periodically as a monthly pension.

   a. Create a new worksheet similar to the one in Figure 3.17. The "accrual phase" uses the FV function to determine the amount of money you will accumulate. The total contribution in cell B7 is a formula based on a percentage of your annual salary, plus a matching contribution from your employer. The 6.2% in our figure corresponds to the percentages that are currently in effect for Social Security. (In actuality, the government currently deducts 7.65% from your paycheck, and allocates 6.2% for Social Security and the remaining 1.45% for Medicare.)

   b. The pension phase takes the amount of money you have accumulated and uses the PMT function to determine the payments you will receive in retirement. The formula in cell E4 is a simple reference to the amount accumulated in cell B10, whereas the formula in cell E7 uses the PMT function to compute your monthly pension. Note that we used a lower interest rate during retirement than during your working years on the assumption that you will want to be more conservative with your investments. Note, too, that the accrual phase uses an annual contribution in its calculations, whereas the pension phase determines a monthly pension.

   c. Add a hyperlink to the page that goes to the Social Security Administration (www.ssa.gov), then compare your calculation to the benefits provided by the government. Add your name to the worksheet, print the worksheet both ways to show displayed values and cell formulas.

Microsoft Excel - Chapter 3 Practice 1 Solution - Calculating Your Retirement

	A	B	C	D	E
1	Calculating Your Retirement				
2					
3	**Accrual Phase**			**Pension Phase**	
4	Annual Salary	**$35,000**		The size of your "nest egg"	$1,124,305
5	Employee contribution	6.20%		Interest rate	6%
6	Employer contribution	6.20%		Years in retirement	25
7	Total contribution	$4,340		**Monthly Pension**	**$7,244**
8	Interest Rate	8%			
9	Years contributing	40			
10	**Future Value**	**$1,124,305**		**Your Name Goes Here**	
11					
12	Click here to compare to Social Security Projection				
13					
14					
15					
16					
17					
18					
19					
20					
21					

FIGURE 3.17 *Calculating Your Retirement (Exercise 1)*

BUILDS ON

HANDS-ON
EXERCISE 3
PAGES 143–152

2. Alternate Grade Book: Figure 3.18 displays an alternate version of the grade book from the third hands-on exercise. The student names have changed as has the professor's grading scheme. Open the partially completed version of this worksheet in the *Chapter 3 Practice 2* workbook, then complete the workbook as follows:

a. Click in cell F4 to compute the test average for the first student. The test average is computed by dropping the student's lowest grade, then giving equal weight to the three remaining tests. Steve Weinstein's test average, for example, is computed by dropping the 70 on test 1, then taking the average of 80, 90, and 100, his grades for tests 2, 3, and 4. You will need to use the SUM and MIN functions to implement this requirement.

b. Students are required to complete a designated number of homework assignments (12 in Figure 3.18), then receive a bonus or penalty for every additional or deficient home assignment. Andrea Carrion completed 9 homeworks, rather than 12, and thus has a 6-point penalty (2 points per each missing assignment). The bonus or penalty is added to the test average to determine the semester average. Enter the formulas for the first student in cells H4 and I4.

c. The grade for the course is based on the semester average and table of grading criteria according to an HLOOKUP function within the worksheet. Enter the formula in cell I4.

d. Copy the formulas in row 4 to the remaining rows in the worksheet.

e. Format the worksheet as shown. Use conditional formatting to display all failing grades and homework penalties in red. Add your name to the worksheet, then print the worksheet twice, once with displayed values and once with cell formulas.

f. Print the worksheet a second time to reflect Maryann's comment. Submit both copies of the worksheet together to your instructor.

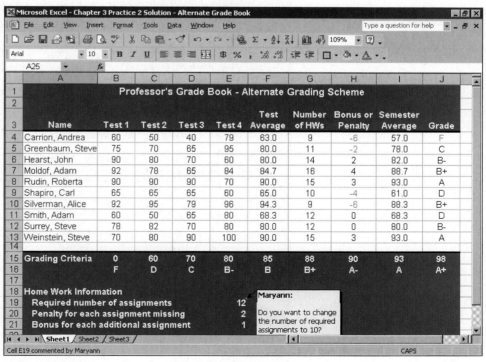

FIGURE 3.18 *Alternate Grade Book (Exercise 2)*

BUILDS ON

CHAPTER 2
PRACTICE
EXERCISE 1
PAGE 98

3. Expanded Payroll: Figure 3.19 displays an expanded version of the payroll example that was used earlier in the text. The assumptions used to determine an individual's net pay are listed at the bottom of the worksheet and repeated below. Proceed as follows:

a. Open the partially completed worksheet, which is found in the *Chapter 3 Practice 3* workbook. Enter the formulas for the first employee in row 2, then copy those formulas to the remaining rows in the worksheet.

b. An employee's regular pay is computed by multiplying the number of regular hours by the hourly wage. The number of regular hours does not appear explicitly in the worksheet and is calculated from the hours worked and the overtime threshold (which is entered in the assumption area). Barber, for example, works a total of 48 hours, 40 regular, and 8 (every hour over the threshold) of overtime.

c. Overtime pay is earned for all hours above the overtime threshold, which is shown as 40 hours. The employee receives the overtime rate (1.5 in this worksheet) times the regular wage for every hour over the threshold.

d. An individual's taxable pay is determined by subtracting the deduction per dependent times the number of dependents.

e. The withholding tax is based on the taxable pay and the tax table. The Social Security/Medicare tax is a fixed percentage of gross pay.

f. Compute the indicated totals in row 10.

g. Format the worksheet as shown in Figure 3.19.

h. Add your name to the worksheet, then print the worksheet to show both displayed values and cell formulas. Be sure to use the appropriate combination of relative and absolute addresses so that your worksheet will reflect changes in any value within the assumption area.

FIGURE 3.19   *Expanded Payroll (Exercise 3)*

4. Fuel Estimates: Figure 3.20 displays a worksheet an airline uses to calculate the fuel requirements and associated cost for available flights. Open the partially completed worksheet in the *Chapter 3 Practice 4* workbook, then complete the worksheet to match our figure. Note the following:

a. Enter the formulas for the first flight in row 4, then copy those formulas to the remainder of the worksheet.

b. The fuel required for each flight is dependent on the type of aircraft and the number of flying hours. Use a VLOOKUP function in the formula to determine the amount of fuel for each flight. (The associated table extends over three columns.)

c. Use the fuel required from part (b) to compute the additional requirements for reserve fuel and holding fuel, which must then be added to the initial fuel requirements to get the total fuel needed for a trip. These parameters are shown at the bottom of the worksheet and are susceptible to change.

d. The estimated fuel cost for each flight is the number of gallons times the price per gallon. There is a price break, however, if the fuel required reaches or exceeds a threshold number of gallons. The Boeing-727 flight from Miami to Los Angeles, for example, requires 71,500 gallons, which exceeds the threshold, and therefore qualifies for the reduced price of fuel.

e. Compute the total, average, and maximum values in rows 11, 12, and 13.

f. Format the worksheet as you see fit. (You need not match our formatting exactly.)

g. Your worksheet should be completely flexible and amenable to change; that is, the hourly fuel requirements, price per gallon, price threshold, and holding and reserve percentages are all subject to change.

h. Add your name to the worksheet, then print the worksheet to show both displayed values and cell formulas.

FIGURE 3.20   *Fuel Estimates (Exercise 4)*

5. Flexibility and Formatting: The worksheet in Figure 3.21 is an improved version of the worksheet developed in the chapter because of its flexibility. (The nicer formatting is secondary.) The spreadsheet is designed so that the user can change the starting interest rate and associated increment—6% and .5%, respectively, in the figure—then have those values reflected in the body of the spreadsheet. The user can also change the number of years for the investment and the associated increment, as well as the annual contribution.

Your assignment is to create the worksheet in Figure 3.21 using mixed references in appropriate fashion. The worksheet is similar to the one in the chapter, except that we have reversed the row and column headings. You can duplicate the formatting in our figure or choose your own design. Print the worksheet two ways, once with displayed values, and once with the cell formulas.

FIGURE 3.21 *Flexibility and Formatting (Exercise 5)*

6. Mortgage Calculator: Figure 3.22 provides another example of mixed references, this time to vary the principal and interest rate in conjunction with the PMT function. The worksheet also provides flexibility in that the user inputs the initial principal and increment (e.g., $150,000 and $5,000) as well as the initial interest rate and its increment (7% and .5%, respectively). The worksheet then computes the associated payment for the different combinations of interest and principal, based on the term of the associated mortgage.

The "trick" to this assignment, as in the previous example, is to develop a formula with the correct mixed references. Click in cell B9 and start to enter the PMT function. You know that the interest rate is in cell B8, but you have to determine the appropriate reference. Ask yourself if the interest rate will always come from column B. (No.) Will it always come from row 8? (Yes.) The answers tell you how to enter the mixed reference within the PMT function. Use similar logic to enter the principal. Once you have the formula for cell B9, you can copy it to the remaining cells in the body of the worksheet.

Your assignment is to create the worksheet in Figure 3.22. You can duplicate the formatting in our figure or choose your own design. Print the worksheet two ways, once with displayed values, and once with the cell formulas.

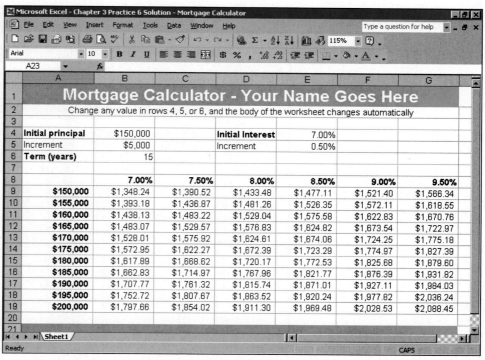

	A	B	C	D	E	F	G
	Mortgage Calculator - Your Name Goes Here						
2	Change any value in rows 4, 5, or 6, and the body of the worksheet changes automatically						
3							
4	Initial principal	$150,000		Initial Interest	7.00%		
5	Increment	$5,000		Increment	0.50%		
6	Term (years)	15					
7							
8		7.00%	7.50%	8.00%	8.50%	9.00%	9.50%
9	$150,000	$1,348.24	$1,390.52	$1,433.48	$1,477.11	$1,521.40	$1,566.34
10	$155,000	$1,393.18	$1,436.87	$1,481.26	$1,526.35	$1,572.11	$1,618.55
11	$160,000	$1,438.13	$1,483.22	$1,529.04	$1,575.58	$1,622.83	$1,670.76
12	$165,000	$1,483.07	$1,529.57	$1,576.83	$1,624.82	$1,673.54	$1,722.97
13	$170,000	$1,528.01	$1,575.92	$1,624.61	$1,674.06	$1,724.25	$1,775.18
14	$175,000	$1,572.95	$1,622.27	$1,672.39	$1,723.29	$1,774.97	$1,827.39
15	$180,000	$1,617.89	$1,668.62	$1,720.17	$1,772.53	$1,825.68	$1,879.60
16	$185,000	$1,662.83	$1,714.97	$1,767.96	$1,821.77	$1,876.39	$1,931.82
17	$190,000	$1,707.77	$1,761.32	$1,815.74	$1,871.01	$1,927.11	$1,984.03
18	$195,000	$1,752.72	$1,807.67	$1,863.52	$1,920.24	$1,977.82	$2,036.24
19	$200,000	$1,797.66	$1,854.02	$1,911.30	$1,969.48	$2,028.53	$2,088.45

FIGURE 3.22   *Mortgage Calculator (Exercise 6)*

BUILDS ON

HANDS-ON
EXERCISE 2
PAGES 124–133

7. Amortization Schedule: Figure 3.23 displays the Print Preview view of a worksheet to compute the amortization (payoff) schedule for a loan. The user enters the principal, interest rate, and length of the loan, and these values are used to determine the monthly payment, which remains constant throughout the life of the loan. Be sure to enter a formula in cell F4, so that your worksheet will adjust automatically if the user changes any of the loan parameters.

   The monthly payment in turn is divided into interest and principal. The amount that goes toward interest decreases each month, while the amount that goes toward principal increases. Two functions, IPMT and PPMT, are used to calculate these amounts for each period. Your assignment is to calculate the amortization schedule as shown in Figure 3.23. There are a total of 180 payments (12 payments a year for 15 years). Note, however, that various rows are hidden within the worksheet so that only selected payments are visible. Thus the worksheet shows the first six payments (in rows 8–13), payment number 12 at the end of the first year, payment number 24 at the end of the second year, and so on. The balance after the last payment is zero, indicating that the loan has been paid off.

   Create the worksheet in Figure 3.23, then print the worksheet two ways, once with displayed values, and once with the cell formulas. Use our formatting or choose your own. Add your name to the worksheet, then submit the assignment to your professor.

8. Information from the Web: The compound document in Figure 3.24 contains a spreadsheet to compute a car payment together with a description and picture of the associated car. The latter two were taken from the Web site, carpoint.msn.com. Choose any car you like, then go to the indicated Web site to obtain the retail price of that car so you can create the spreadsheet. Download a picture and description of the car in order to complete the document. *Be sure to credit the source in your document.* Add your name and submit the assignment to your instructor.

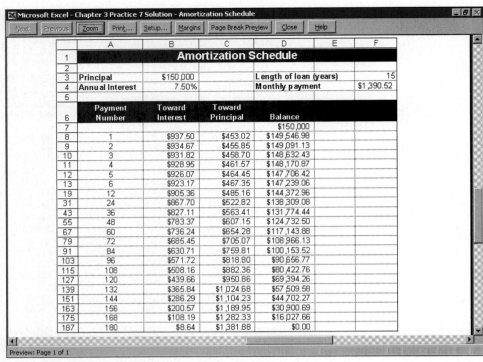

FIGURE 3.23 *Amortization Schedule (Exercise 7)*

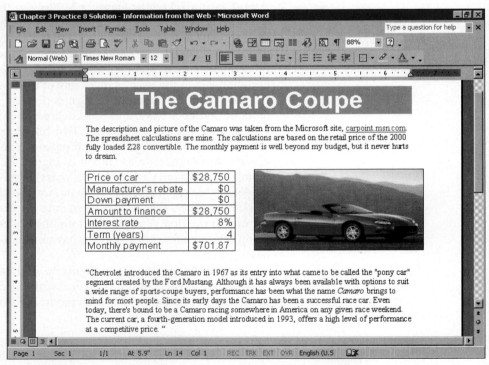

FIGURE 3.24 *Information from the Web (Exercise 8)*

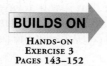

BUILDS ON

HANDS-ON
EXERCISE 3
PAGES 143–152

9. Nested IFs and Other Functions: Figure 3.25 displays a modified version of the expanded grade book, with two additional columns, the Student ID in column C and the Rank in column L. (The Student ID was added since the instructor intends to post this worksheet to the Web and does not want to show the complete Social Security number.) The grading criteria have also been modified with respect to the homework bonus as explained below. Complete the third hands-on exercise in the chapter, then continue with the steps below to create the workbook in Figure 3.25:

a. Insert a new column, Student ID, after column B that contains the students' Social Security numbers. Use the LEFT function in column C to display the first four digits of each student's Social Security number.

b. Sort the worksheet according to the first four digits of the newly created Student ID. Be sure that your results correspond to our figure.

c. Modify the contents of cells H19 through J22 as shown in Figure 3.25. Students are now penalized two points for poor homework, and are rewarded three and five points, for satisfactory (OK) and good homework, respectively. Modify the formula in cell J4 to include a nested IF statement that takes the homework bonus or penalty into account. Change the homework grade for the last three students (after sorting the worksheet) to good, so that you can test the modified formula.

d. Use the Rank function to determine each student's rank in class according to the computed value of his or her semester average. Use the Help menu if necessary to learn more about this function.

e. Add your name to the worksheet as the grading assistant.

f. Hide the first two rows and the first two columns, then print the worksheet from within Excel.

e. Use the Save As Web Page command to save the worksheet as a Web page, open the newly created page using your browser, then print the Web page from your browser. Submit both printouts to your instructor.

Microsoft Excel - Chapter 3 Practice 9 Solution - Nested If and Other Functions

	C	D	E	F	G	H	I	J	K	L	M
3	Student ID	Test 1	Test 2	Test 3	Test 4	Average	Homework	Average	Grade	Rank	
4	1000	60	50	40	79	61.6	OK	64.6	D	14	
5	1112	80	71	70	84	77.8	Poor	75.8	C	11	
6	1234	65	65	65	60	63.0	OK	66.0	D	12	
7	2000	90	90	80	90	88.0	Poor	86.0	B	5	
8	2222	75	70	65	95	80.0	OK	83.0	B	8	
9	3000	92	78	65	84	80.6	OK	83.6	B	6	
10	4444	82	78	62	77	75.2	OK	78.2	C	10	
11	4445	96	98	97	90	94.2	OK	97.2	A	1	
12	5555	92	88	65	78	80.2	OK	83.2	B	7	
13	6666	94	92	86	84	88.0	OK	91.0	A	2	
14	7777	60	50	65	80	67.0	Poor	65.0	D	13	
15	7778	78	81	70	78	77.0	Good	82.0	B	9	
16	8888	90	90	90	70	82.0	Good	87.0	B	4	
17	9999	92	95	79	80	85.2	Good	90.2	A	3	
18											
19	Average	81.9	78.3	71.4	80.6	HW Bonus/Penalty		Grading Criteria			
20	Maximum	96.0	98.0	97.0	95.0	Poor	-2	0	F		
21	Minimum	60.0	50.0	40.0	60.0	OK	3	60	D		
22	Range	36.0	48.0	57.0	35.0	Good	5	70	C		

FIGURE 3.25 *Nested IFs and Other Functions (Exercise 9)*

10. Election 2000: Election 2000 has come and gone, but it will always be remembered as the closest election in our history. You will find a partially completed version of Figure 3.26 in the file, *Chapter 3 Practice 10*. Open the partially completed workbook and proceed as follows:

a. Enter an appropriate IF function in cells D9 and F9 to determine the electoral votes for each candidate. The electoral votes are awarded on an all-or-nothing basis—that is, the candidate with the larger popular vote wins all of that state's electoral votes.

b. Copy the entries in cells D9 and F9 to the remaining rows in the respective columns. Format these columns to display red and blue values, for Bush and Gore, respectively.

c. Enter a function of formula in cell G9 to determine the difference in the popular vote between the two candidates. The result should always appear as a positive number. You can do this in one of two ways, by using either an absolute value function or an appropriate IF function. Copy this formula to the remaining rows in the column.

d. Click in cell H9 and determine the percentage differential in the popular vote. This is the difference in the number of votes divided by the total number of votes.

e. Enter the appropriate SUM functions in cells B4 to C5 to determine the electoral and popular totals for each candidate.

f. Add your name somewhere in the worksheet, then print the completed sheet for your instructor. Be sure your worksheet fits on one page. Print the worksheet a second time to show the cell formulas.

g. Use the Sort function to display the states in a different sequence, such as the smallest (or largest) vote differential. Print the worksheet with the alternate sequence.

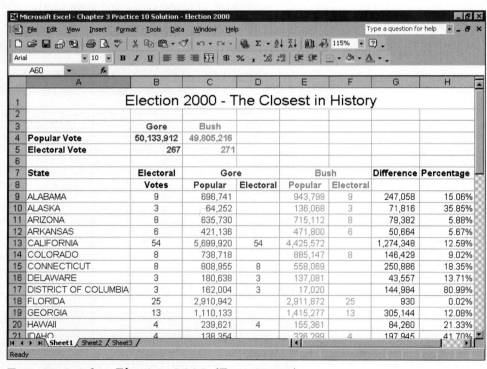

FIGURE 3.26 *Election 2000 (Exercise 10)*

The Financial Consultant

A friend of yours is in the process of buying a home and has asked you to compare the payments and total interest on a 15- and a 30-year loan. You want to do as professional a job as possible and have decided to analyze the loans in Excel, then incorporate the results into a memo written in Microsoft Word. As of now, the principal is $150,000, but it is very likely that your friend will change his mind several times, and so you want to use the OLE capability within Windows to dynamically link the worksheet to the word processing document. Your memo should include a letterhead that takes advantage of the formatting capabilities within Word; a graphic logo would be a nice touch.

The Rule of 72

Delaying your IRA for one year can cost you as much as $64,000 at retirement, depending on when you begin. That may be hard to believe, but you can check the numbers without a calculator, using the "Rule of 72." This financial rule of thumb states that to find out how long it takes money to double, divide the number 72 by the interest rate; e.g., money earning 8% annually will double in approximately 9 years (72 divided by 8). The money doubles again in 18 years, again in 27 years, and so on. Now assume that you start your IRA at age 21, rather than 20, effectively losing 45 years of compound interest for the initial contribution. Use the rule of 72 to determine approximately how much you will lose, assuming an 8% rate of return. Check your calculation by creating a worksheet to determine the exact amount.

Individual Retirement Accounts

There are two types of individual retirement accounts, a Roth IRA and a traditional IRA. The Roth IRA is newer and has been called "the deal of the century." Search the Web to learn the benefits and limitations of each type of account. Which one is better for you? Summarize your findings in a brief note to your instructor.

The Automobile Dealership

The purchase of a car usually entails extensive bargaining between the dealer and the consumer. The dealer has an asking price but typically settles for less. The commission paid to a salesperson depends on how close the selling price is to the asking price. Exotic Motors has the following compensation policy for its sales staff:

- A 5% commission on the actual selling price for cars sold at 98% or more of the asking price
- A 3% commission on the actual selling price for cars sold at 95% or more (but less than 98%) of the asking price.
- A 2% commission on the actual selling price for cars sold at 90% or more (but less than 95%) of the asking price
- A 1% commission on the actual selling price for cars sold at less than 90% of the asking price. The dealer will not go below 85% of his asking price.

The dealer's asking price is based on the dealer's cost plus a 20% markup; for example, the asking price on a car that cost the dealer $20,000 would be $24,000. Develop a worksheet to be used by the dealer that shows his profit (the selling price minus the cost of the car minus the salesperson's commission) on every sale. The worksheet should be completely flexible and allow the dealer to vary the markup or commission percentages without having to edit or recopy any of the formulas. Use the data in the *Automobile Dealership* workbook to test your worksheet.

The Lottery

Many states raise money through lotteries that advertise prizes of several million dollars. In reality, however, the actual value of the prize is considerably less than the advertised value, although the winners almost certainly do not care. One state, for example, recently offered a twenty million dollar prize that was to be distributed in twenty annual payments of one million dollars each. How much was the prize actually worth, assuming a long-term interest rate of seven percent?

A Penny a Day

What if you had a rich uncle who offered to pay you "a penny a day," then double your salary each day for the next month? It does not sound very generous, but you will be surprised at how quickly the amount grows. Create a simple worksheet that enables you to use the Goal Seek command to answer the following questions. On what day of the month (if any) will your uncle pay you more than one million dollars? How much money will your uncle pay you on the 31st day?

CHAPTER 4

Graphs and Charts: Delivering a Message

OBJECTIVES

AFTER READING THIS CHAPTER YOU WILL BE ABLE TO:

1. Distinguish between the different types of charts, stating the advantages and disadvantages of each.
2. Distinguish between a chart embedded in a worksheet and one in a separate chart sheet; explain how many charts can be associated with the same worksheet.
3. Use the Chart Wizard to create and/or modify a chart.
4. Use the Drawing toolbar to enhance a chart by creating lines, objects, and 3-D shapes.
5. Differentiate between data series specified in rows and data series specified in columns.
6. Create a compound document consisting of a word processing memo, a worksheet, and a chart.

OVERVIEW

Business has always known that the graphic representation of data is an attractive, easy-to-understand way to convey information. Indeed, business graphics has become one of the most exciting Windows applications, whereby charts (graphs) are easily created from a worksheet, with just a few simple keystrokes or mouse clicks.

The chapter begins by emphasizing the importance of determining the message to be conveyed by a chart. It describes the different types of charts available within Excel and how to choose among them. It explains how to create a chart using the Chart Wizard, how to embed a chart within a worksheet, and how to create a chart in a separate chart sheet. It also describes how to use the Drawing toolbar to enhance a chart by creating lines, objects, and 3-D shapes.

The second half of the chapter explains how one chart can plot multiple sets of data, and how several charts can be based on the same worksheet. It also describes how to create a compound document, in which a chart and its associated worksheet are dynamically linked to a memo created by a word processor. All told, we think you will find this to be one of the most enjoyable chapters in the text.

CHART TYPES

A *chart* is a graphic representation of data in a worksheet. The chart is based on descriptive entries called *category labels*, and on numeric values called *data points*. The data points are grouped into one or more *data series* that appear in row(s) or column(s) on the worksheet. In every chart there is exactly one data point in each data series for each value of the category label.

The worksheet in Figure 4.1 will be used throughout the chapter as the basis for the charts we will create. Your manager believes that the sales data can be understood more easily from charts than from the strict numerical presentation of a worksheet. You have been given the assignment of analyzing the data in the worksheet and are developing a series of charts to convey that information.

The sales data in the worksheet can be presented several ways—for example, by city, by product, or by a combination of the two. Ask yourself which type of chart is best suited to answer the following questions:

- What percentage of total revenue comes from each city? from each product?
- What is the dollar revenue produced by each city? by each product?
- What is the rank of each city with respect to sales?
- How much revenue does each product contribute in each city?

In every instance, realize that a chart exists only to deliver a message, and that *you cannot create an effective chart unless you are sure of what that message is*. The next several pages discuss various types of business charts, each of which is best suited to a particular type of message.

	A	B	C	D	E	F
1	Superior Software Sales					
2						
3		Miami	Denver	New York	Boston	Total
4	Word Processing	$50,000	$67,500	$9,500	$141,000	$268,000
5	Spreadsheets	$44,000	$18,000	$11,500	$105,000	$178,500
6	Database	$12,000	$7,500	$6,000	$30,000	$55,500
7	Total	$106,000	$93,000	$27,000	$276,000	$502,000

FIGURE 4.1   *Superior Software*

KEEP IT SIMPLE

Keep it simple. This rule applies to both your message and the means of conveying that message. Excel makes it almost too easy to change fonts, styles, type sizes, and colors, but such changes will often detract from, rather than enhance, a chart. More is not necessarily better, and you do not have to use the features just because they are there. Remember that a chart must ultimately succeed on the basis of content, and content alone.

Pie Charts

A *pie chart* is the most effective way to display proportional relationships. It is the type of chart to select whenever words like *percentage* or *market share* appear in the message to be delivered. The pie, or complete circle, denotes the total amount. Each slice of the pie corresponds to its respective percentage of the total.

The pie chart in Figure 4.2a divides the pie representing total sales into four slices, one for each city. The size of each slice is proportional to the percentage of total sales in that city. The chart depicts a single data series, which appears in cells B7 through E7 on the associated worksheet. The data series has four data points corresponding to the total sales in each city.

To create the pie chart, Excel computes the total sales ($502,000 in our example), calculates the percentage contributed by each city, and draws each slice of the pie in proportion to its computed percentage. Boston's sales of $276,000 account for 55 percent of the total, and so this slice of the pie is allotted 55 percent of the area of the circle.

An *exploded pie chart*, as shown in Figure 4.2b, separates one or more slices of the pie for emphasis. Another way to achieve emphasis in a chart is to choose a title that reflects the message you are trying to deliver. The title in Figure 4.2a, for example, *Revenue by Geographic Area*, is neutral and leaves the reader to develop his or her own conclusion about the relative contribution of each area. By contrast, the title in Figure 4.2b, *New York Accounts for Only 5% of Revenue,* is more suggestive and emphasizes the problems in this office. Alternatively, the title could be changed to *Boston Exceeds 50% of Total Revenue* if the intent were to emphasize the contribution of Boston.

Three-dimensional pie charts may be created in exploded or nonexploded format as shown in Figures 4.2c and 4.2d, respectively. Excel also enables you to add arrows and text for emphasis.

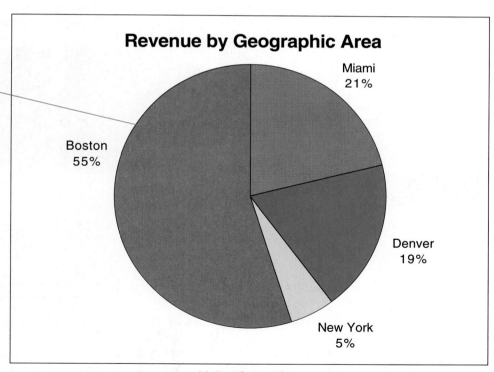

Size of slice is proportional to percentage of total sales from Boston

(a) Simple Pie Chart

FIGURE 4.2   *Pie Charts*

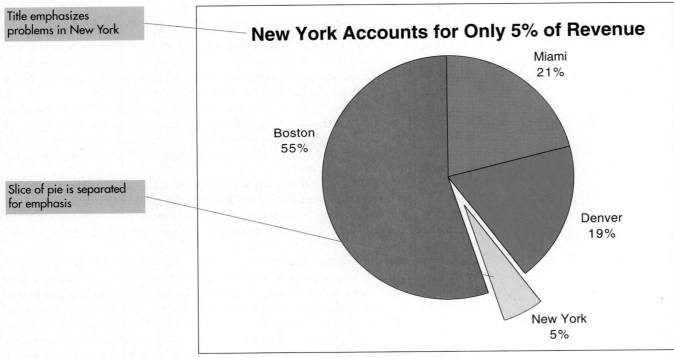

Title emphasizes problems in New York

Slice of pie is separated for emphasis

New York Accounts for Only 5% of Revenue

Miami 21%

Boston 55%

Denver 19%

New York 5%

(b) Exploded Pie Chart

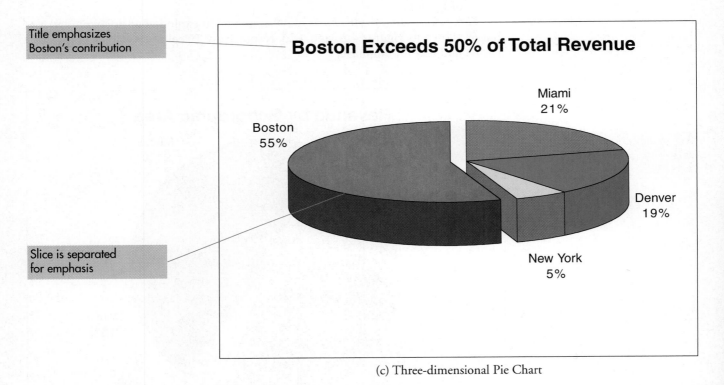

Title emphasizes Boston's contribution

Slice is separated for emphasis

Boston Exceeds 50% of Total Revenue

Miami 21%

Boston 55%

Denver 19%

New York 5%

(c) Three-dimensional Pie Chart

FIGURE 4.2   *Pie Charts (continued)*

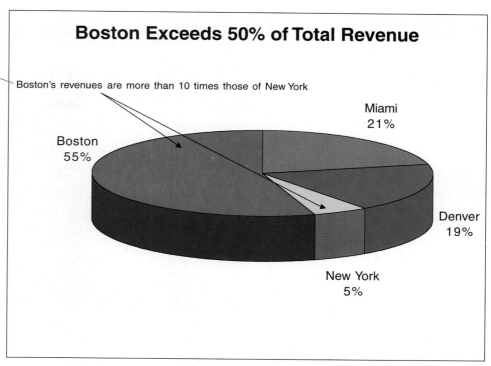

(d) Enhanced Pie Chart

FIGURE 4.2 *Pie Charts (continued)*

A pie chart is easiest to read when the number of slices is limited (i.e., not more than six or seven), and when small categories (percentages less than five) are grouped into a single category called "Other."

EXPLODED PIE CHARTS

Click and drag wedges out of a pie chart to convert an ordinary pie chart to an exploded pie chart. For best results pull the wedge out only slightly from the main body of the pie.

Column and Bar Charts

A *column chart* is used when there is a need to show actual numbers rather than percentages. The column chart in Figure 4.3a plots the same data series as the earlier pie chart, but displays it differently. The category labels (Miami, Denver, New York, and Boston) are shown along the **X** (horizontal) *axis*. The data points (monthly sales) are plotted along the **Y** (vertical) *axis*, with the height of each column reflecting the value of the data point.

A column chart can be given a horizontal orientation and converted to a *bar chart* as in Figure 4.3b. Some individuals prefer the bar chart over the corresponding column chart because the longer horizontal bars accentuate the difference between the items. Bar charts are also preferable when the descriptive labels are long, to eliminate the crowding that can occur along the horizontal axis of a column chart. As with the pie chart, a title can lead the reader and further emphasize the message, as with *Boston Leads All Cities* in Figure 4.3b.

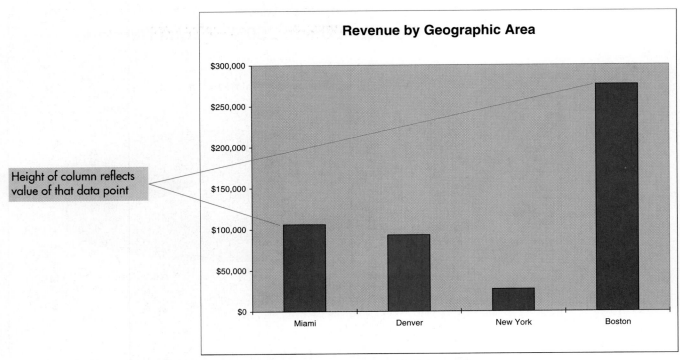

Height of column reflects value of that data point

(a) Column Chart

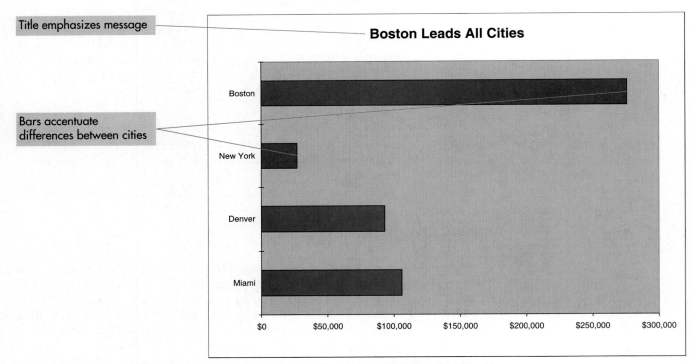

Title emphasizes message

Bars accentuate differences between cities

(b) Horizontal Bar Chart

FIGURE 4.3   *Column/Bar Charts*

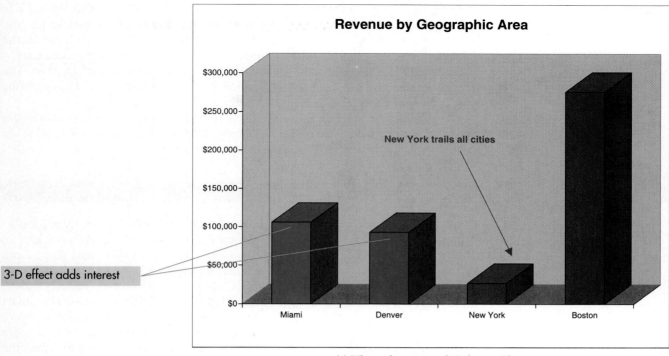

3-D effect adds interest

(c) Three-dimensional Column Chart

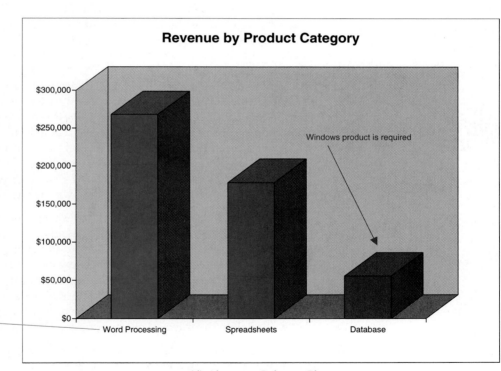

Applications are shown on the X axis, rather than the cities

(d) Alternate Column Chart

FIGURE 4.3   *Column/Bar Charts (continued)*

A three-dimensional effect can produce added interest as shown in Figures 4.3c and 4.3d. Figure 4.3d plots a different set of numbers than we have seen so far (the sales for each product, rather than the sales for each city). The choice between the charts in Figures 4.3c and 4.3d depends on the message you want to convey—whether you want to emphasize the contribution of each city or each product. The title can be used to emphasize the message. Arrows, text, and 3-D shapes can be added to either chart to enhance the message.

As with a pie chart, column and bar charts are easiest to read when the number of categories is relatively small (seven or fewer). Otherwise, the columns (bars) are plotted so close together that labeling becomes impossible.

CREATING A CHART

There are two ways to create a chart in Excel. You can *embed* the chart in a worksheet, or you can create the chart in a separate *chart sheet*. Figure 4.4a displays an embedded column chart. Figure 4.4b shows a pie chart in its own chart sheet. Both techniques are valid. The choice between the two depends on your personal preference.

Regardless of where it is kept (embedded in a worksheet or in its own chart sheet), a chart is linked to the worksheet on which it is based. The charts in Figure 4.4 plot the same data series (the total sales for each city). Change any of these data points on the worksheet, and both charts will be updated automatically to reflect the new data.

Both charts are part of the same workbook (Software Sales) as indicated in the title bar of each figure. The tabs within the workbook have been renamed to indicate the contents of the associated sheet. Additional charts may be created and embedded in the worksheet and/or placed on their own chart sheets. And, as previously stated, if you change the worksheet, the chart (or charts) based upon it will also change.

Study the column chart in Figure 4.4a to see how it corresponds to the worksheet on which it is based. The descriptive names on the X axis are known as category labels and match the entries in cells B3 through E3. The quantitative values (data points) are plotted on the Y axis and match the total sales in cells B7 through E7. Even the numeric format matches; that is, the currency format used in the worksheet appears automatically on the scale of the Y axis.

The *sizing handles* on the *embedded chart* indicate it is currently selected and can be sized, moved, or deleted the same way as any other Windows object:

- To size the selected chart, point to a sizing handle (the mouse pointer changes to a double arrow), then drag the handle in the desired direction.
- To move the selected chart, point to the chart (the mouse pointer is a single arrow), then drag the chart to its new location.
- To copy the selected chart, click the Copy button to copy the chart to the clipboard, click in the workbook where you want the copied chart to go, then click the Paste button to paste the chart at that location.
- To delete the selected chart, press the Del key.

The same operations apply to any of the objects within the chart (such as its title), as will be discussed in the next section on enhancing a chart. Note, too, that both figures contain the chart toolbar that enables you to modify a chart after it has been created.

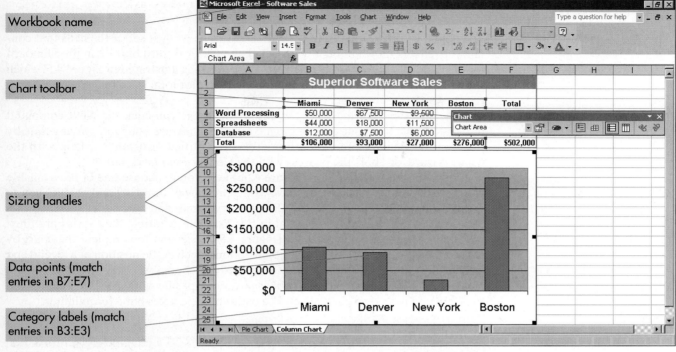

Workbook name

Chart toolbar

Sizing handles

Data points (match entries in B7:E7)

Category labels (match entries in B3:E3)

(a) Embedded Chart

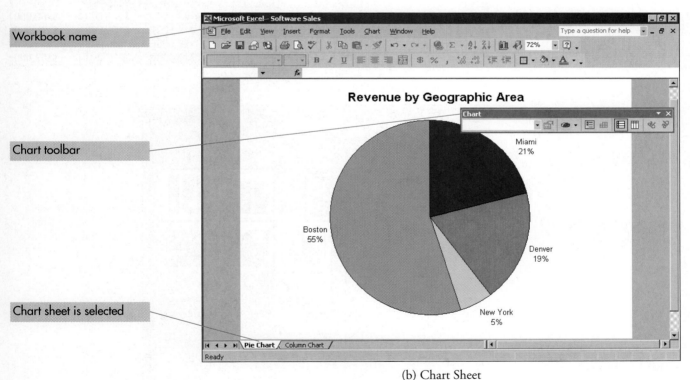

Workbook name

Chart toolbar

Chart sheet is selected

(b) Chart Sheet

FIGURE 4.4   *Creating a Chart*

The Chart Wizard

The **Chart Wizard** is the easiest way to create a chart. Just select the cells that contain the data as shown in Figure 4.5a, click the Chart Wizard button on the Standard toolbar, and let the Wizard do the rest. The process is illustrated in Figure 4.5, which shows how the Wizard creates a column chart to plot total sales by geographic area (city).

The steps in Figure 4.5 appear automatically as you click the Next command button to move from one step to the next. You can retrace your steps at any time by pressing the Back command button, access the Office Assistant for help with the Chart Wizard, or abort the process with the Cancel command button.

Step 1 in the Chart Wizard (Figure 4.5b) asks you to choose one of the available **chart types**. Step 2 (Figure 4.5c) shows you a preview of the chart and enables you to confirm (and, if necessary, change) the category names and data series specified earlier. (Only one data series is plotted in this example. Multiple data series are illustrated later in the chapter.) Step 3 (Figure 4.5d) asks you to complete the chart by entering its title and specifying additional options (such as the position of a legend and gridlines). And finally, step 4 (Figure 4.5e) has you choose whether the chart is to be created as an embedded chart (an object) within a specific worksheet, or whether it is to be created in its own chart sheet. The entire process takes but a few minutes.

Selected cells (B3:E3 and B7:E7)

	A	B	C	D	E	F
1	Superior Software Sales					
2						
3		Miami	Denver	New York	Boston	Total
4	Word Processing	$50,000	$67,500	$9,500	$141,000	$268,000
5	Spreadsheets	$44,000	$18,000	$11,500	$105,000	$178,500
6	Database	$12,000	$7,500	$6,000	$30,000	$55,500
7	Total	$106,000	$93,000	$27,000	$276,000	$502,000

(a) The Worksheet

Available chart types

Available subtypes for selected chart type

Description of selected subtype

(b) Select the Chart Type (step 1)

FIGURE 4.5 *The Chart Wizard*

Preview of chart

Data series (B7:E7)

Category labels (B3:E3)

(c) Check the Data Series (step 2)

Tabs reflect chart options

Chart title

(d) Complete the Chart Options (step 3)

Select to create chart on chart sheet

Select to embed chart on Sheet1 of workbook

(e) Choose the Location (step 4)

FIGURE 4.5   *The Chart Wizard (continued)*

Modifying a Chart

A chart can be modified in several ways after it has been created. You can change the chart type and/or the color, shape, or pattern of the data series. You can add (or remove) gridlines and/or a legend. You can add labels to the data series. You can also change the font, size, color, and style of existing text anywhere in the chart by selecting the text, then changing its format. All of these features are implemented from the Chart menu or by using the appropriate button on the **Chart toolbar**.

You can also use the **Drawing toolbar** to add text boxes, arrows, and other objects for added emphasis. Figure 4.6, for example, contains a three-dimensional arrow with a text box within the arrow to call attention to the word processing sales. It also contains a second text box with a thin arrow in reference to the database product. Each of these objects is created separately using the appropriate tool from the Drawing toolbar. It's easy, as you will see in our next exercise.

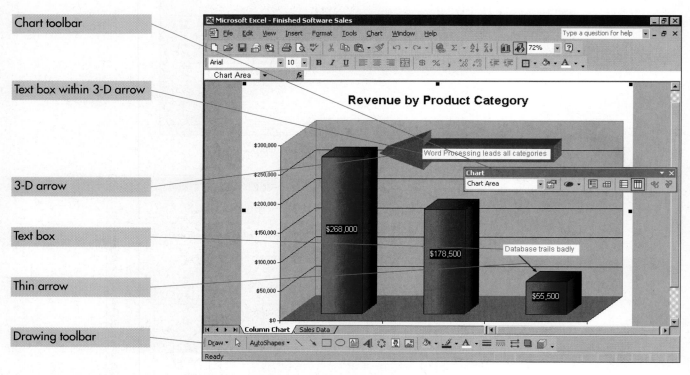

FIGURE 4.6   *Enhancing a Chart*

SET A TIME LIMIT

Excel enables you to customize virtually every aspect of every object within a chart. That is the good news. It's also the bad news, because you can spend inordinate amounts of time for little or no gain. It's fun to experiment, but set a time limit and stop when you reach the allocated time. The default settings are often adequate to convey your message, and further experimentation might prove counterproductive.

THE CHART WIZARD

Objective   To create and modify a chart by using the Chart Wizard; to embed a chart within a worksheet; to enhance a chart to include arrows and text. Use Figure 4.7 as a guide in the exercise.

Step 1:   **The AutoSum Command**

➤ Start Excel. Open the Software Sales workbook in the Exploring Excel folder. Save the workbook as **Finished Software Sales**.

➤ Click and drag to select cells **B7 through E7** (the cells that will contain the total sales for each location). Click the **AutoSum button** on the Standard toolbar to compute the total for each city.

➤ The totals are computed automatically as shown in Figure 4.7a. The formula bar shows that Cell B7 contains the Sum function to total all of the numeric entries immediately above the cell.

➤ Click and drag to select cells **F4 through F7**, then click the **AutoSum button**. The Sum function is entered automatically into these cells to total the entries to the left of the selected cells.

➤ Click and drag to select cells **B4 through F7** to format these cells with the currency symbol and no decimal places.

➤ Boldface the row and column headings and the totals. Add a red border and center the headings.

➤ Save the workbook.

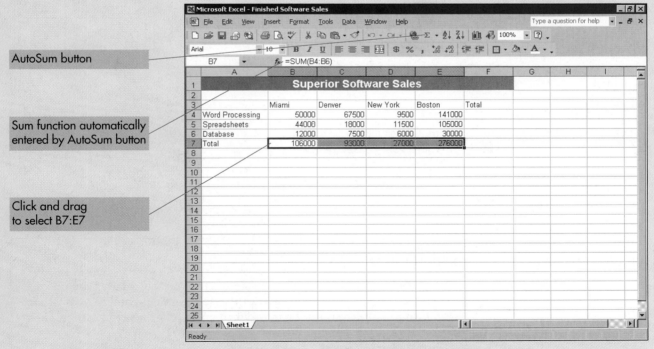

(a) The AutoSum Command (step 1)

FIGURE 4.7   *Hands-on Exercise 1*

Step 2:   **Start the Chart Wizard**

➤ Separate the toolbars if they occupy the same row. Pull down the **Tools menu**, click the **Customize command**, click the **Options tab**, then check the box that displays the toolbars on two rows.

➤ Drag the mouse over cells **B3 through E3** to select the category labels (the names of the cities). Press and hold the **Ctrl key** as you drag the mouse over cells **B7 through E7** to select the data series (the cells containing the total sales for the individual cities).

➤ Check that cells B3 through E3 and B7 through E7 are selected. Click the **Chart Wizard button** on the Standard toolbar to start the wizard. If you don't see the button, pull down the **Insert menu** and click the **Chart command**.

➤ You should see the dialog box for step 1 of the Chart Wizard as shown in Figure 4.7b. The **Column** chart type and **Clustered column** subtype are selected.

➤ Click (and hold) the button to see a sample chart. Click **Next**.

Chart Wizard button

Select category labels (B3:E3)

Select data series (B7:E7)

Click Column

Click Clustered Column subtype

Click to see a sample chart

(b) Start the Chart Wizard (step 2)

FIGURE 4.7   *Hands-on Exercise 1 (continued)*

RETRACE YOUR STEPS

The Chart Wizard guides you every step of the way, but what if you make a mistake or change your mind? Click the Back command button at any time to return to a previous screen in order to enter different information, then continue working with the Wizard.

Step 3: **The Chart Wizard (continued)**

➤ You should see step 2 of the Chart Wizard. Click the **Series tab** in the dialog box so that your screen matches Figure 4.7c. Note that the values (the data being plotted) are in cells B7 through E7, and that the Category labels for the X axis are in cells B3 through E3. Click **Next** to continue.

➤ You should see step 3 of the Chart Wizard. If necessary, click the **Titles tab**, then click in the text box for the Chart title.

➤ Type **Revenue by Geographic Area**. Click the **Legend tab** and clear the box to show a legend. Click **Next**.

➤ You should see step 4 of the Chart Wizard. If necessary, click the option button to place the chart **As object** in Sheet1 (the name of the worksheet in which you are working).

➤ Click **Finish**.

Click the Series tab

Data series is in B7:E7

Category labels are in B3:E3

(c) The Chart Wizard (step 3)

FIGURE 4.7 *Hands-on Exercise 1 (continued)*

THE F11 KEY

The F11 key is the fastest way to create a chart in its own sheet. Select the data, including the legends and category labels, then press the F11 key to create the chart according to the default format built into the Excel column chart. After the chart has been created, you can use the menu bar, Chart toolbar, or shortcut menus to choose a different chart type and/or customize the formatting.

Step 4: **Move and Size the Chart**

➤ You should see the completed chart as shown in Figure 4.7d. The sizing handles indicate that the chart is selected and will be affected by subsequent commands. The Chart toolbar is displayed automatically whenever a chart is selected.

➤ Move and/or size the chart just as you would any other Windows object:
  • To move the chart, click the chart (background) area to select the chart (a ScreenTip, "Chart Area," is displayed), then click and drag (the mouse pointer changes to a four-sided arrow) to move the chart.
  • To size the chart, drag a corner handle (the mouse pointer changes to a double arrow) to change the length and width of the chart simultaneously, keeping the chart in proportion as it is resized.

➤ Click outside the chart to deselect it. The sizing handles disappear and the Chart toolbar is no longer visible.

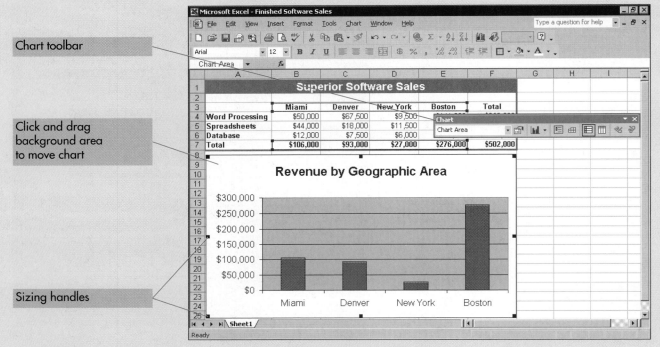

Chart toolbar

Click and drag background area to move chart

Sizing handles

(d) Move and Size the Chart (step 4)

FIGURE 4.7 *Hands-on Exercise 1 (continued)*

EMBEDDED CHARTS

An embedded chart is treated as an object that can be moved, sized, copied, or deleted just as any other Windows object. To move an embedded chart, click the background of the chart to select the chart, then drag it to a new location in the worksheet. To size the chart, select it, then drag any of the eight sizing handles in the desired direction. To delete the chart, select it, then press the Del key. To copy the chart, select it, click the Copy button on the Standard toolbar to copy the chart to the clipboard, click elsewhere in the workbook where you want the copied chart to go, then click the Paste button.

Step 5: **Change the Worksheet**

➤ Any changes in a worksheet are automatically reflected in the associated chart. Click in cell **B4**, change the entry to **$400,000**, and press the **enter key**.

➤ The total sales for Miami in cell B7 change automatically to reflect the increased sales for word processing, as shown in Figure 4.7e. The column for Miami also changes in the chart and is now larger than the column for Boston.

➤ Click in cell **B3**. Change the entry to **Chicago**. Press **enter**. The category label on the X axis changes automatically.

➤ Click the **Undo button** to change the city back to Miami. Click the **Undo button** a second time to return to the initial value of $50,000. The worksheet and chart are restored to their earlier values.

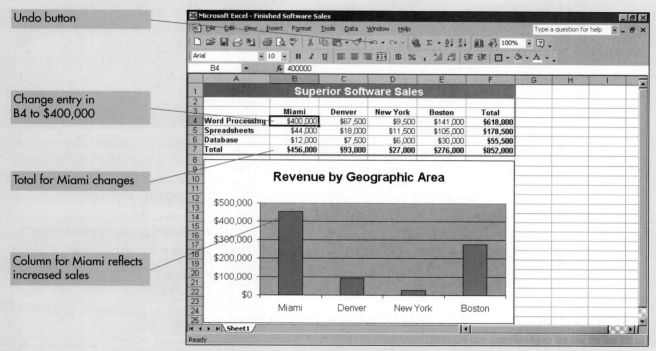

Undo button

Change entry in B4 to $400,000

Total for Miami changes

Column for Miami reflects increased sales

(e) Change the Worksheet (step 5)

FIGURE 4.7   *Hands-on Exercise 1 (continued)*

THE AUTOFORMAT COMMAND

The AutoFormat command does not do anything that could not be done through individual formatting commands, but it does provide inspiration by suggesting several attractive designs. Select the cells you want to format, pull down the Format menu, and click the AutoFormat command to display the AutoFormat dialog box. Select (click) a design, then click the Options button to determine the formats to apply (font, column width, patterns, and so on). Click OK to close the dialog box and apply the formatting. Click the Undo button if you do not like the result. See practice exercise 1 at the end of the chapter.

Step 6: **Change the Chart Type**

➤ Click the chart (background) area to select the chart, click the **drop-down arrow** on the Chart type button on the Chart toolbar, then click the **3-D Pie Chart icon**. The chart changes to a three-dimensional pie chart.

➤ Point to the chart area, click the **right mouse button** to display a shortcut menu, then click the **Chart Options command** to display the Chart Options dialog box shown in Figure 4.7f.

➤ Click the **Data Labels tab**, then click the check boxes for Category name and Percentage. Click **OK** to accept the settings and close the dialog box.

➤ The pie chart changes to reflect the options you just specified. Modify each component as necessary:

  • Select (click) the (gray) **Plot area**. Click and drag the sizing handles to increase the size of the plot area within the embedded chart.

  • Point to any of the labels, click the **right mouse button** to display a shortcut menu, and click **Format Data Labels** to display a dialog box. Click the **Font tab**, and select a smaller point size. It may also be necessary to click and drag each label away from the plot area.

➤ Make other changes as necessary. Save the workbook.

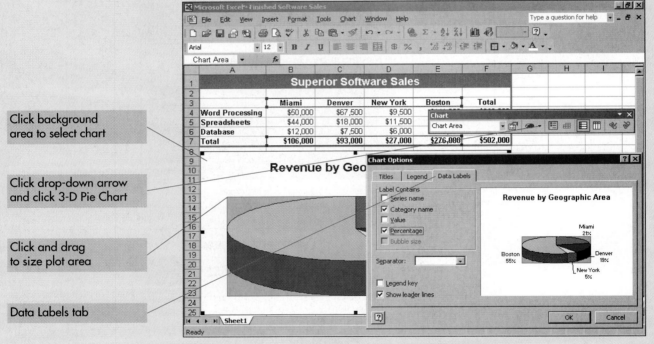

(f) Change the Chart Type (step 6)

FIGURE 4.7 *Hands-on Exercise 1 (continued)*

ADDITIONAL CHART TYPES

Excel offers a total of 14 standard chart types, each with several formats. Line charts are best to display time-related information such as a five-year trend of sales or profit data. A combination chart uses two or more chart types to display different kinds of data or when different scales are required for multiple data series. See practice exercise 6 at the end of the chapter.

Step 7: **Create a Second Chart**

➤ Click and drag to select cells **A4 through A6** in the worksheet. Press and hold the **Ctrl key** as you drag the mouse to select cells **F4 through F6**.

➤ Click the **Chart Wizard button** on the Standard toolbar to start the Chart Wizard and display the dialog box for step 1 as shown in Figure 4.7g. The Column Chart type is already selected. Click the **Clustered column with a 3-D visual effect subtype**. Press and hold the indicated button to preview the chart with your data. Click **Next**.

➤ Click the **Series tab** in the dialog box for step 2 to confirm that you selected the correct data points. The values for series1 should consist of cells F4 through F6. The Category labels for the X axis should be cells A4 through A6. Click **Next**.

➤ You should see step 3 of the Chart Wizard. Click the **Titles tab**, then click in the text box for the Chart title. Type **Revenue by Product Category**. Click the **Legend tab** and clear the box to show a legend. Click **Next**.

➤ You should see step 4 of the Chart Wizard. Select the option button to create the chart **As new sheet** (Chart1). Click **Finish**.

➤ The 3-D column chart has been created in the chart sheet labeled Chart1.

(g) Create a Second Chart (step 7)

FIGURE 4.7   *Hands-on Exercise 1 (continued)*

ANATOMY OF A CHART

A chart is composed of multiple components (objects), each of which can be selected and changed separately. Point to any part of a chart to display a ScreenTip indicating the name of the component, then click the mouse to select that component and display the sizing handles. You can then click and drag the object within the chart and/or click the right mouse button to display a shortcut menu with commands pertaining to the selected object.

Step 8: **Add a Text Box**

➤ Point to any visible toolbar, click the **right mouse button** to display a shortcut menu listing the available toolbars, then click **Drawing** to display the Drawing toolbar as shown in Figure 4.7h.

➤ Click the **Text Box button** on the Drawing toolbar. Click in the chart (the mouse pointer changes to a thin crosshair), then click and drag to create a text box. Release the mouse, then enter the text, **Word Processing leads all categories**.

➤ Point to the thatched border around the text box, then right click the border to display a context-sensitive menu. Click **Format Text Box** to display the Format Text dialog box. Click the **Font tab** and change the font to **12 point bold**. Choose **Red** as the font color.

➤ Click the **Colors and Lines tab** and select **white** as the fill color. Click **OK**. You should see red text on a white background. If necessary, size the text box so that the text fits on one line. Do not worry about the position of the text box.

➤ Click the title of the chart. You will see sizing handles around the title to indicate it has been selected. Click the **drop-down arrow** in the Font Size box on the Formatting toolbar. Click **22** to increase the size of the title. Save the workbook.

Click and drag to create text box

Point to thatched border and right click

Click Format Text Box

Text Box button

Drawing toolbar

(h) Add a Text Box (step 8)

FIGURE 4.7   *Hands-on Exercise 1 (continued)*

FLOATING TOOLBARS

Any toolbar can be docked along the edge of the application window, or it can be displayed as a floating toolbar within the application window. To move a docked toolbar, drag the move handle. To move a floating toolbar, drag its title bar. To size a floating toolbar, drag any border in the direction you want to go. Double click the title bar of any floating toolbar to dock it. A floating toolbar will dim and disappear if it is not used.

Step 9:   **Create a 3-D Shape**

➤ Click on the **AutoShapes button** and, if necessary, click the double arrow to display additional commands. Click **Block Arrows**. Select an arrow style.

➤ Click in the chart (the mouse pointer changes to a thin crosshair), then click and drag to create an arrow. Release the mouse.

➤ Click the **3-D button** on the drawing toolbar and click **3-D Style 1** as shown in Figure 4.7i. Right click the arrow and click the **Format AutoShape** command to display the Format AutoShape dialog box. Click the **Colors and Lines tab**. Choose **Red** as the fill color. Click **OK**, then size the arrow.

➤ Select (click) the text box you created in the previous step, then click and drag the text box out of the way. Select (click) the 3-D arrow and position it next to the word processing column.

➤ Click and drag the text box on top of the arrow. If you do not see the text, right click the arrow, click the **Order command**, and click **Send to Back**.

➤ Save the workbook, but do not print it at this time. Exit Excel if you do not want to continue with the next exercise at this time.

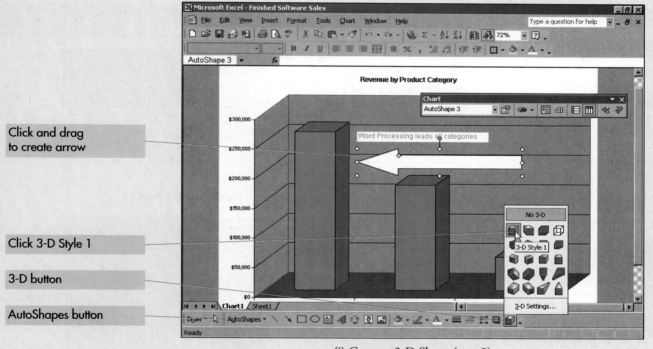

Click and drag to create arrow

Click 3-D Style 1

3-D button

AutoShapes button

(i) Create a 3-D Shape (step 9)

FIGURE 4.7   *Hands-on Exercise 1 (continued)*

FORMAT THE DATA SERIES

Use the Format Data Series command to change the color, shape, or pattern of the columns within the chart. Right click any column to select the data series (be sure that all three columns are selected), then click Format Data Series to display the Format Data Series dialog box. Experiment with the various options, especially those on the Shapes and Patterns tabs within the dialog box. Click OK when you are satisfied with the changes.

The charts presented so far displayed only a single data series such as the total sales by location or the total sales by product category. Although such charts are useful, it is often more informative to view **_multiple data series_** on the same chart. Figure 4.8a displays the worksheet we have been using throughout the chapter. Figure 4.8b displays a side-by-side column chart that plots multiple data series that exist as rows (B4:E4, B5:E5, and B6:E6) within the worksheet. Figure 4.8c displays a chart based on the same data when the series are in columns (B4:B6, C4:C6, D4:D6, and E4:E6).

Both charts plot a total of twelve data points (three product categories for each of four locations), but they group the data differently. Figure 4.8b displays the data by city in which the sales of three product categories are shown for each of four cities. Figure 4.8c is the reverse and groups the data by product category. This time the sales in the four cities are shown for each of three product categories. The choice between the two charts depends on your message and whether you want to emphasize revenue by city or by product category. It sounds complicated, but it's not; Excel will create either chart for you according to your specifications.

A3:E6 is selected

	A	B	C	D	E	F
1		Superior Software Sales				
2						
3		Miami	Denver	New York	Boston	Total
4	Word Processing	$50,000	$67,500	$9,500	$141,000	$268,000
5	Spreadsheets	$44,000	$18,000	$11,500	$105,000	$178,500
6	Database	$12,000	$7,500	$6,000	$30,000	$55,500
7	Total	$106,000	$93,000	$27,000	$276,000	$502,000

(a) Worksheet Data

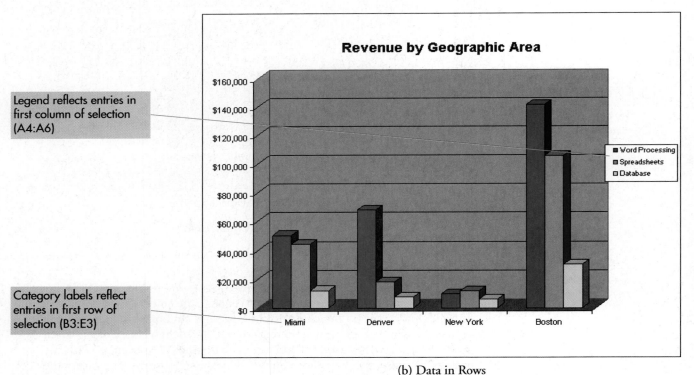

Legend reflects entries in first column of selection (A4:A6)

Category labels reflect entries in first row of selection (B3:E3)

(b) Data in Rows

FIGURE 4.8   *Side-by-Side Column Charts*

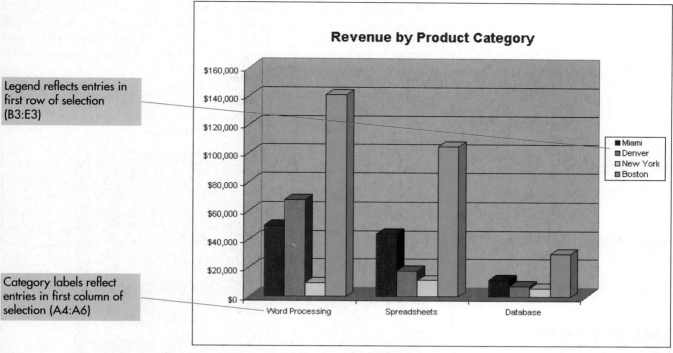

Legend reflects entries in first row of selection (B3:E3)

Category labels reflect entries in first column of selection (A4:A6)

(c) Data in Columns

FIGURE 4.8 *Side-by-Side Column Charts (continued)*

- If you specify that the data series are in rows (Figure 4.8b), the Wizard will:
  - Use the first row (cells B3 through E3) for the category labels
  - Use the remaining rows (rows four, five, and six) for the data series
  - Use the first column (cells A4 through A6) for the legend text
- If you specify the data series are in columns (Figure 4.8c), the Wizard will:
  - Use the first column (cells A4 through A6) for the category labels
  - Use the remaining columns (columns B, C, D, and E) for the data series
  - Use the first row (cells B3 through E3) for the legend text

Stacked Column Charts

The next decision associated with charts that contain multiple data series is the choice between *side-by-side column charts* versus *stacked column charts* such as those shown in Figure 4.9. Stacked column charts also group data in one of two ways, in rows or in columns. Thus Figure 4.9a is a stacked column chart with the data in rows. Figure 4.9b is also a stacked column chart, but the data is in columns.

The choice of side-by-side versus stacked column charts depends on the intended message. If you want the audience to see the individual sales in each city or product category, then the side-by-side columns in Figure 4.8 are more appropriate. If, on the other hand, you want to emphasize the total sales for each city or product category, the stacked columns in Figure 4.9 are preferable. The advantage of the stacked column is that the totals are clearly shown and can be easily compared. The disadvantage is that the segments within each column do not start at the same point, making it difficult to determine the actual sales for the individual categories.

Note, too, that the scale on the y axis in charts is different for charts with side-by-side columns versus charts with stacked columns. The side-by-side columns in Figure 4.8 show the sales of each product category and so the Y axis goes only to $160,000. The stacked columns in Figure 4.9, however, reflect the total sales for all products in each city and thus the scale goes to $300,000. Realize too, that for a stacked column chart to make sense, its numbers must be additive. It would not make sense, for example, to convert a column chart that plots units and dollar sales side by side, to a stacked column chart, because units and dollars should not be added together.

(a) Data in Rows

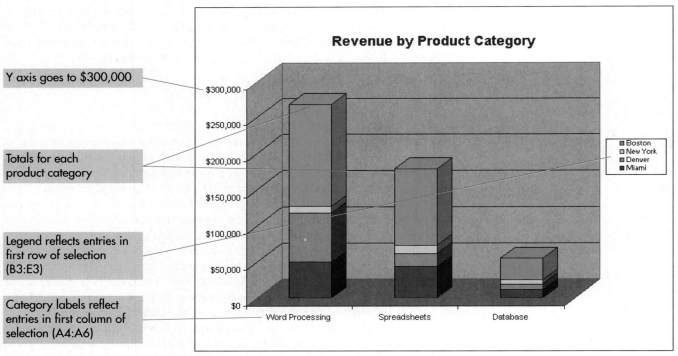

(b) Data in Columns

FIGURE 4.9   *Stacked Column Charts*

HANDS-ON EXERCISE 2

MULTIPLE DATA SERIES

Objective To plot multiple data series in the same chart; to differentiate between data series in rows and columns; to create and save multiple charts that are associated with the same worksheet. Use Figure 4.10 as a guide in the exercise.

Step 1: **Rename the Worksheets**

➤ Open the **Finished Software Sales** workbook from the previous exercise as shown in Figure 4.10a. The workbook contains an embedded chart and a separate chart sheet.

➤ Point to the workbook tab labeled **Sheet1**, click the **right mouse button** to display a shortcut menu, then click the **Rename** command. The name of the worksheet (Sheet1) is selected.

➤ Type **Sales Data** to change the name of the worksheet to the more descriptive name. Press the **enter key**.

➤ Point to the tab labeled **Chart1** (which contains the three-dimensional column chart created in the previous exercise). Click the **right mouse button** to display a shortcut menu.

➤ Click **Rename**. Enter **Column Chart** as the name of the chart sheet. Press the **enter key**.

➤ Save the workbook.

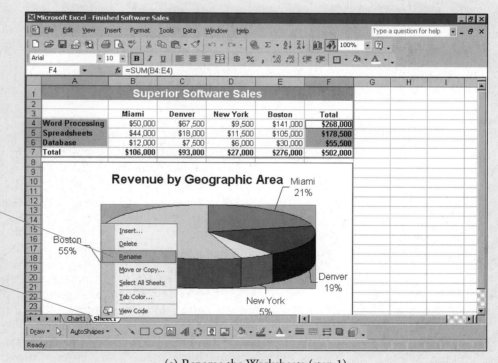

Click Rename

Point to Sheet1 tab and click right mouse button

(a) Rename the Worksheets (step 1)

FIGURE 4.10 *Hands-on Exercise 2*

Step 2: **The Office Assistant**

➤ Click the **Sales Data tab**, then click and drag to select cells **A3 through E6**. Click the **Chart Wizard button** on the Standard toolbar to start the Wizard and display the dialog box shown in Figure 4.10b.

➤ If necessary, click the **Office Assistant button** in the Chart Wizard dialog box to display the Office Assistant and the initial help screen. Click the option button for **Help with this feature**.

➤ The display for the Assistant changes to offer help about the various chart types available. (It's up to you whether you want to explore the advice at this time. You can close the Assistant, or leave it open and drag the title bar out of the way.)

➤ Select **Column** as the chart type and **Clustered column with a 3-D visual effect** as the subtype. Click **Next** to continue with the Chart Wizard.

Chart Wizard button

Click and drag to select A3:E6

Click Column

Click Clustered column with a 3-D visual effect

Office Assistant button

(b) The Office Assistant (step 2)

FIGURE 4.10 *Hands-on Exercise 2 (continued)*

THE OFFICE ASSISTANT

The Office Assistant button is common to all Office applications and is an invaluable source of online help. You can activate the Assistant at any time by clicking its button on the Standard toolbar or from within a specialized dialog box. You can ask the Assistant a specific question and/or you can have the Assistant monitor your work and suggest tips as appropriate. You can tell that the Assistant has a suggestion when you see a lightbulb appear adjacent to the character.

Step 3: **View the Data Series**

➤ You should see step 2 of the Chart Wizard as shown in Figure 4.10c. The help supplied by the Office Assistant changes automatically with the steps in the Chart Wizard.

➤ The data range should be specified as **Sales Data!$A$3:$E$6** as shown in Figure 4.10c. The option button for **Series in Rows** should be selected. Click the **Series tab**:

  • The series list box shows three data series (Word Processing, Spreadsheets, and Database) corresponding to the legends for the chart.
  • The **Word Processing** series is selected by default. The legend in the sample chart shows that the data points in the series are plotted in blue. The values are taken from cells B4 through E4 in the Sales Data Worksheet.
  • Click **Spreadsheets** in the series list box. The legend shows that the series is plotted in red. The values are taken from cells B5 through E5 in the Sales Data worksheet.
  • Click **Database** in the series list box. The legend shows that the series is plotted in yellow. The values are taken from cells B6 through E6 in the Sales Data worksheet.

➤ Click **Next** to continue creating the chart. You should see step 3 of the Chart Wizard. Click the **Titles tab**. Click the text box for Chart title. Type **Revenue by City**. Click **Next**.

➤ You should see step 4 of the Chart Wizard. Click the option button for **As new sheet**. Type **Revenue by City** in the associated text box to give the chart sheet a meaningful name. Click **Finish**.

➤ Excel creates the new chart in its own sheet named Revenue by City. Click **No** to tell the Assistant that you don't need further help. Right click the Assistant. Click **Hide**. Save the workbook.

(c) View the Data Series (step 3)

FIGURE 4.10   *Hands-on Exercise 2 (continued)*

Step 4: **Copy the Chart**

➤ Point to the tab named **Revenue by City**. Click the **right mouse button**. Click **Move or Copy** to display the dialog box in Figure 4.10d.
➤ Click **Sales Data** in the Before Sheet list box. Check the box to **Create a Copy**. Click **OK**.
➤ A duplicate worksheet called Revenue by City(2) is created and appears before (to the left of) the Sales Data worksheet. (You can also press and hold the Ctrl key as you drag the worksheet tab to create a copy of the worksheet.)
➤ Double click the newly created worksheet tab to select the name. Enter **Revenue by Product** as the new name.
➤ Save the workbook.

(d) Copy the Chart (step 4)

FIGURE 4.10 *Hands-on Exercise 2 (continued)*

MOVING AND COPYING A WORKSHEET

The fastest way to move or copy a chart sheet is to drag its tab. To move a sheet, point to its tab, then click and drag the tab to its new position. To copy a sheet, press and hold the Ctrl key as you drag the tab to the desired position for the second sheet. Rename the copied sheet (or any sheet for that matter) by double clicking its tab to select the existing name. Enter a new name for the worksheet, then press the enter key. You can also right click the worksheet tab to change its color. See practice exercise 1 at the end of the chapter.

Step 5: **Change the Source Data**

➤ Click the **Revenue by Product tab** to make it the active sheet. Click anywhere in the title of the chart, drag the mouse over the word **City** to select the text, then type **Product Category** to replace the selected text. Click outside the title to deselect it.

➤ Pull down the **Chart menu**. If necessary, click the double arrow to see more commands, click **Source Data** (you will see the Sales Data worksheet), then click the **Columns option button** so that your screen matches Figure 4.10e.

➤ Click the **Series tab** and note the following:
  • The current chart plots the data in rows. There are three data series (one series for each product).
  • The new chart (shown in the dialog box) plots the data in columns. There are four data series (one for each city as indicated in the Series list box).

➤ Click **OK** to close the Source Data dialog box.

➤ Save the workbook.

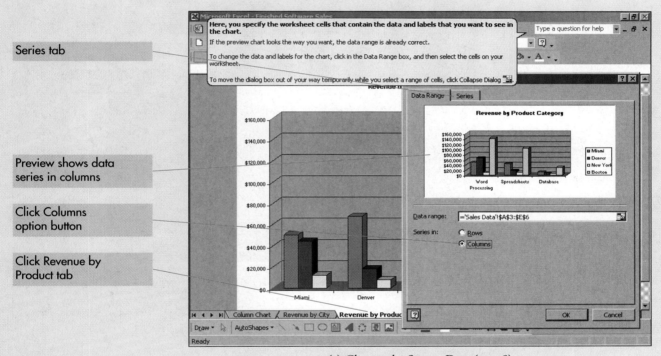

Series tab

Preview shows data series in columns

Click Columns option button

Click Revenue by Product tab

(e) Change the Source Data (step 5)

FIGURE 4.10 *Hands-on Exercise 2 (continued)*

THE HORIZONTAL SCROLL BAR

The horizontal scroll bar contains four scrolling buttons to scroll through the sheet tabs in a workbook. Click ◄ or ► to scroll one tab to the left or right. Click ◄ or ► to scroll to the first or last tab in the workbook. Once the desired tab is visible, click the tab to select it. Change the color of any tab by right clicking the tab and selecting Tab Color from the context-sensitive menu. See practice exercise 1 at the end of the chapter.

Step 6: **Change the Chart Type**

➤ Point to the chart area, click the **right mouse button** to display a shortcut menu, then click the **Chart Type command** to display the Chart Type dialog box. (You can also access the command from the Chart menu.)
➤ Select the **Stacked Column with a 3-D visual effect chart** (the middle entry in the second row). Click **OK**. The chart changes to a stacked column chart as shown in Figure 4.10f.
➤ Save the workbook.
➤ Pull down the **File menu**, click the **Print command**, then click the option button to print the **Entire Workbook**. Click **OK**.
➤ Submit the workbook to your instructor as proof that you completed the exercise. Close the workbook. Exit Excel if you do not want to continue with the next exercise at this time.

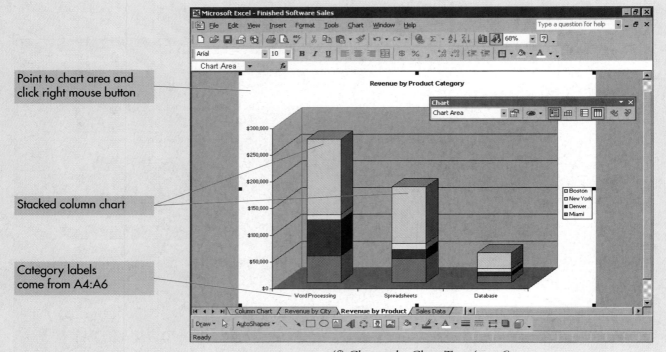

Point to chart area and click right mouse button

Stacked column chart

Category labels come from A4:A6

(f) Change the Chart Type (step 6)

FIGURE 4.10 *Hands-on Exercise 2 (continued)*

THE RIGHT MOUSE BUTTON

Point to a cell (or group of selected cells), a chart or worksheet tab, a toolbar, or chart (or a selected object on the chart), then click the right mouse button to display a shortcut menu. All shortcut menus are context-sensitive and display commands appropriate for the selected item. Right clicking a toolbar, for example, enables you to display (hide) additional toolbars. Right clicking a sheet tab enables you to rename, move, copy, or delete the sheet.

The applications within Microsoft Office enable you to create a document in one application that contains data (objects) from another application. The memo in Figure 4.11, for example, was created in Microsoft Word and it contains *objects* (a worksheet and a chart) that were developed in Microsoft Excel. The Excel objects are *linked* to the Word document, so that any changes to the Excel workbook are automatically reflected in the Word document.

The following exercise uses *object linking and embedding (OLE)* to create a Word document containing an Excel worksheet and chart. As you do the exercise, both applications (Word and Excel) will be open, and it will be necessary to switch back and forth between them. This in turn demonstrates the *multitasking* capability within Windows and the use of the *taskbar* to switch between the open applications.

Superior Software

Miami, Florida

To: Mr. White
          Chairman, Superior Software

From: Heather Bond
          Vice President, Marketing

Subject: May Sales Data

The May sales data clearly indicate that Boston is outperforming our other geographic areas. It is my feeling that Ms. Brown, the office supervisor, is directly responsible for its success and that she should be rewarded accordingly. In addition, we may want to think about transferring her to New York, as they are in desperate need of new ideas and direction. I will be awaiting your response after you have time to digest the information presented.

Superior Software Sales					
	Miami	Denver	New York	Boston	Total
Word Processing	$50,000	$67,500	$200,000	$141,000	**$458,500**
Spreadsheets	$44,000	$18,000	$11,500	$105,000	**$178,500**
Database	$12,000	$7,500	$6,000	$30,000	**$55,500**
Total	**$106,000**	**$93,000**	**$217,500**	**$276,000**	**$692,500**

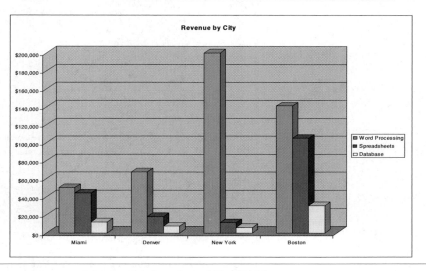

FIGURE 4.11   *Object Linking and Embedding*

OBJECT LINKING AND EMBEDDING

Objective To create a compound document consisting of a memo, worksheet, and chart. Use Figure 4.12 as a guide in the exercise.

Step 1: **Open the Software Sales Document**

➤ Click the **Start button** on the taskbar to display the Start menu. Click (or point to) the **Programs menu**, then click **Microsoft Word 2002** to start the program. Hide the Office Assistant if it appears.

➤ If necessary, click the **Maximize button** in the application window so that Word takes the entire desktop as shown in Figure 4.12a. (The Open dialog box is not yet visible.)

➤ Pull down the **File menu** and click **Open** (or click the **Open button** on the Standard toolbar).

- Click the **drop-down arrow** in the Look In list box. Click the appropriate drive, drive C or drive A, depending on the location of your data.
- Double click the **Exploring Excel folder** (we placed the Word memo in the Exploring Excel folder) to open the folder. Double click the **Software Memo** to open the document.
- Save the document as **Finished Software Memo**.

➤ Pull down the **View menu**. Click **Print Layout** to change to the Print Layout view. Pull down the **View menu**. Click **Zoom**. Click **Page Width**.

➤ The software memo is open on your desktop.

Open button

Click drop-down arrow to select drive/folder

Double click to open Software Memo

Start button

(a) Open the Software Sales Document (step 1)

FIGURE 4.12 *Hands-on Exercise 3*

Step 2:   **Copy the Worksheet**

➤ Open the **Finished Software Sales workbook** from the previous exercise.
  • If you did not close Microsoft Excel at the end of the previous exercise, you will see its button on the taskbar. Click the **Microsoft Excel button** to return to the Finished Software Sales workbook.
  • If you closed Microsoft Excel, click the **Start button** to start Excel, then open the Finished Software Sales workbook.
➤ The taskbar should now contain a button for both Microsoft Word and Microsoft Excel. Click either button to move back and forth between the open applications. End by clicking the **Microsoft Excel button**.
➤ Click the tab for **Sales Data**. Click and drag to select **A1 through F7** to select the entire worksheet as shown in Figure 4.12b.
➤ Point to the selected area and click the **right mouse button** to display the short-cut menu. Click **Copy**.
➤ A moving border appears around the entire worksheet, indicating that it has been copied to the clipboard.

Click and drag
to select A1:F7

Point to selected area
and right click

Click Copy

Click Sales Data tab

Taskbar contains buttons
for both Word and Excel

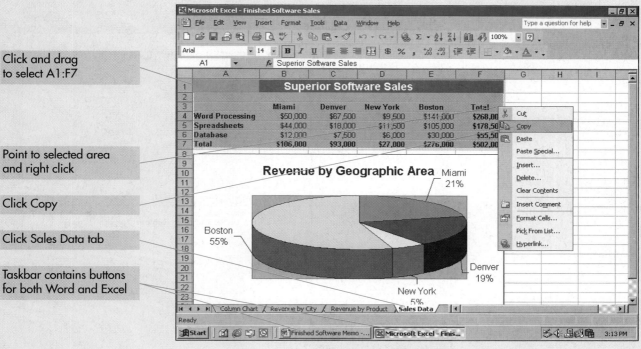

(b) Copy the Worksheet (step 2)

FIGURE 4.12   *Hands-on Exercise 3 (continued)*

THE WINDOWS TASKBAR

Multitasking, the ability to run multiple applications at the same time, is one of the primary advantages of the Windows environment. Each button on the taskbar appears automatically when its application or folder is opened, and disappears upon closing. (The buttons are resized automatically according to the number of open windows.) The taskbar can be moved to the left or right edge of the desktop, or to the top of the desktop, by dragging a blank area of the taskbar to the desired position.

Step 3:   **Create the Link**

➤ Click the **Microsoft Word button** on the taskbar to return to the memo as shown in Figure 4.12c. Press **Ctrl+End** to move to the end of the memo, which is where you will insert the Excel worksheet.

➤ Pull down the **Edit menu**. If necessary, click the **double arrow** to see more commands, then click **Paste Special** to display the dialog box in Figure 4.12c.

➤ Click **Microsoft Excel Worksheet Object** in the As list. Click the **Paste Link** option **button**. Click **OK** to insert the worksheet into the document.

➤ Right click the worksheet to display a context-sensitive menu, click **Format Object** to display the associated dialog box, and click the **Layout tab**.

➤ Choose **Square** in the Wrapping Style area, then click the option button to **Center** the object. Click **OK** to accept the settings and close the dialog box.

➤ Save the memo.

(c) Create the Link (step 3)

FIGURE 4.12   *Hands-on Exercise 3 (continued)*

THE COMMON USER INTERFACE

The common user interface provides a sense of familiarity from one Office application to the next. The applications share a common menu structure with consistent ways to execute commands from those menus. The Standard and Formatting toolbars are present in both applications. Many keyboard shortcuts are also common, such as Ctrl+Home and Ctrl+End to move to the beginning and end of a document, respectively.

Step 4: **Copy the Chart**

➤ Click the **Microsoft Excel button** on the taskbar to return to the worksheet. Click outside the selected area (cells A1 through F7) to deselect the cells. Press **Esc** to remove the moving border.

➤ Click the **Revenue by City tab** to select the chart sheet. Point to the chart area, then click the left mouse button to select the chart.

➤ Be sure you have selected the entire chart and that you see the same sizing handles as in Figure 4.12d.

➤ Pull down the **Edit menu** and click **Copy** (or click the **Copy button** on the Standard toolbar). A moving border appears around the entire chart, indicating that the chart has been copied to the clipboard.

Copy button

Click chart to select it

Click Revenue by City tab

Click Excel button

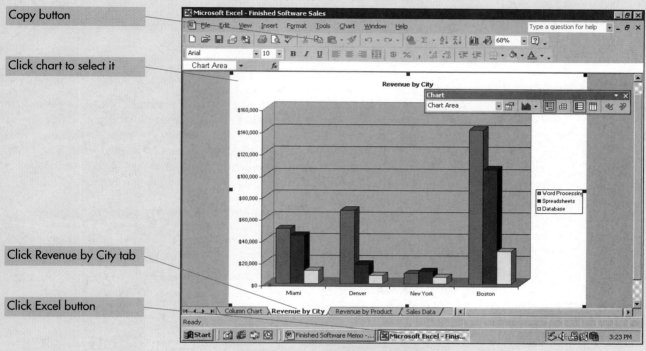

(d) Copy the Chart (step 4)

FIGURE 4.12 *Hands-on Exercise 3 (continued)*

ALT+TAB STILL WORKS

Alt+Tab was a treasured shortcut in Windows 3.1 that enabled users to switch back and forth between open applications. The shortcut also works in all subsequent versions of Windows. Press and hold the Alt key while you press and release the Tab key repeatedly to cycle through the open applications, whose icons are displayed in a small rectangular window in the middle of the screen. Release the Alt key when you have selected the icon for the application you want.

Step 5: Add the Chart

➤ Click the **Microsoft Word button** on the taskbar to return to the memo. If necessary, press **Ctrl+End** to move to the end of the Word document. Press the **enter key** to add a blank line.

➤ Pull down the **Edit menu**. Click **Paste Special**. Click the **Paste link option button**. If necessary, click **Microsoft Excel Chart Object**. Click **OK** to insert the chart into the document.

➤ Right click the chart to display a context-sensitive menu, click **Format Object**, click the **Layout tab**, and choose **Square** in the Wrapping Style area.

➤ Zoom to **Whole Page** to facilitate moving and sizing the chart. You need to reduce its size so that it fits on the same page as the memo. Thus, scroll to the chart and click the chart to select it. This displays the sizing handles as shown in Figure 4.12e.

➤ Click and drag a corner sizing handle inward to make the chart smaller. Move the chart to the first page and center it on the page.

➤ Zoom to **Page Width**. Look carefully at the worksheet and chart in the document. The sales for Word Processing in New York are currently $9,500, and the chart reflects this amount. Save the memo.

➤ Point to the **Microsoft Excel button** on the taskbar and click the **right mouse button** to display a shortcut menu. Click **Close** to close Excel. Click **Yes** if prompted to save the changes to the Finished Software Sales workbook.

➤ Pull down the **File menu** and click the **Exit command**. The Microsoft Excel button disappears from the taskbar, indicating that Excel has been closed. Word is now the only open application.

Zoom button

Sizing handles

Click chart to select it

Right click on Excel button

Click Word button

(e) Add the Chart (step 5)

FIGURE 4.12 *Hands-on Exercise 3 (continued)*

Step 6: **Modify the Worksheet**

➤ Click anywhere in the worksheet to select the worksheet and display the sizing handles as shown in Figure 4.12f.
➤ The status bar indicates that you can double click to edit the worksheet. Double click anywhere within the worksheet to reopen Excel in order to change the data.
➤ The system pauses as it loads Excel and reopens the Finished Software Sales workbook. If necessary, click the **Maximize button** to maximize the Excel window. Hide the Office Assistant if it appears.
➤ If necessary, click the **Sales Data tab** within the workbook. Click in **cell D4**. Type **$200,000**. Press **enter**.
➤ Click the ◀| **button** to scroll to the first tab. Click the **Revenue by City tab** to select the chart sheet. The chart has been modified automatically and reflects the increased sales for New York.

Click worksheet to select it; double click to open Excel and modify data

Word is only open application

(f) Modify the Worksheet (step 6)

FIGURE 4.12 *Hands-on Exercise 3 (continued)*

LINKING VERSUS EMBEDDING

A linked object maintains its connection to the source file. An embedded object does not. Thus, a linked object can be placed in any number of destination files, each of which maintains a pointer (link) to the same source file. Any change to the object in the source file is reflected automatically in every destination file containing that object.

Step 7: **Update the Links**

➤ Click the **Microsoft Word button** on the taskbar to return to the Software memo. The worksheet and chart should be updated automatically. If not:
   - Pull down the **Edit menu**. Click **Links to** display the Links dialog box in Figure 4.12g.
   - Select the link(s) to update. (You can press and hold the **Ctrl key** to select multiple links simultaneously.)
   - Click the **Update Now button** to update the selected links.
   - Close the Links dialog box.
➤ The worksheet and chart should both reflect $200,000 for word processing sales in New York.
➤ Zoom to the **Whole Page** to view the completed document. Click and drag the worksheet and/or the chart within the memo to make any last-minute changes. Save the memo a final time.
➤ Print the completed memo and submit it to your instructor. Exit Word. Exit Excel. Save the changes to the Finished Software Sales workbook.

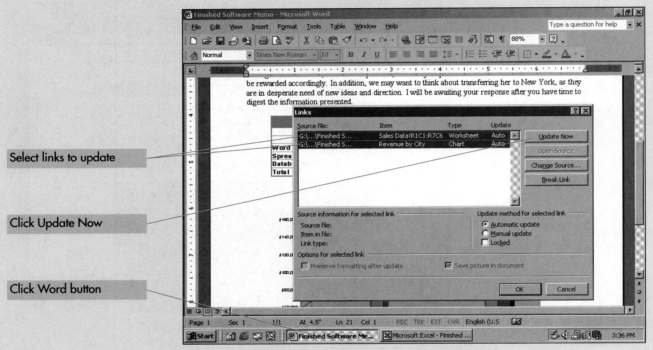

Select links to update

Click Update Now

Click Word button

(g) Update the Links (step 7)

FIGURE 4.12 *Hands-on Exercise 3 (continued)*

LINKING WORKSHEETS

A Word document can be linked to an Excel chart and/or worksheet; that is, change the chart in Excel, and the Word document changes automatically. The chart itself is linked to the underlying worksheet; change the worksheet, and the chart changes. Worksheets can also be linked to one another; for example, a summary worksheet for the corporation as a whole can reflect data from detail worksheets for individual cities. See practice exercise 5 at the end of the chapter.

A chart is a graphic representation of data in a worksheet. The type of chart chosen depends on the message to be conveyed. A pie chart is best for proportional relationships. A column or bar chart is used to show actual numbers rather than percentages. A line chart is preferable for time-related data. A combination chart uses two or more chart types when different scales are required for different data series. The title of a chart can help to convey the message.

The Chart Wizard is an easy way to create a chart. Once created, a chart can be enhanced with arrows and text boxes found on the Drawing toolbar. These objects can be moved or sized and/or modified with respect to their color and other properties. The chart itself can also be modified using various commands from the Chart menu or tools on the Chart toolbar.

A chart may be embedded in a worksheet or created in a separate chart sheet. An embedded chart may be moved within a worksheet by selecting it and dragging it to its new location. An embedded chart may be sized by selecting it and dragging any of the sizing handles in the desired direction.

Multiple data series may be specified in either rows or columns. If the data is in rows, the first row is assumed to contain the category labels, and the first column is assumed to contain the legend. Conversely, if the data is in columns, the first column is assumed to contain the category labels, and the first row the legend. The Chart Wizard makes it easy to switch from rows to columns and vice versa.

Object Linking and Embedding enables the creation of a compound document containing data (objects) from multiple applications. The essential difference between linking and embedding is whether the object is stored within the compound document (embedding) or in its own file (linking). An embedded object is stored in the compound document, which in turn becomes the only user (client) of that object. A linked object is stored in its own file, and the compound document is one of many potential clients of that object. The same chart can be linked to a Word document and a PowerPoint presentation.

It is important that charts are created accurately and that they do not mislead the reader. Stacked column charts should not add dissimilar quantities such as units and dollars.

KEY TERMS

Bar chart (p. 171)
Category label (p. 168)
Chart (p. 168)
Chart sheet (p. 174)
Chart toolbar (p. 178)
Chart type (p. 176)
Chart Wizard (p. 176)
Column chart (p. 171)
Combination chart (p. 184)
Common user interface (p. 200)
Data point (p. 168)
Data series (p. 168)
Docked toolbar (p. 186)

Drawing toolbar (p. 178)
Embedded chart (p. 174)
Embedded object (p. 203)
Exploded pie chart (p. 169)
Floating toolbar (p. 186)
Line chart (p. 184)
Linked object (p. 203)
Linking (p. 197)
Multiple data series (p. 188)
Multitasking (p. 197)
Object (p. 197)
Object Linking and Embedding
  (OLE) (p. 197)

Pie chart (p. 169)
Side-by-side column charts (p. 189)
Sizing handles (p. 174)
Stacked column charts (p. 189)
Taskbar (p. 197)
Three-dimensional column chart
  (p. 173)
Three-dimensional pie chart
  (p. 169)
X axis (p. 171)
Y axis (p. 171)

1. Which type of chart is best to portray proportion or market share?
   (a) Pie chart
   (b) Line
   (c) Column chart
   (d) Combination chart

2. Which of the following is a true statement about the Chart Wizard?
   (a) It is accessed via a button on the Standard toolbar
   (b) It enables you to choose the type of chart you want as well as specify the location for that chart
   (c) It enables you to retrace your steps via the Back command button
   (d) All of the above

3. Which of the following chart types is *not* suitable to display multiple data series?
   (a) Pie chart
   (b) Horizontal bar chart
   (c) Column chart
   (d) All of the above are equally suitable

4. Which of the following is best to display additive information from multiple data series?
   (a) A column chart with the data series stacked one on top of another
   (b) A column chart with the data series side by side
   (c) Both (a) and (b) are equally appropriate
   (d) Neither (a) nor (b) is appropriate

5. A workbook must contain:
   (a) A separate chart sheet for every worksheet
   (b) A separate worksheet for every chart sheet
   (c) Both (a) and (b)
   (d) Neither (a) nor (b)

6. Which of the following is true regarding an embedded chart?
   (a) It can be moved elsewhere within the worksheet
   (b) It can be made larger or smaller
   (c) Both (a) and (b)
   (d) Neither (a) nor (b)

7. Which of the following will produce a shortcut menu?
   (a) Pointing to a workbook tab and clicking the right mouse button
   (b) Pointing to an embedded chart and clicking the right mouse button
   (c) Pointing to a selected cell range and clicking the right mouse button
   (d) All of the above

8. Which of the following is done *prior* to invoking the Chart Wizard?
   (a) The data series are selected
   (b) The location of the embedded chart within the worksheet is specified
   (c) Both (a) and (b)
   (d) Neither (a) nor (b)

9. Which of the following will display sizing handles when selected?
   (a) An embedded chart
   (b) The title of a chart
   (c) A text box or arrow
   (d) All of the above

10. How do you switch between open applications?
   (a) Click the appropriate button on the taskbar
   (b) Use Alt+Tab to cycle through the applications
   (c) Both (a) and (b)
   (d) Neither (a) nor (b)

11. You want to create a Word document that is linked to an Excel worksheet and associated chart. Which of the following best describes the way the documents are stored on disk?
   (a) There is a single file that contains the Word document, the Excel worksheet, and the associated chart
   (b) There are two files—one for the Word document and one for the Excel workbook, which contains both the worksheet and associated chart
   (c) There are three files—one for the Word document, one for the Excel worksheet, and one for the Excel chart
   (d) None of the above

12. In order to represent multiple data series on the same chart:
   (a) The data series must be in rows and the rows must be adjacent to one another on the worksheet
   (b) The data series must be in columns and the columns must be adjacent to one another on the worksheet
   (c) The data series may be in rows or columns so long as they are adjacent to one another
   (d) The data series may be in rows or columns with no requirement to be next to one another

13. If multiple data series are selected and rows are specified:
   (a) The first row will be used for the category (X axis) labels
   (b) The first column will be used for the legend
   (c) Both (a) and (b)
   (d) Neither (a) nor (b)

14. If multiple data series are selected and columns are specified:
   (a) The first column will be used for the category (X axis) labels
   (b) The first row will be used for the legend
   (c) Both (a) and (b)
   (d) Neither (a) nor (b)

15. Which of the following is true about the scale on the Y axis in a column chart that plots multiple data series side-by-side versus one that stacks the values one on top of another?
   (a) The scale for the stacked columns will contain larger values than if the columns are plotted side-by-side
   (b) The scale for the side-by-side columns will contain larger values than if the columns are stacked
   (c) The values on the scale will be the same regardless of whether the columns are stacked or side-by-side
   (d) The values on the scale will be different but it is not possible to tell which chart will contain the higher values

ANSWERS

1. a	**6.** c	**11.** b
2. d	**7.** d	**12.** d
3. a	**8.** a	**13.** c
4. a	**9.** d	**14.** c
5. d	**10.** c	**15.** a

1. Theme Park Admissions: A partially completed version of the worksheet in Figure 4.13 is available in the Exploring Excel folder as *Chapter 4 Practice 1*. Follow the directions in steps (a) and (b) to compute the totals and format the worksheet, then create each of the charts listed below.

   a. Use the AutoSum command to enter the formulas to compute the total number of admissions for each region and each quarter.

   b. Select the entire worksheet (cells A1 through F8), then use the AutoFormat command to format the worksheet. You do not have to accept the entire design nor do you have to use the design we selected. You can also modify the design after it has been applied to the worksheet by changing the font size of selected cells and/or changing boldface and italics.

   c. A column chart showing the total number of admissions in each quarter as shown in Figure 4.13. Add the graphic shown in the figure for emphasis.

   d. A pie chart showing the percentage of the total number of admissions in each region. Create this chart in its own chart sheet with an appropriate name.

   e. A stacked column chart showing the total number of admissions for each region and the contribution of each quarter within each region. Create this chart in its own chart sheet with an appropriate name.

   f. A stacked column chart showing the total number of admissions for each quarter and the contribution of each region within each quarter. Create this chart in its own chart sheet with an appropriate name.

   g. Change the color of each of the worksheet tabs.

   h. Print the entire workbook, consisting of the worksheet in Figure 4.13 plus the three additional sheets that you create. Submit the completed assignment to your instructor.

   i. This workbook is also the basis for a PowerPoint presentation in practice exercise 9.

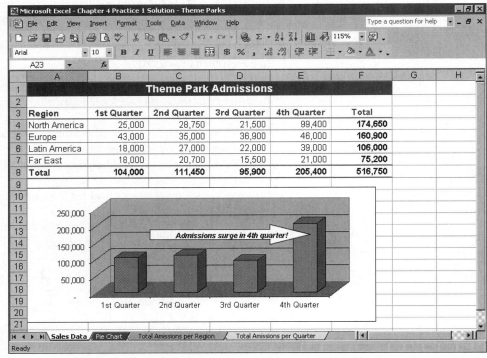

FIGURE 4.13 *Theme Park Admissions (Exercise 1)*

2. **Rows versus Columns:** Figure 4.14 displays the Page Preview view of a worksheet with two similar charts, one that plots data by rows and the other by columns. The distinction depends on the message you want to deliver. Both charts are correct. Your assignment is to open the partially completed worksheet in the *Chapter 4 Practice 2* workbook and do the following:
   a. Complete the worksheet by computing the total number of visits for each pet category and each quarter, then format the worksheet attractively. (You need not follow our formatting.)
   b. Create each of the charts in Figure 4.14. You can embed the charts in the same worksheet as the data, or you can place the charts on separate worksheets.
   c. Add your name to the worksheet, then print the entire workbook for your instructor. Use the Page Setup command to add a header or footer that contains the name of your course and instructor.

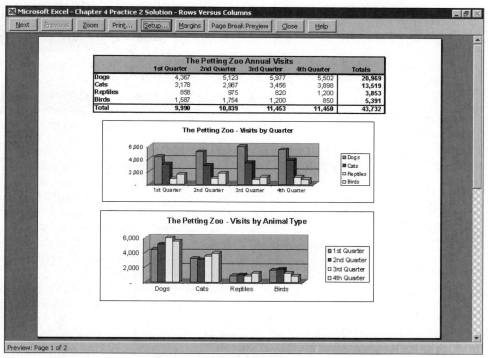

FIGURE 4.14   *Rows versus Columns (Exercise 2)*

3. **Exploded Pie Charts:** Tom Liquer Men's Wear is a privately owned chain of four stores in various cities. Your assignment is to open the partially completed workbook in *Chapter 4 Practice 3* workbook in order to create the worksheet and associated chart in Figure 4.15.
   a. Use the AutoSum and AutoFormat commands to compute the totals and format the worksheet appropriately. You do not have to match our formatting exactly and are free to modify the suggested designs as you see fit.
   b. Create the exploded pie chart in the figure that shows the percentage of total sales that is attributed to each city. Use the Help command as necessary to learn about pulling one slice out of the pie.
   c. Create a second three-dimensional pie chart in its own sheet that shows the percentage of sales that is attributed to each product line.
   d. Add your name to the worksheet, then print the entire workbook for your instructor. Use the Page Setup command to add an appropriate header or footer to each worksheet.

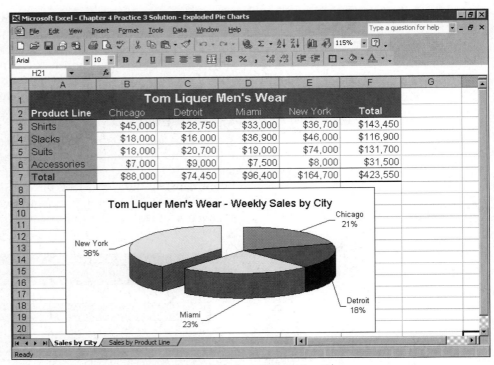

Product Line	Chicago	Detroit	Miami	New York	Total
Shirts	$45,000	$28,750	$33,000	$36,700	$143,450
Slacks	$18,000	$16,000	$36,900	$46,000	$116,900
Suits	$18,000	$20,700	$19,000	$74,000	$131,700
Accessories	$7,000	$9,000	$7,500	$8,000	$31,500
Total	$88,000	$74,450	$96,400	$164,700	$423,550

FIGURE 4.15 *Exploded Pie Charts (Exercise 3)*

4. Page Break Preview: Open the partially completed workbook in *Chapter 4 Practice 4* and create the four charts shown in Figure 4.16. Use the AutoSum and AutoFormat commands to complete the worksheet. Select cells A2 through E6 as the basis for each of the four charts in the figure. The charts should all appear as embedded objects on the worksheet, but do not worry about the placement of the charts until you have completed all four.

   a. The first chart is a side-by-side column chart that emphasizes the sales in each city (the data is in rows).

   b. The second chart is a stacked column version of the chart in part (a).

   c. The third chart (that begins in column H of the worksheet) is a side-by-side column chart that emphasizes the sale of each product line (the data is in columns).

   d. The last chart is a stacked column version of the chart in part c.

   e. Pull down the View command, then change to the Page Break Preview view as shown in Figure 4.16. You will see one or more dashed lines that show where the page breaks will occur. You will also see the message in Figure 4.16 indicating that you can change the location of the page breaks. Click OK after you have read the message.

   f. You can change the position of a page break and/or remove the break entirely by clicking and dragging the line that indicates the break. You can insert horizontal or vertical page breaks by clicking the appropriate cell, pulling down the Insert menu, and selecting Page Break. Pull down the View menu and click Normal view to return to the normal view.

   g. Add your name to the completed worksheet, then print the worksheet and four embedded charts on one page. If necessary, change to landscape printing for a more attractive layout.

   h. Write a short note to your instructor that describes the differences between the charts. Suggest a different title for one or more charts that helps to convey a specific message.

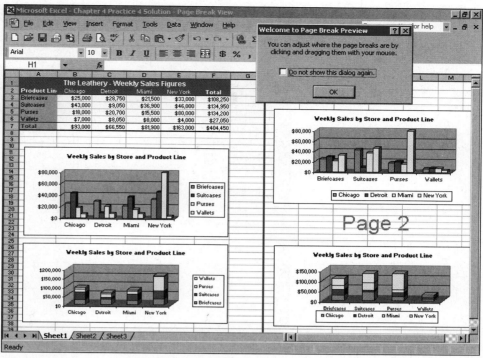

FIGURE 4.16   *Page Break Preview (Exercise 4)*

5. Linking Worksheets: This chapter described how a chart is linked to the data in an underlying worksheet. It is also possible to link the data from one worksheet to another as can be seen in Figure 4.16. The figure contains a table, which at first glance is similar to the example that was used throughout the chapter. Look closely, however, and you will see that the workbook contains individual worksheets for each city, in addition to a worksheet for the corporation as a whole.

   The numbers in the corporate worksheet are linked to the numbers in the worksheets for the individual cities. The entry in cell B4 of the Corporate worksheet contains the formula =Phoenix!F2 to indicate that the entry comes from cell F2 in the Phoenix worksheet. Other cells in the table reference other cells in the Phoenix worksheet as well as cells in the other worksheets.

a. Open the *Chapter 4 Practice 5* workbook. Check that you are in the Corporate worksheet, then click in cell B4 of this worksheet. Type an = sign, click the Phoenix worksheet tab, click in cell F2 of this worksheet, and press the enter key. Click in cell C4, type an = sign, click the Minneapolis tab, click in cell F2 of that worksheet, and press enter.

b. Repeat the process to enter the sales for San Francisco and Los Angeles. Do you see how the worksheet name is reflected in the cell formula?

c. Click and drag cells B4 through E4, then drag the fill handle to row 6 to copy the formulas for the other product lines. The copy operation works because the worksheet references are absolute, but the cell references are relative.

d. Use the AutoSum button to compute the totals for the corporation as a whole.

e. Use the completed worksheet in Figure 4.17 as the basis for a side-by-side column chart with the data plotted in rows.

f. Plot a second side-by-side chart with the data in columns. Put each chart in a separate chart sheet.

g. Print the entire workbook for your instructor.

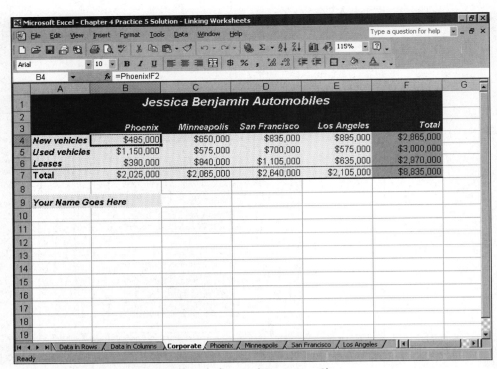

FIGURE 4.17 *Linking Worksheets (Exercise 5)*

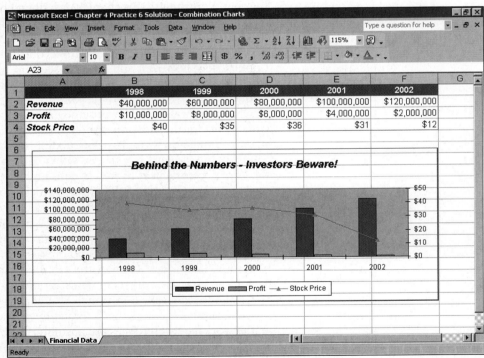

FIGURE 4.18 *Combination Charts (Exercise 6)*

6. Combination Charts: Figure 4.18 on the previous page contains a combination chart, which uses two or more chart types to display different kinds of information and/or different scales for multiple data series. A stacked column chart type is specified for both the revenue and profits, while a line chart is used for the stock price. Two different scales are necessary.

   a. Open the partially completed workbook in *Chapter 4 Practice 6* and format the worksheet appropriately.

   b. Select the entire worksheet (cells A1 through F4), then invoke the Chart Wizard. Click the Custom Types tab in step 1 of the Chart Wizard, choose Line-Column on 2 Axis as the chart type, then in step 2 specify the data in rows. The Chart Wizard will do the rest.

   c. Modify the completed chart so that its appearance is similar to our figure. We made the chart wider and moved the legend to the bottom. (Right click the legend, click the Format Legend command, click the Placement tab, then click the bottom option button.) To place a border around the chart, right click the completed chart, choose the Format Chart Area command, click the Patterns tab, then choose the style, thickness, and color of the border.

   d. Add your name to the worksheet, then submit the completed worksheet.

7. Object Linking and Embedding: The document in Figure 4.19 is based on the partially completed worksheet in the *Chapter 4 Practice 7* workbook. Your assignment is to open the partially completed workbook, compute the sales totals for each individual salesperson as well as the totals for each quarter, then format the resulting worksheet in an attractive fashion. You can use our formatting or develop your own. In addition, you are to create a stacked column chart comparing quarterly sales for each salesperson. Save the workbook.

   a. You will find the text of the document in the Exploring Excel folder in the file *Chapter 4 Practice 7 Memo*.

   b. Use object linking and embedding to link the Excel worksheet to the Word document as described in the chapter. Repeat the process to link the Excel chart to the word document.

   c. Save the Word document, then print the completed document.

BUILDS ON

CHAPTER 3
HANDS-ON
EXERCISE 2
PAGES 130–133

8. Investment Strategies: An IRA (Individual Retirement Account) is a wise investment for your future. In essence, you save a fixed amount each year (up to $2,000 in today's environment) and can invest that money in any way you choose. The money grows over time and the amount at retirement may surprise you. For example, $2000 a year, invested for 40 years and earning 8% a year, will grow to more than $518,000 as shown in Figure 4.20. If you are able to save for 45 years rather than 40 (i.e., you began saving at age 20 rather than 25), the amount at retirement exceeds $750,000.

   a. Open the partially completed workbook in *Chapter 4 Practice 8*, which contains the table shown in Figure 4.20. We have supplied the formula to obtain the future value for an investment earning 6% for 10 years. All you need to do is copy that formula to the remaining rows and columns in the worksheet, then format the worksheet appropriately. We highlighted the row showing the return at 8% since that is the historical rate of return in the stock market.

   b. Create a line chart that shows the growth of your investment over time as an embedded object in the same worksheet. Save the worksheet.

   c. You will find the text of the memo in a Word document, *Chapter 4 Practice 8 memo*, in the Exploring Excel folder. Open the Word document, then use object linking and embedding to link the worksheet and the line chart to the Word document.

   d. Add your name to the memo after the salutation, "To the New Graduate", then print the completed memo and submit it to your instructor. Compound interest has been called the eighth wonder of the world. Use it to your advantage!

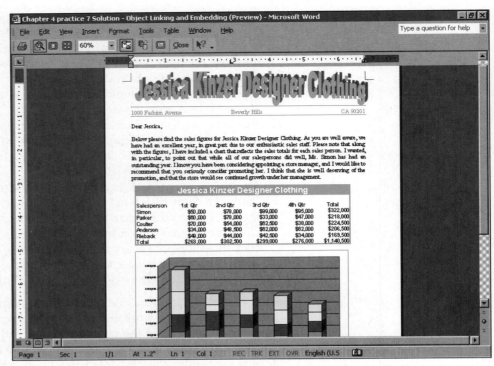

FIGURE 4.19   *Object Linking and Embedding (Exercise 7)*

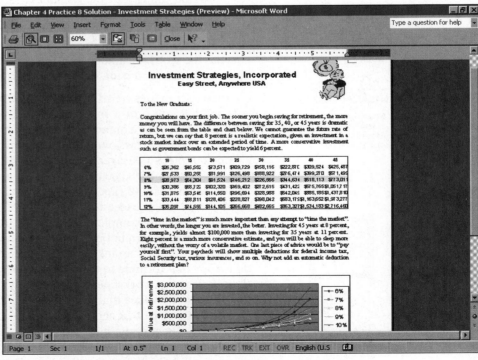

FIGURE 4.20   *Investment Strategies (Exercise 8)*

9. PowerPoint Presentations: The third hands-on exercise in the chapter showed you how to create a Word document containing an Excel chart and/or worksheet. You can use the same technique to create a PowerPoint presentation similar to those in Figure 4.21. The objective of this exercise is to show you how you can link an object such as an Excel chart or worksheet to other Office documents.

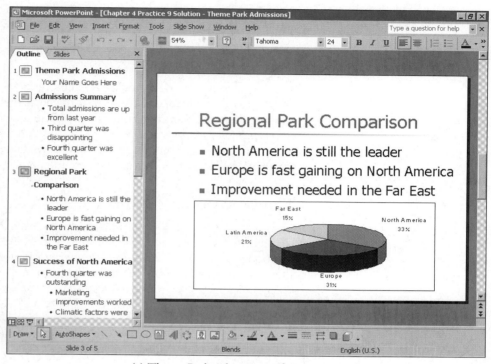

BUILDS ON

PRACTICE
EXERCISE 1
PAGE 208

(a) Theme Park Admissions (from exercise 1)

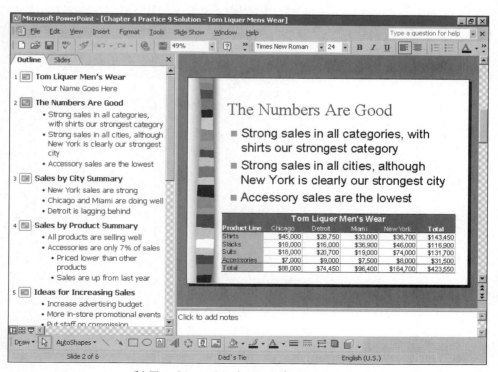

BUILDS ON

PRACTICE
EXERCISE 3
PAGE 209

(b) Tom Liquer Men's Wear (from exercise 3)

FIGURE 4.21   *PowerPoint Presentations (Exercise 9)*

The Census Bureau

Use your favorite search engine to locate the home page of the United States Census Bureau, then download one or more series of population statistics of interest to you. Use the data to plot one or more charts that describe the population growth of the United States. There is an abundance of information available, and you are free to choose any statistics you deem relevant.

UMC Theatres

You are currently working for UMC Theatres, a local chain of movie theatres. Your current assignment is to create a series of charts that show how the ticket sales in the various theatres compare to one another. The assignment is open ended in that you can create any chart you like based on the data in the *UMC Theatres Workbook*. Open the partially completed workbook, format the worksheet attractively, and then create at least two charts based on the data.

The Convention Planner

Your first task as a convention planner is to evaluate the hotel capacity for the host city in order to make recommendations as to where to host the convention. The data can be found in the *Convention Planner* workbook, which contains a single worksheet showing the number of rooms in each hotel, divided into standard and deluxe categories, together with the associated room rates. Open the workbook and format the worksheet in attractive fashion. Create a stacked column chart that shows the total capacity for each hotel, then create a second chart that shows the percentage of total capacity for each hotel. Store each chart in its own worksheet, then print the entire workbook for your instructor.

Irrational Exuberance

Your brother-in-law has called you with a stock tip based on sales and profit data found in the file *Irrational Exuberance*. Open the file, examine the data and associated chart that your brother-in-law has created, and then respond with a short note on what you think of the investment. Be sure to comment on the chart that accompanies the data.

Essentials of
Microsoft® Windows®

OBJECTIVES

AFTER READING THIS SUPPLEMENT YOU WILL BE ABLE TO:

1. Describe the objects on the Windows desktop; use the icons on the desktop to start the associated applications.
2. Explain the significance of the common user interface; identify the elements that are present in every window.
3. Explain in general terms the similarities and differences between various versions of Windows.
4. Use the Help command to learn about Windows.
5. Format a floppy disk.
6. Differentiate between a program file and a data file; explain the significance of the icons that appear next to a file in My Computer and Windows Explorer.
7. Explain how folders are used to organize the files on a disk; use the View menu and/or the Folder Options command to change the appearance of a folder.
8. Distinguish between My Computer and Windows Explorer with respect to viewing files and folders; explain the advantages of the hierarchical view available within Windows Explorer.
9. Use Internet Explorer to download a file; describe how to view a Web page from within Windows Explorer.
10. Copy and/or move a file from one folder to another; delete a file, then recover the deleted file from the Recycle Bin.

OVERVIEW

Microsoft® Windows is a computer program (actually many programs) that controls the operation of a computer and its peripherals. The Windows environment provides a common user interface and consistent command structure for every application. You have seen the interface many times, but do you really understand it? Can you move and copy files with confidence? Do you know how to back up the Excel spreadsheets, Access databases, and other Office documents that you work so hard to create? If not, now is the time to learn. This section is written for you, the computer novice, and it assumes no previous knowledge.

We begin with an introduction to the Windows desktop, the graphical user interface that enables you to work in intuitive fashion by pointing at icons and clicking the mouse. We identify the basic components of a window and describe how to execute commands and supply information through different elements in a dialog box. We introduce you to My Computer, an icon on the Windows desktop, and show you how to use My Computer to access the various components of your system. We also describe how to access the Help command.

The supplement concentrates, however, on disk and file management. We present the basic definitions of a file and a folder, then describe how to use My Computer to look for a specific file or folder. We introduce Windows Explorer, which provides a more efficient way of finding data on your system, then show you how to move or copy a file from one folder to another. We discuss other basic operations, such as renaming and deleting a file. We also describe how to recover a deleted file (if necessary) from the Recycle Bin.

There are also four hands-on exercises, which enable you to apply the conceptual discussion in the text at the computer. The exercises refer to a set of practice files (data disk) that we have created for you. You can obtain these files from our Web site (www.prenhall.com/grauer) or from a local area network if your professor has downloaded the files for you.

THE DESKTOP

Windows 95 was the first of the so-called "modern Windows" and was followed by Windows NT, Windows 98, Windows 2000, Windows Me (Millennium edition), and most recently, by Windows XP. Each of these systems is still in use. Windows 98 and its successor, Windows Me, are geared for the home user and provide extensive support for games and peripheral devices. Windows NT, and its successor Windows 2000, are aimed at the business user and provide increased security and reliability. Windows XP is the successor to all current breeds of Windows. It has a slightly different look, but maintains the conventions of its various predecessors. Hence we have called this module "Essentials of Microsoft Windows" and refer to Windows in a generic sense. (The screens were taken from Windows 2000 Professional, but could just as easily have been taken from other versions of the operating system.)

All versions of Windows create a working environment for your computer that parallels the working environment at home or in an office. You work at a desk. Windows operations take place on the *desktop* as shown in Figure 1. There are physical objects on a desk such as folders, a dictionary, a calculator, or a phone. The computer equivalents of those objects appear as icons (pictorial symbols) on the desktop. Each object on a real desk has attributes (properties) such as size, weight, and color. In similar fashion, Windows assigns properties to every object on its desktop. And just as you can move the objects on a real desk, you can rearrange the objects on the Windows desktop.

Figure 1a displays the typical desktop that appears when Windows is installed on a new computer. It has only a few objects and is similar to the desk in a new office, just after you move in. This desktop might have been taken from any of five systems—Windows 95, Windows NT, Windows 98, Windows 2000, or Windows Me—and is sometimes called "Classic Windows." The icons on this desktop are opened by double clicking. (It is possible to display an alternate desktop with underlined icons that are opened by single clicking, but that option is rarely used.) Figure 1b shows the new Windows XP desktop as it might appear on a home computer, where individual accounts are established for different users.

Double click an icon to open it

(a) Windows 95, Windows NT, Windows 98, Windows Me, and Windows 2000

Click to open Start menu

Individual desktops are established for different users

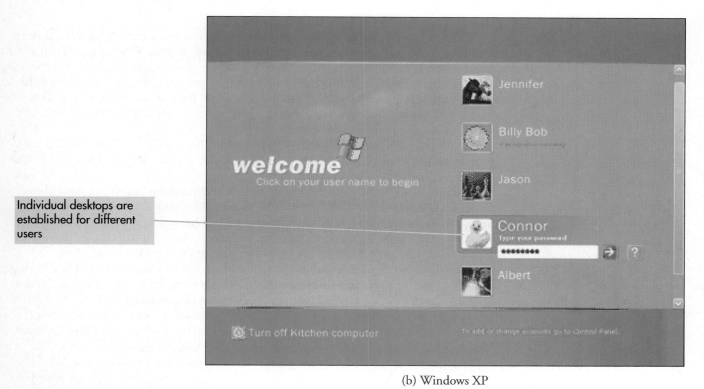

(b) Windows XP

FIGURE 1 *The Different Faces of Windows*

My Computer window

Buttons for open programs

Taskbar

(c) A Working Desktop (all versions of Windows)

FIGURE 1   *The Different Faces of Windows (continued)*

Do not be concerned if your desktop is different from ours. Your real desk is arranged differently from those of your friends, just as your Windows desktop will also be different. Moreover, you are likely to work on different systems—at school, at work, or at home, and thus it is important that you recognize the common functionality that is present on all desktops. The *Start button,* as its name suggests, is where you begin. Click the Start button and you see a menu that lets you start any program installed on your computer.

Look now at Figure 1c, which displays an entirely different desktop, one with four open windows that is similar to a desk in the middle of a working day. Each window in Figure 1c displays a program that is currently in use. The ability to run several programs at the same time is known as *multitasking*, and it is a major benefit of the Windows environment. Multitasking enables you to run a word processor in one window, create a spreadsheet in a second window, surf the Internet in a third window, play a game in a fourth window, and so on. You can work in a program as long as you want, then change to a different program by clicking its window.

You can also change from one program to another by using the taskbar at the bottom of the desktop. The *taskbar* contains a button for each open program, and it enables you to switch back and forth between those programs by clicking the appropriate button. The taskbar in Figure 1a does not contain any buttons (other than the Start button) since there are no open applications. The taskbar in Figure 1c, however, contains four additional buttons, one for each open window.

The icons on the desktop are used to access programs or other functions. The *My Computer* icon is the most basic. It enables you to view the devices on your system, including the drives on a local area network to which you have direct access. Open My Computer in either Figure 1a or 1b, for example, and you see the objects in the My Computer window of Figure 1c. The contents of My Computer depend on the hardware of the specific computer system. Our system, for example, has one floppy drive, three local (hard or fixed) disks, a removable disk (an Iomega Zip drive), a CD-ROM, and access to various network drives. The My Computer window also contains the Control Panel folder that provides access to functions that control other elements of your computing environment. (These capabilities are not used by beginners, are generally "off limits" in a lab environment, and thus are not discussed further.)

The other icons on the desktop are also noteworthy. The **My Documents** folder is a convenient place in which to store the documents you create. **My Network Places** extends the view of your computer to include the other local area networks (if any) that your computer can access, provided you have a valid username and password. The **Recycle Bin** enables you to restore a file that was previously deleted. The Internet Explorer icon starts **Internet Explorer**, the Web browser that is built into the Windows operating system.

THE DOJ (DEPARTMENT OF JUSTICE) VERSUS MICROSOFT

A simple icon is at the heart of the multibillion dollar lawsuit brought by 19 states against Microsoft. In short, Microsoft is accused of integrating its Internet Explorer browser into the Windows operating system with the goal of dominating the market and eliminating the competition. Is Internet Explorer built into every current version of Microsoft Windows? Yes. Can Netscape Navigator run without difficulty under every current version of Microsoft Windows? The answer is also yes. As of this writing the eventual outcome of the case against Microsoft has yet to be determined.

THE COMMON USER INTERFACE

All Windows applications share a **common user interface** and possess a consistent command structure. This means that every Windows application works essentially the same way, which provides a sense of familiarity from one application to the next. In other words, once you learn the basic concepts and techniques in one application, you can apply that knowledge to every other application. Consider, for example, Figure 2, which shows open windows for My Computer and My Network Places, and labels the essential elements in each.

The contents of the two windows are different, but each window has the same essential elements. The **title bar** appears at the top of each window and displays the name of the window, My Computer and My Network Places in Figure 2a and 2b, respectively. The icon at the extreme left of the title bar identifies the window and also provides access to a control menu with operations relevant to the window such as moving it or sizing it. The **minimize button** shrinks the window to a button on the taskbar, but leaves the window in memory. The **maximize button** enlarges the window so that it takes up the entire desktop. The **restore button** (not shown in either figure) appears instead of the maximize button after a window has been maximized, and restores the window to its previous size. The **close button** closes the window and removes it from memory and the desktop.

The **menu bar** appears immediately below the title bar and provides access to **pull-down menus**. One or more **toolbars** appear below the menu bar and let you execute a command by clicking a button as opposed to pulling down a menu. The **status bar** at the bottom of the window displays information about the window as a whole or about a selected object within a window.

A vertical (or horizontal) **scroll bar** appears at the right (or bottom) border of a window when its contents are not completely visible and provides access to the unseen areas. A scroll bar does not appear in Figure 2a since all of the objects in the window are visible at the same time. A vertical scroll bar is found in Figure 2b, however, since there are other objects in the window.

Title bar

Menu bar

Toolbars

Minimize button

Maximize button

Close button

Status bar

(a) My Computer

Title bar

Menu bar

Toolbars

Minimize button

Maximize button

Close button

Scroll bar

Status bar

(b) My Network Places

FIGURE 2   *Anatomy of a Window*

Moving and Sizing a Window

A window can be sized or moved on the desktop through appropriate actions with the mouse. To **size a window**, point to any border (the mouse pointer changes to a double arrow), then drag the border in the direction you want to go—inward to shrink the window or outward to enlarge it. You can also drag a corner (instead of a border) to change both dimensions at the same time. To **move a window** while retaining its current size, click and drag the title bar to a new position on the desktop.

Pull-Down Menus

The menu bar provides access to **pull-down menus** that enable you to execute commands within an application (program). A pull-down menu is accessed by clicking the menu name or by pressing the Alt key plus the underlined letter in the menu name; for example, press Alt+V to pull down the View menu. (You may have to press the Alt key in order to see the underlines.) Three pull-down menus associated with My Computer are shown in Figure 3.

Commands within a menu are executed by clicking the command or by typing the underlined letter. Alternatively, you can bypass the menu entirely if you know the equivalent keystrokes shown to the right of the command in the menu (e.g., Ctrl+X, Ctrl+C, or Ctrl+V to cut, copy, or paste as shown within the Edit menu). A dimmed command (e.g., the Paste command in the Edit menu) means the command is not currently executable; some additional action has to be taken for the command to become available.

An ellipsis (...) following a command indicates that additional information is required to execute the command; for example, selection of the Format command in the File menu requires the user to specify additional information about the format-

FIGURE 3 *Pull-Down Menus*

ting process. This information is entered into a dialog box (discussed in the next section), which appears immediately after the command has been selected.

A check next to a command indicates a toggle switch, whereby the command is either on or off. There is a check next to the Status Bar command in the View menu of Figure 3, which means the command is in effect (and thus the status bar will be displayed). Click the Status Bar command and the check disappears, which suppresses the display of the status bar. Click the command a second time and the check reappears, as does the status bar in the associated window.

A bullet next to an item (e.g., Large Icons in Figure 3) indicates a selection from a set of mutually exclusive choices. Click another option within the group (e.g., Small Icons) and the bullet will disappear from the previous selection (Large Icons) and appear next to the new selection (Small Icons).

An arrowhead after a command (e.g., the Arrange Icons command in the View menu) indicates that a submenu (also known as a cascaded menu) will be displayed with additional menu options.

Dialog Boxes

A *dialog box* appears when additional information is necessary to execute a command. Click the Print command in Internet Explorer, for example, and you are presented with the Print dialog box in Figure 4, requesting information about precisely what to print and how. The information is entered into the dialog box in different ways, depending on the type of information that is required. The tabs at the top of the dialog box provide access to different sets of options. The General and Paper tabs are selected in Figures 4a and 4b, respectively.

Option (Radio) buttons indicate mutually exclusive choices, one of which must be chosen, such as the page range in Figure 4a. You can print all pages, the selection (highlighted text), the current page, or a specific set of pages (such as pages 1–4), but you can choose one and only one option. Click a button to select an option, which automatically deselects the previously selected option.

A *text box* enters specific information such as the pages that will be printed in conjunction with selecting the radio button for pages. A flashing vertical bar (an I-beam) appears within the text box when the text box is active, to mark the insertion point for the text you will enter.

A *spin button* is another way to enter specific information such as the number of copies. Click the Up or Down arrow to increase or decrease the number of pages, respectively. You can also enter the information explicitly by typing it into a spin box, just as you would a text box.

Check boxes are used instead of option buttons if the choices are not mutually exclusive or if an option is not required. The Collate check box is checked in Figure 4a, whereas the Print to file box is not checked. Individual options are selected and cleared by clicking the appropriate check box, which toggles the box on and off.

A *list box* such as the Size is list box in Figure 4b displays some or all of the available choices, any one of which is selected by clicking the desired item. Just click the Down arrow on the list box to display the associated choices such as the paper source in Figure 4b. (A scroll bar appears within an open list box if all of the choices are not visible and provides access to the hidden choices.)

The *Help button* (a question mark at the right end of the title bar) provides help for any item in the dialog box. Click the button, then click the item in the dialog box for which you want additional information. The Close button (the X at the extreme right of the title bar) closes the dialog box without executing the command.

Tabs provide access to different sets of options

Spin buttons

Check box is clear if option is not required

Option buttons indicate mutually exclusive choices

Text box enters specific information

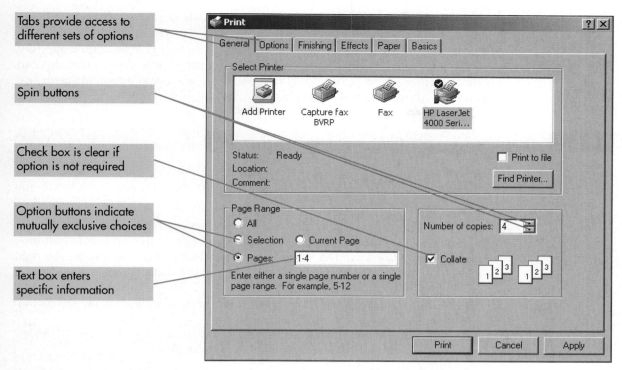

(a) General Tab

Help button

Close button

List box displays some or all available choices

Click down arrow to display associated choices

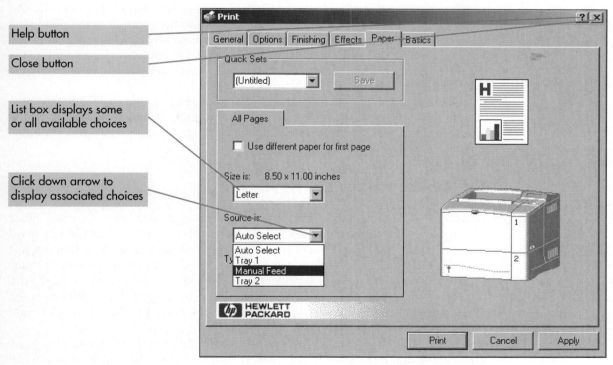

(b) Paper Tab

FIGURE 4   *Dialog Boxes*

All dialog boxes also contain one or more ***command buttons***, the function of which is generally apparent from the button's name. The Print button, in Figure 4a, for example, initiates the printing process. The Cancel button does just the opposite, and ignores (cancels) any changes made to the settings, then closes the dialog box without further action. An ellipsis (three dots) on a command button indicates that additional information will be required if the button is selected.

THE MOUSE

The mouse is indispensable to Windows and is referenced continually in the hands-on exercises throughout the text. There are five basic operations with which you must become familiar:

- To ***point*** to an object, move the mouse pointer onto the object.
- To ***click*** an object, point to it, then press and release the left mouse button.
- To ***right click*** an object, point to the object, then press and release the right mouse button. Right clicking an object displays a context-sensitive menu with commands that pertain to the object.
- To ***double click*** an object, point to it and then quickly click the left button twice in succession.
- To ***drag*** an object, move the pointer to the object, then press and hold the left button while you move the mouse to a new position.

You may also encounter a mouse with a wheel between the left and right buttons that lets you scroll through a document by rotating the wheel forward or backward. The action of the wheel, however, may change, depending on the application in use. In any event, the mouse is a pointing device—move the mouse on your desk and the mouse pointer, typically a small arrowhead, moves on the monitor. The mouse pointer assumes different shapes according to the location of the pointer or the nature of the current action. You will see a double arrow when you change the size of a window, an I-beam as you insert text, a hand to jump from one help topic to the next, or a circle with a line through it to indicate that an attempted action is invalid.

The mouse pointer will also change to an hourglass to indicate Windows is processing your command, and that no further commands may be issued until the action is completed. The more powerful your computer, the less frequently the hourglass will appear.

The Mouse versus the Keyboard

Almost every command in Windows can be executed in different ways, using either the mouse or the keyboard. Most people start with the mouse and add keyboard shortcuts as they become more proficient. There is no right or wrong technique, just different techniques, and the one you choose depends entirely on personal preference in a specific situation. If, for example, your hands are already on the keyboard, it is faster to use the keyboard equivalent. Other times, your hand will be on the mouse and that will be the fastest way. Toolbars provide still other ways to execute common commands.

In the beginning, you may wonder why there are so many different ways to do the same thing, but you will eventually recognize the many options as part of Windows' charm. It is not necessary to memorize anything, nor should you even try; just be flexible and willing to experiment. The more you practice, the faster all of this will become second nature to you.

All versions of Windows include extensive documentation with detailed information about virtually every function in Windows. It is accessed through the **Help command** on the Start menu, which provides different ways to search for information.

The **Contents tab** in Figure 5a is analogous to the table of contents in an ordinary book. The topics are listed in the left pane and the information for the selected topic is displayed in the right pane. The list of topics can be displayed in varying amounts of detail, by opening and closing the various book icons that appear. (The size of the left pane can be increased or decreased by dragging the border between the left and right pane in the appropriate direction.)

A closed book such as "Troubleshooting and Maintenance" indicates the presence of subtopics, which are displayed by opening (clicking) the book. An open book, on the other hand, such as "Internet, E-mail, and Communications," already displays its subtopics. Each subtopic is shown with one of two icons—a question mark to indicate "how to" information, or an open book to indicate conceptual information. Either way, you can click any subtopic in the left pane to view its contents in the right pane. Underlined entries in the right pane (e.g., Related Topics) indicate a hyperlink, which in turn displays additional information. Note, too, that you can print the information in the right pane by pulling down the Options menu and selecting the Print command.

The **Index tab** in Figure 5b is analogous to the index of an ordinary book. You enter the first several letters of the topic to look up, such as "floppy disk," choose a topic from the resulting list, and then click the Display button to view the information in the right pane. The underlined entries in the right pane represent hyperlinks, which you can click to display additional topics. And, as in the Contents window, you can print the information in the right pane by pulling down the Options menu and selecting the Print command.

The **Search tab** (not shown in Figure 5) displays a more extensive listing of entries than does the Index tab. It lets you enter a specific word or phrase and then it returns every topic containing that word or phrase.

The **Favorites tab** enables you to save the information within specified help topics as bookmarks, in order to return to those topics at a later date, as explained in the following hands-on exercise.

FORMATTING A FLOPPY DISK

You will soon begin to work on the computer, which means that you will be using various applications to create different types of documents. Each document is saved in its own file and stored on disk, either on a local disk (e.g., drive C) if you have your own computer, or on a floppy disk (drive A) if you are working in a computer lab at school.

All disks have to be formatted before they can hold data. The formatting process divides a disk into concentric circles called tracks, and then further divides each track into sectors. You don't have to worry about formatting a hard disk, as that is done at the factory prior to the machine being sold. You typically don't even have to format a floppy disk, since most floppies today are already formatted when you buy them. Nevertheless, it is very easy to format a floppy disk and it is a worthwhile exercise. Be aware, however, that formatting erases any data that was previously on a disk, so be careful not to format a disk with important data (e.g., one containing today's homework assignment). Formatting is accomplished through the **Format command**. The process is straightforward, as you will see in the hands-on exercise that follows.

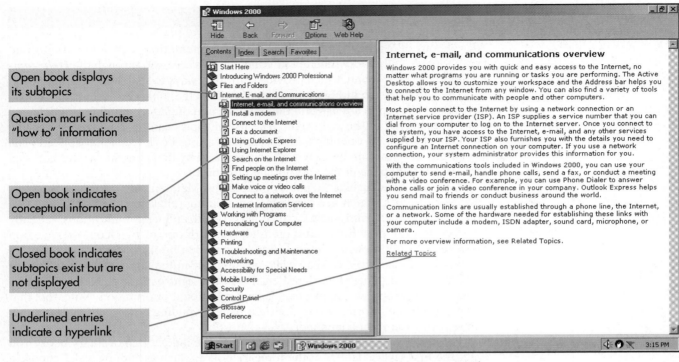

Open book displays
its subtopics

Question mark indicates
"how to" information

Open book indicates
conceptual information

Closed book indicates
subtopics exist but are
not displayed

Underlined entries
indicate a hyperlink

(a) Contents Tab

Enter topic to look up

Underlined entries
represent hyperlinks to
additional information

Click topic

Click Display button

(b) Index Tab

FIGURE 5   *The Help Command*

WELCOME TO WINDOWS

Objective   To turn on the computer, start Windows, and open My Computer; to move and size a window; to format a floppy disk and use the Help command. Use Figure 6 as a guide in the exercise.

Step 1:   **Open My Computer**

> ➤ Start the computer by turning on the various switches appropriate to your system. Your system will take a minute or so to boot up, after which you may be asked for a **user name** and **password**.
> ➤ Enter this information, after which you should see the desktop in Figure 6a. It does not matter if you are using a different version of Windows.
> ➤ Close the Getting Started with Windows 2000 window if it appears. Do not be concerned if your desktop differs from ours.
> ➤ The way in which you open My Computer (single or double clicking) depends on the options in effect as described in step 2. Either way, however, you can **right click** the **My Computer icon** to display a context-sensitive menu, then click the **Open command**.
> ➤ The My Computer window will open on your desktop, but the contents of your window and/or its size and position will be different from ours. You are ready to go to work.

Right click My Computer and click Open from the context-sensitive menu

Click to close Getting Started with Windows 2000 window

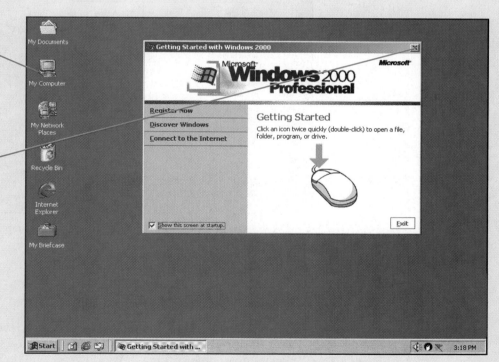

(a) Open My Computer (step 1)

FIGURE 6   *Hands-on Exercise 1*

Step 2: **Set the Folder Options**

➤ Pull down the **Tools menu** and click the **Folder Options command** to display the Folder Options dialog box. Click the **General tab**, then set the options as shown in Figure 6b. (Your network administrator may have disabled this command, in which case you will use the default settings.)

- The Active desktop enables you to display Web content directly on the desktop. We suggest that you disable this option initially.
- Enabling Web content in folders displays the template at the left side of the window. The Windows classic option does not contain this information.
- Opening each successive folder within the same window saves space on the desktop as you browse the system. We discuss this in detail later on.
- The choice between clicking underlined items and double clicking an icon (without the underline) is personal. We prefer to double click.

➤ Click **OK** to accept the settings and close the Folder Options dialog box. The My Computer window on your desktop should be similar to ours.

General tab

Set the options as shown

Click OK

(b) Set the Folder Options (step 2)

FIGURE 6   *Hands-on Exercise 1 (continued)*

IT'S DIFFERENT IN WINDOWS 98

The Folder Options command is under the View menu in Windows 98, whereas it is found in the Tools menu in Windows 2000. Thus, to go from clicking to double clicking in Windows 98, pull down the View menu, click Folder Options, click the General tab, then choose Web style or Classic style, respectively. The procedure to display Web content in a folder is also different in Windows 98; you need to pull down the View menu and toggle the As Web Page command on.

Step 3: **Move and Size a Window**

➤ If necessary, pull down the **View menu** and click **Large Icons** so that your My Computer window more closely resembles the window in Figure 6c.
➤ Move and size the My Computer window on your desktop to match the display in Figure 6c.
  • To change the width or height of the window, click and drag a border (the mouse pointer changes to a double arrow) in the direction you want to go.
  • To change the width and height at the same time, click and drag a corner rather than a border.
  • To change the position of the window, click and drag the title bar.
➤ Click the **minimize button** to shrink the My Computer window to a button on the taskbar. My Computer is still active in memory, however. Click the **My Computer button** on the taskbar to reopen the window.
➤ Click the **maximize button** so that the My Computer window expands to fill the entire screen. Click the **restore button** (which replaces the maximize button and is not shown in Figure 6c) to return the window to its previous size.

Click and drag title bar to move window

Minimize button

Maximize button

Click and drag border or corner to size window

(c) Move and Size a Window (step 3)

FIGURE 6 *Hands-on Exercise 1 (continued)*

MINIMIZING VERSUS CLOSING AN APPLICATION

Minimizing an application leaves the application open in memory and available at the click of the taskbar button. Closing it, however, removes the application from memory, which also causes it to disappear from the taskbar. The advantage of minimizing an application is that you can return to the application immediately. The disadvantage is that leaving too many applications open simultaneously may degrade performance.

Step 4: **Use the Pull-Down Menus**

➤ Pull down the **View menu**, then click the **Toolbars command** to display a cascaded menu as shown in Figure 6d. If necessary, check the commands for the **Standard Buttons** and **Address Bar**, and clear the commands for Links and Radio.

➤ Pull down the **View menu** to make or verify the following selections. (You have to pull down the View menu each time you make an additional change.)

- The **Status Bar command** should be checked. The Status Bar command functions as a toggle switch. Click the command and the status bar is displayed; click the command a second time and the status bar disappears.)
- Click the **Details command** to change to this view. Notice that the different views are grouped within the menu and that only one view at a time can be selected.

➤ Pull down the **View menu** once again, click (or point to) the **Explorer Bar command**, and verify that none of the options is checked.

Standard Buttons and Address Bar should be checked

Status Bar should be checked

Details should be selected

(d) Use the Pull-Down Menus (step 4)

FIGURE 6   *Hands-on Exercise 1 (continued)*

DESIGNATING THE DEVICES ON A SYSTEM

The first (usually only) floppy drive is always designated as drive A. (A second floppy drive, if it were present, would be drive B.) The first hard (local) disk on a system is always drive C, whether or not there are one or two floppy drives. Additional local drives, if any, a Zip (removable storage) drive, a network drive, and/or the CD-ROM are labeled from D on.

Step 5: **Format a Floppy Disk**

➤ Place a floppy disk in drive A. Select (click) drive A, then pull down the **File menu** and click the **Format command** to display the dialog box in Figure 6e.
  • Set the **Capacity** to match the floppy disk you purchased (1.44MB for a high-density disk and 720KB for a double-density disk).
  • Click the **Volume label text box** if it's empty or click and drag over the existing label. Enter a new label (containing up to 11 characters).
  • You can check the **Quick Format box** if the disk has been previously formatted, as a convenient way to erase the contents of the disk.
➤ Click the **Start button**, then click **OK** after you have read the warning. The formatting process erases anything that is on the disk, so be sure that you do not need anything on the disk you are about to format.
➤ Click **OK** after the formatting is complete. Close the Format dialog box, then save the formatted disk for use with various exercises later in the text.
➤ Close the My Computer window.

Click to select appropriate capacity

Enter a Volume label

Quick Format box

Click OK

(e) Format a Floppy Disk (step 5)

FIGURE 6   *Hands-on Exercise 1 (continued)*

THE HELP BUTTON

The Help button (a question mark) appears in the title bar of almost every dialog box. Click the question mark, then click the item you want information about (which then appears in a pop-up window). To print the contents of the pop-up window, click the right mouse button inside the window, and click Print Topic. Click outside the pop-up window to close the window and continue working.

Step 6: **The Help Command**

➤ Click the **Start button** on the taskbar, then click the **Help command** to display the Help window in Figure 6f. Maximize the Help window.

➤ Click the **Contents tab**, then click a closed book such as **Hardware** to open the book and display the associated topics. Click any one of the displayed topics such as **Hardware overview** in Figure 6f.

➤ Pull down the **Options menu** and click the **Print command** to display the Print Topics dialog box. Click the option button to print the selected topic, click **OK**, then click the **Print button** in the resulting dialog box.

➤ Click the **Index tab**, type **format** (the first several letters in "Formatting disks," the topic you are searching for). Double click this topic within the list of index items. Pull down the **Options menu** and click the **Print command** to print this information as well.

➤ Submit the printed information to your instructor. Close the Help window.

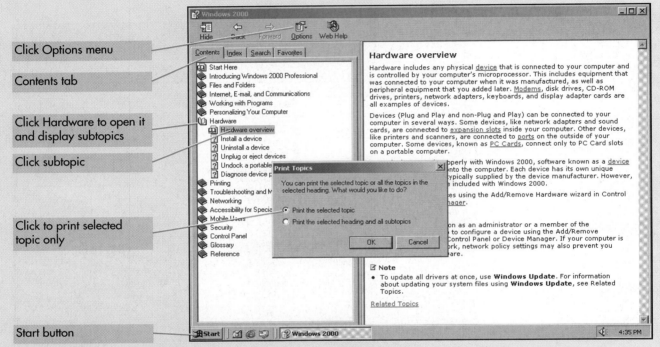

(f) The Help Command (step 6)

FIGURE 6   *Hands-on Exercise 1 (continued)*

THE FAVORITES TAB

Do you find yourself continually searching for the same Help topic? If so, you can make life a little easier by adding the topic to a list of favorite Help topics. Start Help, then use the Contents, Index, or Search tabs to locate the desired topic. Now click the Favorites tab in the Help window, then click the Add button to add the topic. You can return to the topic at any time by clicking the Favorites tab, then double clicking the bookmark to display the information.

Step 7: **Shut Down the Computer**

➤ It is very important that you shut down your computer properly as opposed to just turning off the power. This enables Windows to properly close all of its system files and to save any changes that were made during the session.

➤ Click the **Start button**, click the **Shut Down command** to display the Shut Down Windows dialog box in Figure 6g. Click the **drop-down arrow** to display the desired option:

   • Logging off ends your session, but leaves the computer running at full power. This is the typical option you select in a laboratory setting.
   • Shutting down the computer ends the session and also closes Windows so that you can safely turn the power off. (Some computers will automatically turn the power off for you if this option is selected.)
   • Restarting the computer ends your sessions, then closes and restarts Windows to begin a new session.

➤ Welcome to Windows 2000!

Click to display
shutdown options

Start button

(g) Shut Down the Computer (step 7)

FIGURE 6   *Hands-on Exercise 1 (continued)*

THE TASK MANAGER

The Start button is the normal way to exit Windows. Occasionally, however, an application may "hang"—in which case you want to close the problem application but leave Windows open. Press Ctrl+Alt+Del to display the Windows Security dialog box, then click the Task Manager command button. Click the Applications tab, select the problem application, and click the End Task button.

A *file* is a set of instructions or data that has been given a name and stored on disk. There are two basic types of files, *program files* and *data files*. Microsoft Word and Microsoft Excel are examples of program files. The documents and workbooks created by these programs are examples of data files.

A *program file* is an executable file because it contains instructions that tell the computer what to do. A *data file* is not executable and can be used only in conjunction with a specific program. As a typical student, you execute (run) program files, then you use those programs to create and/or modify the associated data files.

Every file has a *file name* that identifies it to the operating system. The file name may contain up to 255 characters and may include spaces. (File names cannot contain the following characters: \, /, :, *, ?, ", <, >, or |. We suggest that you try to keep file names simple and restrict yourself to the use of letters, numbers, and spaces.) Long file names permit descriptive entries such as *Term Paper for Western Civilization* (as distinct from a more cryptic *TPWCIV* that was required under MS-DOS and Windows 3.1).

Files are stored in *folders* to better organize the hundreds (thousands, or tens of thousands) of files on a hard disk. A Windows folder is similar in concept to a manila folder in a filing cabinet into which you put one or more documents (files) that are somehow related to each other. An office worker stores his or her documents in manila folders. In Windows, you store your files (documents) in electronic folders on disk.

Folders are the keys to the Windows storage system. Some folders are created automatically; for example, the installation of a program such as Microsoft Office automatically creates one or more folders to hold the various program files. Other folders are created by the user to hold the documents he or she creates. You could, for example, create one folder for your word processing documents and a second folder for your spreadsheets. Alternatively, you can create a folder to hold all of your work for a specific class, which may contain a combination of word processing documents and spreadsheets. The choice is entirely up to you, and you can use any system that makes sense to you. Anything at all can go into a folder—program files, data files, even other folders.

Figure 7 displays the contents of a hypothetical Homework folder with six documents. Figure 7a enables Web content, and so we see the colorful logo at the left of the folder, together with links to My Documents, My Network Places, and My Computer. Figure 7b is displayed without the Web content, primarily to gain space within the window. The display or suppression of the Web content is determined by a setting in the Folder Options command.

Figures 7a and 7b are displayed in different views. Figure 7a uses the *Large Icons view*, whereas Figure 7b is displayed in the *Details view*, which shows additional information for each file. (Other possible views include Small Icons, List, and Thumbnail.) The file icon, whether large or small, indicates the *file type* or application that was used to create the file. The History of Computers file, for example, is a Microsoft Word document. The Grade Book is a Microsoft Excel workbook.

Regardless of the view and options in effect, the name of the folder (Homework) appears in the title bar next to the icon of an open folder. The minimize, maximize, and Close buttons appear at the right of the title bar. A menu bar with six pull-down menus appears below the title bar. The Standard Buttons toolbar appears below the menu, and the Address Bar (indicating the drive and folder) appears below the toolbar. A status bar appears at the bottom of both windows, indicating that the Homework folder contains six objects (documents) and that the total file size is 525KB.

Folder name

Menu bar

Standard Buttons toolbar

Address bar

Web content view
displays colorful logo

Status bar

(a) Large Icons View with Web Content Enabled

Folder name

Menu bar

Standard Buttons toolbar

Address bar

Icon indicates an Excel file

Icon indicates a Word
document

Status bar

(b) Details View without Web Content

FIGURE 7   *The Homework Folder*

CHANGE THE VIEW

Look closely at the address bar in Figures 7a and 7b to see that both figures
display the Homework folder on drive C, although the figures are very different in appearance. Figure 7a displays Web content to provide direct links to
three other folders, and the contents of the Homework folder are displayed in
the Large Icons view to save space. Figure 7b suppresses the Web content and
uses the Details view to provide the maximum amount of information for each
file in the Homework folder. You are free to choose whichever options you
prefer.

My Computer enables you to browse through the various drives and folders on a system in order to locate a document and go to work. Let's assume that you're looking for a document called "History of Computers" that you saved previously in the Homework folder on drive C. To get to this document, you would open My Computer, from where you would open drive C, open the Homework folder, and then open the document. It's a straightforward process that can be accomplished in two different ways, as shown in Figure 8.

The difference between the two figures is whether each drive or folder is opened in its own window, as shown in Figure 8a, or whether the same window is used for every folder, as in Figure 8b. (This is another option that is set through the Folder Options command.) In Figure 8a you begin by double clicking the My Computer icon on the desktop to open the My Computer window, which in turn displays the devices on your system. Next, you double click the icon for drive C to open a second window that displays the folders on drive C. From there, you double click the icon for the Homework folder to open a third window containing the documents in the Homework folder. Once in the Homework folder, you can double click the icon of an existing document, which starts the associated application and opens the document.

The process is identical in Figure 8b except that each object opens in the same window. The Back arrow on the Standard Buttons toolbar is meaningful in Figure 8b because you can click the button to return to the previous window (drive C), then click it again to go back to My Computer. Note, however, that the button is dimmed in all three windows in Figure 8a because there is no previous window, since each folder is opened in its own window.

THE EXPLORING OFFICE PRACTICE FILES

There is only one way to master the file operations inherent in Windows and that is to practice at the computer. To do so requires that you have a series of files with which to work. We have created these files for you, and we reference them in the next several hands-on exercises. Your instructor will make these files available to you in a variety of ways:

- The files can be downloaded from our Web site, assuming that you have access to the Internet and that you have a basic proficiency with Internet Explorer. Software and other files that are downloaded from the Internet are typically compressed (made smaller) to reduce the amount of time it takes to transmit the file. In essence, you will download a *compressed file* (which may contain multiple individual files) from our Web site and then uncompress the file onto a local drive as described in the next hands-on exercise.
- The files might be on a network drive, in which case you can use My Computer (or Windows Explorer, which is discussed later in the chapter) to copy the files from the network drive to a floppy disk. The procedure to do this is described in the third hands-on exercise.
- There may be an actual "data disk" in the computer lab. Go to the lab with a floppy disk, then use the Copy Disk command (on the File menu of My Computer) to duplicate the data disk and create a copy for yourself.

It doesn't matter how you obtain the practice files, only that you are able to do so. Indeed, you may want to try different techniques in order to gain additional practice with Windows.

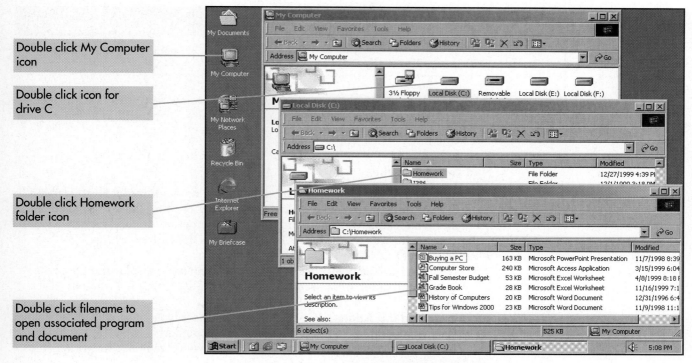

Double click My Computer icon

Double click icon for drive C

Double click Homework folder icon

Double click filename to open associated program and document

(a) Multiple Windows

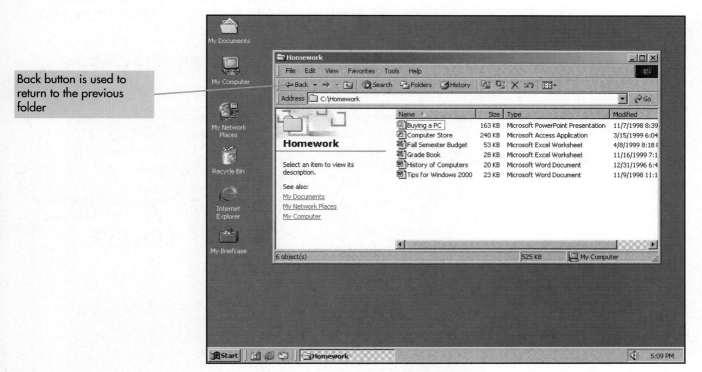

Back button is used to return to the previous folder

(b) One Window

FIGURE 8 *Browsing My Computer*

THE PRACTICE FILES VIA THE WEB

Objective To download a file from the Web. The exercise requires a formatted floppy disk and access to the Internet. Use Figure 9 as a guide in the exercise.

Step 1: **Start Internet Explorer**

> ➤ Start Internet Explorer, perhaps by double clicking the **Internet Explorer icon** on the desktop, or by clicking the **Start button**, clicking the **Programs command**, then locating the command to start the program. If necessary, click the **maximize button** so that Internet Explorer takes the entire desktop.
> ➤ Enter the address of the site you want to visit:
> • Pull down the **File menu**, click the **Open command** to display the Open dialog box, and enter **www.prenhall.com/grauer** (the http:// is assumed). Click **OK**.
> • *Or, c*lick in the **Address bar** below the toolbar, which automatically selects the current address (so that whatever you type replaces the current address). Enter the address of the site you want to visit, **www.prenhall.com/grauer** (the http:// is assumed). Press **enter**.
> ➤ You should see the *Exploring Office Series* home page as shown in Figure 9a. Click the book for **Office XP**, which takes you to the Office XP home page.
> ➤ Click the **Student Resources link** (at the top of the window) to go to the Student Resources page.

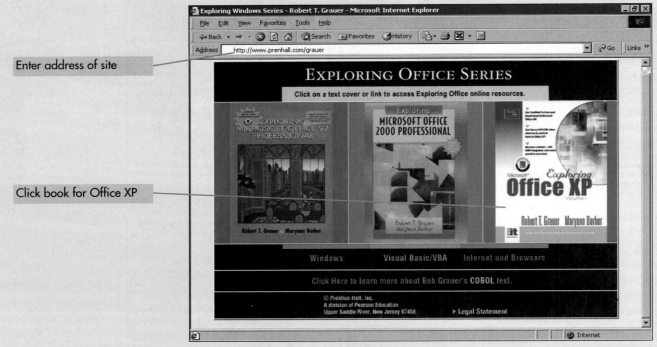

Enter address of site

Click book for Office XP

(a) Start Internet Explorer (step 1)

FIGURE 9   *Hands-on Exercise 2*

Step 2:   **Download the Practice Files**

➤ Click the link to **Student Data Disk** (in the left frame), then scroll down the page until you can see **Essentials of Microsoft Windows**.

➤ Click the indicated link to download the practice files. The Save As dialog box is not yet visible.

➤ You will see the File Download dialog box asking what you want to do. The option button to save this program to disk is selected. Click **OK**. The Save As dialog box appears as shown in Figure 9b.

➤ Place a formatted floppy disk in drive A, click the **drop-down arrow** on the Save in list box, and select (click) **drive A**. Click **Save** to begin downloading the file.

➤ The File Download window will reappear on your screen and show you the status of the downloading operation. If necessary, click **OK** when you see the dialog box indicating that the download is complete.

➤ Close Internet Explorer.

Click link to Student Resources

Click to select drive A

(b) Download the Practice Files (step 2)

FIGURE 9   *Hands-on Exercise 2 (continued)*

REMEMBER THE LOCATION

It's easy to download a file from the Web. The only tricky part, if any, is remembering where you have saved the file. This exercise is written for a laboratory setting, and thus we specified drive A as the destination, so that you will have the file on a floppy disk at the end of the exercise. If you have your own computer, however, it's faster to save the file to the desktop or in a temporary folder on drive C. Just remember where you save the file so that you can access it after it has been downloaded.

Step 3: **Open My Computer**

➤ Double click the My Computer icon on the desktop to open My Computer. If necessary, customize My Computer to match Figure 9c.
  • Pull down the **View menu** and change to the **Details view**.
  • Pull down the **View menu** a second time, click (or point to) the **Toolbars command**, then check the **Standard buttons** and **Address Bar** toolbars.

➤ Pull down the **Tools menu** and click the **Folder Options command** to verify the settings in effect so that your window matches ours. Be sure to **Enable Web content in folders** (in the Web View area), to **Open each folder in the same window** (in the Browse Folders area), and **Double Click to open an item** (in the Click Items area).

➤ Click the icon for **drive A** to select it. The description of drive A appears at the left of the window.

➤ Double click the icon for **drive A** to open this drive. The contents of the My Computer window are replaced by the contents of drive A.

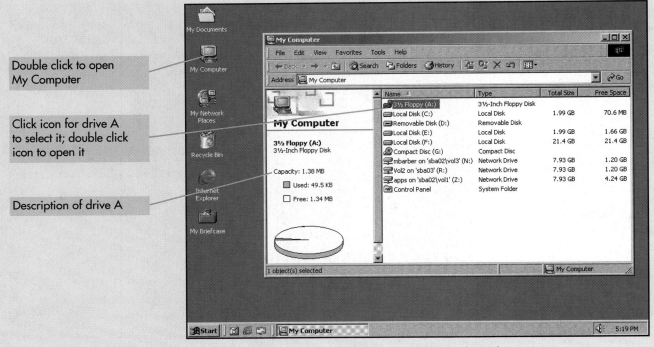

(c) Open My Computer (step 3)

FIGURE 9   *Hands-on Exercise 2 (continued)*

THE RIGHT MOUSE BUTTON

Point to any object on the Windows desktop or within an application window, then click the right mouse button to see a context-sensitive menu with commands pertaining to that object. You could, for example, right click the icon for drive A, then select the Open command from the resulting menu. The right mouse button is one of the most powerful Windows shortcuts and one of its best-kept secrets. Use it!

Step 4: **Install the Practice Files**

➤ You should see the contents of drive A as shown in Figure 9d. (If your desktop displays two windows rather than one, it is because you did not set the folder options correctly. Pull down the **Tools menu**, click the **Folder Options command**, and choose the option to **Open each folder in the same window**.)

➤ Double click the **Win2000data file** to install the data disk. You will see a dialog box thanking you for selecting the *Exploring Windows* series. Click **OK**.

• Check that the Unzip To Folder text box specifies **A:** to extract the files to the floppy disk. (You may enter a different drive and/or folder.)

• Click the **Unzip button** to extract the practice files and copy them onto the designated drive. Click **OK** after you see the message indicating that the files have been unzipped successfully. Close the WinZip dialog box.

➤ The practice files have been extracted to drive A and should appear in the Drive A window. If you do not see the files, pull down the **View menu** and click the **Refresh command**.

Double click icon for Win2000data file

A:\ should be specified as Unzip To Folder

Click Unzip

(d) Install the Practice Files (step 4)

FIGURE 9   *Hands-on Exercise 2 (continued)*

DOWNLOADING A FILE

Software and other files are typically compressed to reduce the amount of storage space the files require on disk and/or the time it takes to download the files. In essence, you download a compressed file (which may contain multiple individual files), then you uncompress (expand) the file on your local drive in order to access the individual files. After the file has been expanded, it is no longer needed and can be deleted.

Step 5: Delete the Compressed File

➤ If necessary, pull down the **View menu** and click **Details** to change to the Details view in Figure 9e. (If you do not see the descriptive information about drive A at the left of the window, pull down the **Tools menu**, click the **Folder Options command**, and click the option button to **Enable Web content in folders**.)

➤ You should see a total of six files in the Drive A window. Five of these are the practice files on the data disk. The sixth file is the original file that you downloaded earlier. This file is no longer necessary, since it has been already been expanded.

➤ Select (click) the **Win2000data file**. Pull down the **File menu** and click the **Delete command**, or click the **Delete button** on the toolbar. Pause for a moment to be sure you want to delete this file, then click **Yes** when asked to confirm the deletion as shown in Figure 9e.

➤ The Win2000Data file is permanently deleted from drive A. (Items deleted from a floppy disk or network drive are not sent to the Recycle Bin, and cannot be recovered.)

Delete button

Click to select Win2000data

Double click Windows 2000 Overview to open it

Click Yes

(e) Delete the Compressed File (step 5)

FIGURE 9   *Hands-on Exercise 2 (continued)*

SORT BY NAME, DATE, FILE TYPE, OR SIZE

Files can be displayed in ascending or descending sequence by name, date modified, file type, or size by clicking the appropriate column heading. Click Size, for example, to display files in the order of their size. Click the column heading a second time to reverse the sequence; that is, to switch from ascending to descending, and vice versa.

Step 6: **Modify a Document**

➤ Double click the **Windows 2000 Overview** document from within My Computer to open the document as shown in Figure 9f. (The document will open in the WordPad accessory if Microsoft Word is not installed on your machine.) If necessary, maximize the window for Microsoft Word.

➤ If necessary, click inside the document window, then press **Ctrl+End** to move to the end of the document. Add the sentence shown in Figure 9h followed by your name.

➤ Pull down the **File menu**, click **Print**, then click **OK** to print the document and prove to your instructor that you did the exercise.

➤ Pull down the **File menu** and click **Exit** to close the application. Click **Yes** when prompted to save the file.

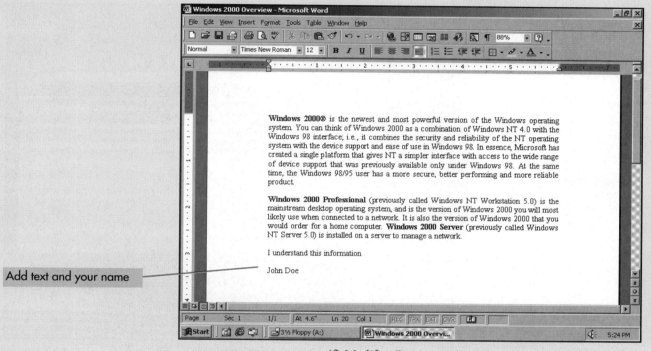

Add text and your name

(f) Modify a Document (step 6)

FIGURE 9 *Hands-on Exercise 2 (continued)*

THE DOCUMENT, NOT THE APPLICATION

All versions of Windows are document oriented, meaning that you are able to think in terms of the document rather than the application that created it. You can still open a document in traditional fashion by starting the application that created the document, then using the File Open command in that program to retrieve the document. It's often easier, however, to open the document from within My Computer (or Windows Explorer) by double clicking its icon. Windows then starts the application and opens the data file. In other words, you can open a document without explicitly starting the application.

Step 7: **Check Your Work**

➤ You should be back in the My Computer window as shown in Figure 9g. If necessary, click the **Views button** to change to the Details view.

➤ Look closely at the date and time that is displayed next to the Windows 2000 Overview document. It should show today's date and the current time (give or take a minute) since that is when the document was last modified.

➤ Look closely and see that Figure 9g also contains a sixth document, called "Backup of Windows 2000 Overview". This is a backup copy of the original document that will be created automatically by Microsoft Word if the appropriate options are in effect. (See the boxed tip below.)

➤ Exit Windows or, alternatively, continue with steps 8 and 9 to return to our Web site and explore additional resources.

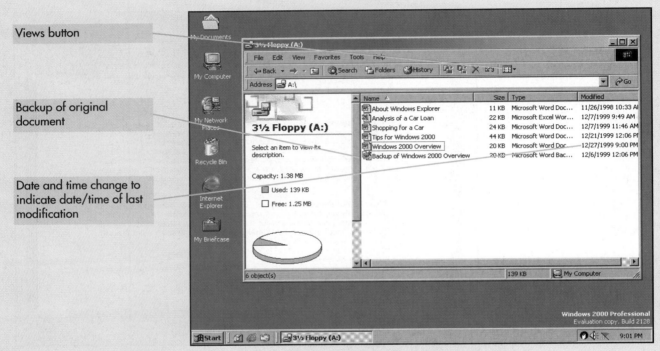

Views button

Backup of original document

Date and time change to indicate date/time of last modification

(g) Check Your Work (step 7)

FIGURE 9 *Hands-on Exercise 2 (continued)*

USE WORD TO CREATE A BACKUP COPY

Microsoft Word enables you to automatically create a backup copy of a document in conjunction with the Save command. The next time you are in Microsoft Word, pull down the Tools menu, click the Options command, click the Save tab, then check the box to always create a backup copy. Every time you save a file from this point on, the previously saved version is renamed "Backup of document," and the document in memory is saved as the current version. The disk will contain the two most recent versions of the document, enabling you to retrieve the previous version if necessary.

Step 8: **Download the PowerPoint Lecture**

➤ Restart Internet Explorer and connect to **www.prenhall.com/grauer**. Click the book for **Office XP**, click the link to **Student Resources**, then choose **PowerPoint Lectures** to display the screen in Figure 9h.

➤ Click the down arrow until you can click the link to the PowerPoint slides for **Essentials of Windows**. The File Download dialog box will appear with the option to save the file to disk selected by default. Click **OK**.

➤ Click the **drop-down arrow** on the Save in list box, and select **drive A**. Be sure that the floppy disk is still in drive A, then click **Save** to begin downloading the file. Click **OK** when you see the dialog box indicating that the download is complete.

➤ Click the taskbar button to return to the **My Computer window** for drive A. You should see all of the files that were previously on the floppy disk plus the file you just downloaded.

➤ Double click the **Win2000ppt file**, then follow the onscreen instructions to unzip the file to drive A.

Click the Student Resources tab

Click the link to PowerPoint Lectures

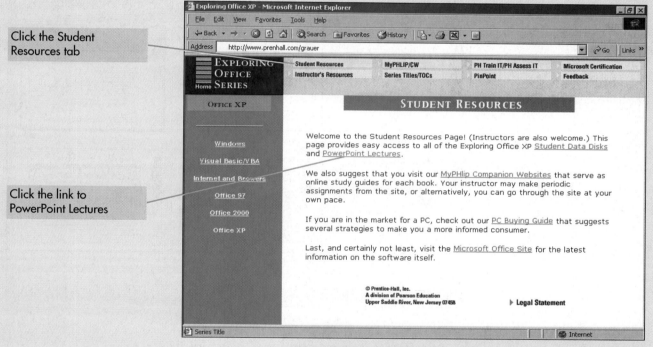

(h) Download the PowerPoint Lecture (step 8)

FIGURE 9 *Hands-on Exercise 2 (continued)*

THE MyPHLIP WEB SITE

The MyPHLIP (Prentice Hall Learning on the Internet Partnership) Web site is another resource that is available for the Exploring Office series. Click the MyPHLIP tab at the top of the screen, which takes you to www.prenhall.com/myphlip, where you will register and select the text you are using. See exercise 3 at the end of the chapter.

Step 9: **Show Time**

➤ Drive A should now contain a PowerPoint file in addition to the self-extracting file. (Pull down the **View menu** and click the **Refresh command** if you do not see the PowerPoint file.)

➤ Double click the PowerPoint file to open the presentation, then click the button to Enable Macros (if prompted). You should see the PowerPoint presentation in Figure 9i. (You must have PowerPoint installed on your computer in order to view the presentation.)

➤ Pull down the **View menu** and click **Slide Show** to begin the presentation, which is intended to review the material in this supplement. Click the left mouse button (or press the **PgDn key**) to move to the next slide.

➤ Click the left mouse button continually to move from one slide to the next. Close PowerPoint at the end of the presentation.

➤ Exit Windows if you do not want to continue with the next exercise at this time.

Pull down the View menu and click the Slide Show command

The presentation reviews the material on Windows

(i) Show Time (step 9)

FIGURE 9   *Hands-on Exercise 2 (continued)*

MISSING POWERPOINT—WHICH VERSION OF OFFICE DO YOU HAVE?

You may have installed Microsoft Office on your computer, but you may not have PowerPoint. That is because Microsoft has created several different versions of Microsoft Office, each with a different set of applications. Unfortunately, PowerPoint is not included in every configuration and may be missing from the suite that is shipped most frequently with new computers.

Windows has two different programs to manage the files and folders on a system, My Computer and Windows Explorer. My Computer is intuitive, but less efficient, as you have to open each folder in succession. Windows Explorer is more sophisticated, as it provides a hierarchical view of the entire system in a single window. A beginner might prefer My Computer, whereas a more experienced user will most likely opt for Windows Explorer.

Assume, for example, that you are taking four classes this semester, and that you are using the computer in each course. You've created a separate folder to hold the work for each class and have stored the contents of all four folders on a single floppy disk. Assume further that you need to retrieve your third English assignment so that you can modify the assignment, then submit the revised version to your instructor. Figure 10 illustrates how Windows Explorer could be used to locate your assignment.

The Explorer window in Figure 10a is divided into two panes. The left pane contains a tree diagram (or hierarchical view) of the entire system showing all drives and, optionally, the folders in each drive. The right pane shows the contents of the active drive or folder. Only one object (a drive or folder) can be active in the left pane, and its contents are displayed automatically in the right pane.

Look carefully at the icon for the English folder in the left pane of Figure 10a. The folder is open, whereas the icon for every other folder is closed. The open folder indicates that the English folder is the active folder. (The name of the active folder also appears in the title bar of Windows Explorer and in the Address bar.) The contents of the active folder (three Word documents in this example) are displayed in the right pane. The right pane is displayed in Details view, but could just as easily have been displayed in another view (e.g., Large Icons).

As indicated, only one folder can be open (active) at a time in the left pane. Thus, to see the contents of a different folder such as Accounting, you would open (click on) the Accounting folder, which automatically closes the English folder. The contents of the Accounting folder would then appear in the right pane. You should organize your folders in ways that make sense to you, such as a separate folder for every class you are taking. You can also create folders within folders; for example, a correspondence folder may contain two folders of its own, one for business correspondence and one for personal letters.

Windows Explorer can also be used to display a Web page, as shown in Figure 10b. All you do is click the icon for Internet Explorer in the left pane to start the program and display its default home page. Alternatively, you can click in the Address bar and enter the address of any Web page directly; for example, click in the Address bar and type www.microsoft.com to display the home page for Microsoft. Once you are browsing pages on the Web, it's convenient to close the left pane so that the page takes the complete window. You can reopen the Folders window by pulling down the View menu, clicking the Explorer Bar command, and toggling Folders on.

THE SMART TOOLBAR

The toolbar in Windows Explorer recognizes whether you are viewing a Web page or a set of files and folders, and changes accordingly. The icons that are displayed when viewing a Web page are identical to those in Internet Explorer and include the Search, Favorites, and History buttons. The buttons that are displayed when viewing a file or folder include the Undo, Delete, and Views buttons that are used in file management.

Name of active folder

Minus indicates object is expanded

Active folder

Plus sign indicates object is collapsed

Contents of active folder

(a) Drive A

Enter address of desired site

Click to close left pane

Click icon for Internet Explorer

Web page is displayed

(b) A Web Page

FIGURE 10   *Windows Explorer*

Expanding and Collapsing a Drive or Folder

The tree diagram in Windows Explorer displays the devices on your system in hierarchical fashion. The desktop is always at the top of the hierarchy, and it contains icons such as My Computer, the Recycle Bin, Internet Explorer, and My Network Places. My Computer in turn contains the various drives that are accessible from your system, each of which contains folders, which in turn contain documents and/or additional folders. Each object may be expanded or collapsed by clicking the plus or minus sign, respectively. Click either sign to toggle to the other. Clicking a plus sign, for example, expands the drive, then displays a minus sign next to the drive to indicate that its subordinates are visible.

Look closely at the icon next to My Computer in either Figure 10a or 10b. It is a minus sign (as opposed to a plus sign) and it indicates that My Computer has been expanded to show the devices on the system. There is also a minus sign next to the icon for drive A to indicate that it too has been expanded to show the folders on the disk. Note, however, the plus sign next to drives C and D, indicating that these parts of the tree are currently collapsed and thus their subordinates (in this case, folders) are not visible.

Any folder may contain additional folders, and thus individual folders may also be expanded or collapsed. The minus sign next to the Finance folder, for example, indicates that the folder has been expanded and contains two additional folders, for Assignments and Class Notes, respectively. The plus sign next to the Accounting folder, however, indicates the opposite; that is, the folder is collapsed and its subordinate folders are not currently visible. A folder with neither a plus nor a minus sign, such as Art History, does not contain additional folders and cannot be expanded or collapsed.

The hierarchical view within Windows Explorer, and the ability to expand and collapse the various folders on a system, enables you to quickly locate a specific file or folder. If, for example, you want to see the contents of the Art History folder, you click its icon in the left pane, which automatically changes the display in the right pane to show the documents in that folder. Thus, Windows Explorer is ideal for moving or copying files from one folder or drive to another. You simply select (open) the folder that contains the files, use the scroll bar in the left pane (if necessary) so that the destination folder is visible, then click and drag the files from the right pane to the destination folder.

The Folder Options command functions identically in Windows Explorer and in My Computer. You can decide whether you want to single or double click the icons and/or whether to display Web content within a folder. You can also use the View menu to select the most appropriate view. Our preferences are to double click the icons, to omit Web content, and to use the Details view.

CONVERGENCE OF THE EXPLORERS

Windows Explorer and Internet Explorer are separate programs, but each includes some functionality of the other. You can use Windows Explorer to display a Web page by clicking the Internet Explorer icon within the tree structure in the left pane. Conversely, you can use Internet Explorer to display a local drive, document, or folder. Start Internet Explorer in the usual fashion, click in the Address bar, then enter the appropriate address, such as C:\ to display the contents of drive C.

THE PRACTICE FILES VIA A LOCAL AREA NETWORK

Objective To use Windows Explorer to copy the practice files from a network drive to a floppy disk. The exercise requires a formatted floppy disk and access to a local area network. Use Figure 11 as a guide in the exercise.

Step 1: **Start Windows Explorer**

➤ Click the **Start Button**, click **Programs**, click **Accessories**, then click **Windows Explorer**. Click the **maximize button** so that Windows Explorer takes the entire desktop as shown in Figure 11a. Do not be concerned if your desktop is different from ours.

➤ Make or verify the following selections using the **View menu**. You have to pull down the View menu each time you choose a different command.
  • The **Standard buttons** and **Address bar** toolbars should be selected.
  • The **Status Bar command** should be checked.
  • The **Details view** should be selected.

➤ Click (select) the **Desktop icon** in the left pane to display the contents of the desktop in the right pane. Your desktop may have different icons from ours, but your screen should almost match Figure 11a. We set additional options in the next step.

(a) Start Windows Explorer (step 1)

FIGURE 11 *Hands-on Exercise 3*

Step 2:   **Change the Folder Options**

➤ Click the **minus** (or the **plus**) **sign** next to My Computer to collapse (or expand) My Computer and hide (or display) the objects it contains. Toggle the signs back and forth a few times for practice. End with a minus sign next to My Computer as shown in Figure 11b.

➤ Place a newly formatted floppy disk in drive A. Click the drive icon next to drive A to select the drive and display its contents in the right pane. The disk does not contain any files since zero bytes are used.

➤ Displaying Web content at the left of a folder (as is done in Figure 11b) is fine when a drive or folder does not contain a large number of files. It is generally a waste of space, however, and so we want to change the folder options.

➤ Pull down the **Tools menu** and click the **Folder Options command** to display the Folder Options dialog box in Figure 11a. Click the option to **Use Windows classic folders**. Click **OK**.

Select Use Windows classic folders

Click minus and plus to practice; end with minus sign

Click to select drive A

Click plus sign next to network drive containing files to be copied

Floppy disk is empty

(b) Change the Folder Options (step 2)

FIGURE 11   *Hands-on Exercise 3 (continued)*

THE PLUS AND MINUS SIGN

Any drive, be it local or on the network, may be expanded or collapsed to display or hide its folders. A minus sign indicates that the drive has been expanded and that its folders are visible. A plus sign indicates the reverse; that is, the device is collapsed and its folders are not visible. Click either sign to toggle to the other. Clicking a plus sign, for example, expands the drive, then displays a minus sign next to the drive to indicate that the folders are visible. Clicking a minus sign has the reverse effect.

Step 3:   **Select the Network Drive**

➤ Click the **plus sign** for the network drive that contains the files you are to copy (e.g., drive **R** in Figure 11c). Select (click) the **Exploring Windows 2000 folder** to open this folder.

➤ You may need to expand other folders on the network drive (such as the Datadisk folder on our network) as per instructions from your professor. Note the following:

• The Exploring Windows 2000 folder is highlighted in the left pane, its icon is an open folder, and its contents are displayed in the right pane.

• The status bar indicates that the folder contains five objects and the total file size is 119KB.

➤ Click the icon next to any other folder to select the folder, which in turn deselects the Exploring Windows 2000 folder. (Only one folder in the left pane is active at a time.) Reselect (click) the **Exploring Windows 2000 folder**.

Expand other folders
as necessary

Click Exploring
Windows 2000

Status bar

(c) Select the Network Drive (step 3)

FIGURE 11   *Hands-on Exercise 3 (continued)*

CUSTOMIZE WINDOWS EXPLORER

Increase or decrease the size of the left pane within Windows Explorer by dragging the vertical line separating the left and right panes in the appropriate direction. You can also drag the right border of the various column headings (Name, Size, Type, and Modified) in the right pane to increase or decrease the width of the column. And best of all, you can click any column heading to display the contents of the selected folder in sequence by that column. Click the heading a second time and the sequence changes from ascending to descending and vice versa.

Step 4: **Copy the Individual Files**

➤ Select (click) the file called **About Windows Explorer**, which highlights the file as shown in Figure 11d. Click and drag the selected file in the right pane to the **drive A icon** in the left pane:

- You will see the ⊘ symbol as you drag the file until you reach a suitable destination (e.g., until you point to the icon for drive A). The ⊘ symbol will change to a plus sign when the icon for drive A is highlighted, indicating that the file can be copied successfully.
- Release the mouse to complete the copy operation. You will see a pop-up window, which indicates the status of the copy operation.

➤ Select (click) the file **Tips for Windows 2000**, which automatically deselects the previously selected file. Copy the selected file to drive A by dragging its icon from the right pane to the drive A icon in the left pane.

➤ Copy the three remaining files to drive A as well. Select (click) drive **A** in the left pane, which in turn displays the contents of the floppy disk in the right pane. You should see the five files you have copied to drive A.

Click About Windows Explorer and drag it to icon for drive A in left pane

Pop-up window with status of copy operation

(d) Copy the Individual Files (step 4)

FIGURE 11   *Hands-on Exercise 3 (continued)*

SELECT MULTIPLE FILES

Selecting one file automatically deselects the previously selected file. You can, however, select multiple files by clicking the first file, then pressing and holding the Ctrl key as you click each additional file. Use the Shift key to select multiple files that are adjacent to one another by clicking the first file, then pressing and holding the Shift key as you click the last file.

Step 5: **Display a Web Page**

➤ This step requires an Internet connection. Click the **minus sign** next to the network drive to collapse that drive. Click the **minus sign** next to any other expanded drive so that the left pane is similar to Figure 11e.

➤ Click the **Internet Explorer icon** to start Internet Explorer and display the starting page for your configuration. The page you see will be different from ours, but you can click in the Address bar near the top of the window to enter the address of any Web site.

➤ Look closely at the icons on the toolbar, which have changed to reflect the tools associated with viewing a Web page. Click the **Back button** to return to drive A, the previously displayed item in Windows Explorer. The icons on the toolbar return to those associated with a folder.

➤ Close Windows Explorer. Shut down the computer if you do not want to continue with the next exercise at this time.

(e) Display a Web Page (step 5)

FIGURE 11   *Hands-on Exercise 3 (continued)*

SERVER NOT RESPONDING

Two things have to occur in order for Internet Explorer to display the requested document—it must locate the server on which the document is stored, and it must be able to connect to that computer. If you see a message similar to "Server too busy or not responding", it implies that Internet Explorer has located the server but was unable to connect because the site is busy or is temporarily down. Try to connect again, in a minute or so, or later in the day.

As you grow to depend on the computer, you will create a variety of files using applications such as Microsoft Word or Excel. Learning how to manage those files is one of the most important skills you can acquire. The previous hands-on exercises provided you with a set of files with which to practice. That way, when you have your own files you will be comfortable executing the various file management commands you will need on a daily basis. This section describes the basic file operations you will need, then presents another hands-on exercise in which you apply those commands.

Moving and Copying a File

The essence of file management is to move and copy a file or folder from one location to another. This can be done in different ways, most easily by clicking and dragging the file icon from the source drive or folder to the destination drive or folder, within Windows Explorer. There is one subtlety, however, in that the result of dragging a file (i.e., whether the file is moved or copied) depends on whether the source and destination are on the same or different drives. Dragging a file from one folder to another folder on the same drive moves the file. Dragging a file to a folder on a different drive copies the file. The same rules apply to dragging a folder, where the folder and every file in it are moved or copied as per the rules for an individual file.

This process is not as arbitrary as it may seem. Windows assumes that if you drag an object (a file or folder) to a different drive (e.g., from drive C to drive A), you want the object to appear in both places. Hence, the default action when you click and drag an object to a different drive is to copy the object. You can, however, override the default and move the object by pressing and holding the Shift key as you drag.

Windows also assumes that you do not want two copies of an object on the same drive, as that would result in wasted disk space. Thus, the default action when you click and drag an object to a different folder on the same drive is to move the object. You can override the default and copy the object by pressing and holding the Ctrl key as you drag. It's not as complicated as it sounds, and you get a chance to practice in the hands-on exercise, which follows shortly.

Deleting a File

The **Delete command** deletes (erases) a file from a disk. The command can be executed in different ways, most easily by selecting a file, then pressing the Del key. It's also comforting to know that you can usually recover a deleted file, because the file is not (initially) removed from the disk, but moved instead to the Recycle Bin, from where it can be restored to its original location. Unfortunately, files deleted from a floppy disk are not put in the Recycle Bin and hence cannot be recovered.

The **Recycle Bin** is a special folder that contains all files that were previously deleted from any hard disk on your system. Think of the Recycle Bin as similar to the wastebasket in your room. You throw out (delete) a report by tossing it into a wastebasket. The report is gone (deleted) from your desk, but you can still get it back by taking it out of the wastebasket as long as the basket wasn't emptied. The Recycle Bin works the same way. Files are not deleted from the hard disk per se, but moved instead to the Recycle Bin from where they can be restored to their original location.

The Recycle Bin will eventually run out of space, in which case the files that have been in the Recycle Bin the longest are permanently deleted to make room for additional files. Accordingly, once a file is removed from the Recycle Bin it can no longer be restored, as it has been physically deleted from the hard disk. Note, too, that the protection afforded by the Recycle Bin does not extend to files deleted from a floppy disk. Such files can be recovered, but only through utility programs outside of Windows 2000.

Renaming a File

Every file or folder is assigned a name at the time it is created, but you may want to change that name at some point in the future. Point to a file or a folder, click the right mouse button to display a menu with commands pertaining to the object, then click the *Rename command*. The name of the file or folder will be highlighted with the insertion point (a flashing vertical line) positioned at the end of the name. Enter a new name to replace the selected name, or click anywhere within the name to change the insertion point and edit the name.

Backup

It's not a question of if it will happen, but when—hard disks die, files are lost, or viruses may infect a system. It has happened to us and it will happen to you, but you can prepare for the inevitable by creating adequate backup *before* the problem occurs. The essence of a *backup strategy* is to decide which files to back up, how often to do the backup, and where to keep the backup. Once you decide on a strategy, follow it, and follow it faithfully!

Our strategy is very simple—back up what you can't afford to lose, do so on a daily basis, and store the backup away from your computer. You need not copy every file, every day. Instead, copy just the files that changed during the current session. Realize, too, that it is much more important to back up your data files than your program files. You can always reinstall the application from the original disks or CD, or if necessary, go to the vendor for another copy of an application. You, however, are the only one who has a copy of your term paper.

Write Protection

A floppy disk is normally *write-enabled* (the square hole is covered with the movable tab) so that you can change the contents of the disk. Thus, you can create (save) new files to a write-enabled disk and/or edit or delete existing files. Occasionally, however, you may want to *write-protect* a floppy disk (by sliding the tab to expose the square hole) so that its contents cannot be modified. This is typically done with a backup disk where you want to prevent the accidental deletion of a file and/or the threat of virus infection.

Our Next Exercise

Our next exercise begins with the floppy disk containing the five practice files in drive A. We ask you to create two folders on drive A (step 1) and to move the various files into these folders (step 2). Next, you copy a folder from drive A to the My Documents folder (step 3), modify one of the files in the My Documents folder (step 4), then copy the modified file back to drive A (step 5). We ask you to delete a file in step 6, then recover it from the Recycle Bin in step 7. We also show you how to write-protect a floppy disk in step 8. Let's get started.

FILE MANAGEMENT

Objective Use Windows Explorer to move, copy, and delete a file; recover a deleted file from the Recycle Bin; write-protect a floppy disk. Use Figure 12 as a guide in the exercise.

Step 1: **Create a New Folder**

➤ Start Windows Explorer, maximize its window, and if necessary, change to **Details view**. Place the floppy disk from Exercise 2 or 3 in drive A.

➤ Select (click) the icon for **drive A** in the left pane of the Explorer window. Drive A should contain the files shown in Figure 12a.

➤ You will create two folders on drive A, using two different techniques:

- Point to a blank area anywhere in the **right pane**, click the **right mouse button** to display a context-sensitive menu, click (or point to) the **New command**, then click **Folder** as the type of object to create.
- The icon for a new folder will appear with the name of the folder (New Folder) highlighted. Type **John Doe's Documents** (use your own name) to change the name of the folder. Press **Enter**.
- Click the icon for **drive A** in the left pane. Pull down the **File menu**, click (or point to) the **New command**, and click **Folder** as the type of object to create. Type **Automobile** to change the name of the folder. Press **Enter**. The right pane should now contain five documents and two folders.

➤ Pull down the **View menu**. Click the **Arrange icons command**, then click the **By Name command** to display the folders in alphabetical order.

(a) Create a New Folder (step 1)

FIGURE 12 *Hands-on Exercise 4*

Step 2:   **Move a File**

➤ Click the **plus sign** next to drive A to expand the drive as shown in Figure 12b. Note the following:
  • The left pane shows that drive A is selected. The right pane displays the contents of drive A (the selected object in the left pane).
  • There is a minus sign next to the icon for drive A in the left pane, indicating that it has been expanded and that its folders are visible. Thus, the folder names also appear under drive A in the left pane.
➤ Click and drag the icon for the file **About Windows Explorer** from the right pane, to the **John Doe's Documents folder** in the left pane, to move the file into that folder.
➤ Click and drag the **Tips for Windows 2000** and **Windows 2000 Overview** documents to the **John Doe's Documents folder** in similar fashion.
➤ Click the **John Doe's Documents folder** in the left pane to select the folder and display its contents in the right pane. You should see the three files that were just moved.
➤ Click the icon for **Drive A** in the left pane, then click and drag the remaining files, **Analysis of a Car** and **Shopping for a Car**, to the **Automobile folder**.

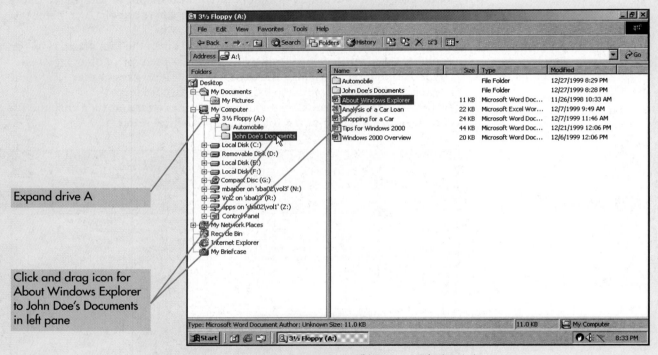

Expand drive A

Click and drag icon for About Windows Explorer to John Doe's Documents in left pane

(b) Move a File (step 2)

FIGURE 12   *Hands-on Exercise 4*

RIGHT CLICK AND DRAG

Click and drag with the right mouse button to display a shortcut menu asking whether you want to copy or move the file. This simple tip can save you from making a careless (and potentially serious) error. Use it!

Step 3: **Copy a Folder**

➤ Point to **John Doe's Documents folder** in either pane, click the **right mouse button**, and drag the folder to the **My Documents folder** in the left pane, then release the mouse to display a shortcut menu. Click the **Copy Here command**.
- You may see a Copy files message box as the individual files within John Doe's folder are copied to the My Documents folder.
- If you see the Confirm Folder Replace dialog box, it means that you already copied the files or a previous student used the same folder when he or she did this exercise. Click the **Yes to All button** so that your files replace the previous versions in the My Documents folder.

➤ Click the **My Documents folder** in the left pane. Pull down the **View menu** and click the **Refresh command** (or press the **F5 key**) so that the tree structure shows the newly copied folder. (Please remember to delete John Doe's Documents folder at the end of the exercise.)

Click Copy Here

Right click and drag the file to My Documents folder

(c) Copy a Folder (step 3)

FIGURE 12 *Hands-on Exercise 4 (continued)*

THE MY DOCUMENTS FOLDER

The My Documents folder is created by default with the installation of Microsoft Windows. There is no requirement that you store your documents in this folder, but it is convenient, especially for beginners who may lack the confidence to create their own folders. The My Documents folder is also helpful in a laboratory environment where the network administrator may prevent you from modifying the desktop and/or from creating your own folders on drive C, in which case you will have to use the My Documents folder.

Step 4: **Modify a Document**

➤ Click **John Doe's Documents folder** within the My Documents folder to make it the active folder and to display its contents in the right pane. Change to the **Details view**.

➤ Double click the **About Windows Explorer** document to start Word and open the document. Do not be concerned if the size and/or position of the Microsoft Word window are different from ours.

➤ If necessary, click inside the document window, then press **Ctrl+End** to move to the end of the document. Add the sentence shown in Figure 12d.

➤ Pull down the **File menu** and click **Save** to save the modified file (or click the **Save button** on the Standard toolbar). Pull down the **File menu** and click **Exit**.

➤ Pull down the **View menu** in Windows Explorer and click **Refresh** (or press the **F5 key**) to update the contents of the right pane. The date and time associated with the About Windows Explorer file has been changed to indicate that the file has just been modified.

Double click About Windows Explorer to open it

Click John Doe's Documents folder within My Documents folder

Add text and your name

(d) Modify a Document (step 4)

FIGURE 12 *Hands-on Exercise 4 (continued)*

KEYBOARD SHORTCUTS

Ctrl+B, Ctrl+I, and Ctrl+U are shortcuts to boldface, italicize, and underline, respectively. Ctrl+X (the X is supposed to remind you of a pair of scissors), Ctrl+C, and Ctrl+V correspond to Cut, Copy, and Paste, respectively. Ctrl+Home and Ctrl+End move to the beginning or end of a document. These shortcuts are not unique to Microsoft Word, but are recognized in virtually every Windows application. See practice exercise 11 at the end of the chapter.

Step 5: **Copy (Back Up) a File**

➤ Verify that **John Doe's folder** within My Documents is the active folder, as denoted by the open folder icon. Click and drag the icon for the **About Windows Explorer** file from the right pane to John Doe's Documents folder on **Drive A** in the left pane.

➤ You will see the message in Figure 12e, indicating that the folder (on drive A) already contains a file called About Windows Explorer and asking whether you want to replace the existing file. Click **Yes** because you want to replace the previous version of the file on drive A with the updated version from the My Documents folder.

➤ You have just backed up the file; in other words, you have created a copy of the file on the disk in drive A. Thus, you can use the floppy disk to restore the file in the My Documents folder should anything happen to it.

John Doe's Documents folder within My Documents is active

Click and drag About Windows Explorer to the John Doe's Documents folder on drive A

Click Yes

(e) Copy (Back Up) a File (step 5)

FIGURE 12 *Hands-on Exercise 4 (continued)*

FILE EXTENSIONS

Long-time DOS users remember a three-character extension at the end of a file name to indicate the file type; for example, DOC or XLS to indicate a Word document or Excel workbook, respectively. The extensions are displayed or hidden according to a setting in the Folder Options command. Pull down the Tools menu, click the Folder Options command to display the Folder Options dialog box, click the View tab, then check (or clear) the box to hide (or show) file extensions for known file types. Click OK to accept the setting and exit the dialog box.

Step 6: **Delete a Folder**

➤ Select (click) **John Doe's Documents folder** within the My Documents folder in the left pane. Pull down the **File menu** and click **Delete** (or press the **Del key**).

➤ You will see the dialog box in Figure 12f asking whether you are sure you want to delete the folder (i.e., send the folder and its contents to the Recycle Bin). Note the recycle logo within the box, which implies that you will be able to restore the file.

➤ Click **Yes** to delete the folder. The folder disappears from drive C. Pull down the **Edit menu**. Click **Undo Delete**. The deletion is cancelled and the folder reappears in the left pane. If you don't see the folder, pull down the **View menu** and click the **Refresh command**.

Click John Doe's Documents folder within My Documents to select it

Recycle logo

Click Yes

(f) Delete a Folder (step 6)

FIGURE 12 *Hands-on Exercise 4 (continued)*

THE UNDO COMMAND

The Undo command is present not only in application programs such as Word or Excel, but in Windows Explorer as well. You can use the Undo command to undelete a file provided you execute the command immediately (within a few commands) after the Delete command. To execute the Undo command, right-click anywhere in the right pane to display a shortcut menu, then select the Undo action. You can also pull down the Edit menu and click Undo to reverse (undo) the last command. Some operations cannot be undone (in which case the command will be dimmed), but Undo is always worth a try.

Step 7:   **The Recycle Bin**

➤ Select John Doe's Documents folder within the My Documents folder in the left pane. Select (click) the **About Windows Explorer** file in the right pane. Press the **Del key**, then click **Yes**.

➤ Click the **Down arrow** in the vertical scroll bar in the left pane until you see the icon for the **Recycle Bin**. Click the icon to make the Recycle Bin the active folder and display its contents in the right pane.

➤ You will see a different set of files from those displayed in Figure 12g. Pull down the **View menu**, click (or point to) **Arrange icons**, then click **By Delete Date** to display the files in this sequence.

➤ Click in the **right pane**. Press **Ctrl+End** or scroll to the bottom of the window. Point to the **About Windows Explorer** file, click the **right mouse button** to display the shortcut menu in Figure 12g, then click **Restore**.

➤ The file disappears from the Recycle bin because it has been returned to John Doe's Documents folder.

Click icon for Recycle Bin

Point to About Windows Explorer and click right mouse button to display context-sensitive menu

Click Restore

Show Desktop button

(g) The Recycle Bin (step 7)

FIGURE 12   *Hands-on Exercise 4 (continued)*

THE SHOW DESKTOP BUTTON

The Show Desktop button on the taskbar enables you to minimize all open windows with a single click. The button functions as a toggle switch. Click it once and all windows are minimized. Click it a second time and the open windows are restored to their positions on the desktop. If you do not see the Show Desktop button, right click a blank area of the taskbar to display a context-sensitive menu, click Toolbars, then check the Quick Launch toolbar.

Step 8: **Write-Protect a Floppy Disk**

➤ Remove the floppy disk from drive A, then move the built-in tab on the disk so that the square hole on the disk is open. Return the disk to the drive.

➤ If necessary, expand drive A in the left pane, select the **Automobile folder**, select the **Analysis of a Car Loan document** in the right pane, then press the **Del key**. Click **Yes** when asked whether to delete the file.

➤ You will see the message in Figure 12h indicating that the file cannot be deleted because the disk has been write-protected. Click **OK**. Remove the write-protection by moving the built-in tab to cover the square hole.

➤ Repeat the procedure to delete the **Analysis of a Car Loan document**. Click **Yes** in response to the confirmation message asking whether you want to delete the file.

➤ The file disappears from the right pane, indicating it has been deleted. The **Automobile folder** on drive A should contain only one file.

➤ Delete **John Doe's Documents folder** from My Documents as a courtesy to the next student. Exit Windows Explorer. Shut down the computer.

(h) Write-Protect a Floppy Disk (step 8)

FIGURE 12   *Hands-on Exercise 4 (continued)*

BACK UP IMPORTANT FILES

We cannot overemphasize the importance of adequate backup and urge you to copy your data files to floppy disks and store those disks away from your computer. You might also want to write-protect your backup disks so that you cannot accidentally erase a file. It takes only a few minutes, but you will thank us, when (not if) you lose an important file and don't have to wish you had another copy.

Microsoft Windows controls the operation of a computer and its peripherals. Windows 98 and its successor, Windows Me, are geared for the home user and provide extensive support for games and peripheral devices. Windows NT and its successor, Windows 2000, are aimed at the business user and provide increased security and reliability. Windows XP replaces all current versions of Windows. All versions of Windows follow the same conventions and have the same basic interface.

All Windows operations take place on the desktop. Every window on the desktop contains the same basic elements, which include a title bar, a control-menu box, a minimize button, a maximize or restore button, and a close button. Other elements that may be present include a menu bar, vertical and/or horizontal scroll bars, a status bar, and various toolbars. All windows may be moved and sized. The Help command in the Start menu provides access to detailed information.

Multitasking is a major benefit of the Windows environment as it enables you to run several programs at the same time. The taskbar contains a button for each open program and enables you to switch back and forth between those programs by clicking the appropriate button.

A dialog box supplies information needed to execute a command. Option buttons indicate mutually exclusive choices, one of which must be chosen. Check boxes are used if the choices are not mutually exclusive or if an option is not required. A text box supplies descriptive information. A (drop-down or open) list box displays multiple choices, any of which may be selected. A tabbed dialog box provides access to multiple sets of options.

A floppy disk must be formatted before it can store data. Formatting is accomplished through the Format command within the My Computer window. My Computer enables you to browse the disk drives and other devices attached to your system. The contents of My Computer depend on the specific configuration.

A file is a set of data or set of instructions that has been given a name and stored on disk. There are two basic types of files, program files and data files. A program file is an executable file, whereas a data file can be used only in conjunction with a specific program. Every file has a file name and a file type. The file name can be up to 255 characters in length and may include spaces.

Files are stored in folders to better organize the hundreds (or thousands) of files on a disk. A folder may contain program files, data files, and/or other folders. There are two basic ways to search through the folders on your system, My Computer and Windows Explorer. My Computer is intuitive but less efficient than Windows Explorer, as you have to open each folder in succession. Windows Explorer is more sophisticated, as it provides a hierarchical view of the entire system.

Windows Explorer is divided into two panes. The left pane displays all of the devices and, optionally, the folders on each device. The right pane shows the contents of the active (open) drive or folder. Only one drive or folder can be active in the left pane. Any device, be it local or on the network, may be expanded or collapsed to display or hide its folders. A minus sign indicates that the drive has been expanded and that its folders are visible. A plus sign indicates that the device is collapsed and its folders are not visible.

The result of dragging a file (or folder) from one location to another depends on whether the source and destination folders are on the same or different drives. Dragging the file to a folder on the same drive moves the file. Dragging the file to a folder on a different drive copies the file. It's easier, therefore, to click and drag with the right mouse button to display a context-sensitive menu from which you can select the desired operation.

The Delete command deletes (removes) a file from a disk. If, however, the file was deleted from a local (fixed or hard) disk, it is not really gone, but moved instead to the Recycle Bin from where it can be subsequently recovered.

Backup strategy (p. 42)
Check box (p. 8)
Close button (p. 5)
Command button (p. 10)
Common user interface (p. 5)
Compressed file (p. 22)
Contents tab (p. 11)
Copy a file (p. 47)
Data file (p. 20)
Delete a file (p. 41)
Desktop (p. 2)
Details view (p. 20)
Dialog box (p. 8)
Favorites tab (p. 18)
File (p. 20)
Filename (p. 20)
File type (p. 20)
Folder (p. 20)
Folder Options command (p. 14)
Format command (p. 17)
Help command (p. 18)

Index tab (p. 14)
Internet Explorer (p. 40)
List box (p. 8)
Maximize button (p. 5)
Menu bar (p. 5)
Minimize button (p. 5)
Mouse operations (p. 10)
Move a file (p. 44)
Move a window (p. 15)
Multitasking (p. 4)
My Computer (p. 22)
My Documents folder (p. 45)
My Network Places (p. 5)
New command (p. 43)
Option button (p. 8)
Program file (p. 20)
Pull-down menu (p. 7)
Radio button (p. 8)
Recycle Bin (p. 49)
Rename command (p. 42)
Restore a file (p. 5)

Restore button (p. 5)
Scroll bar (p. 5)
Size a window (p. 15)
Spin button (p. 8)
Start button (p. 4)
Status bar (p. 5)
Taskbar (p. 4)
Text box (p. 8)
Task Manager (p. 19)
Title bar (p. 5)
Toolbar (p. 5)
Undo command (p. 48)
Windows 2000 (p. 2)
Windows 95 (p. 2)
Windows 98 (p. 2)
Windows Explorer (p. 33)
Windows Me (p. 2)
Windows NT (p. 2)
Windows XP (p. 2)
Write-enabled (p. 42)
Write-protected (p. 42)

MULTIPLE CHOICE

1. Which versions of the Windows operating system were intended for the home computer?
   (a) Windows NT and Windows 98
   (b) Windows NT and Windows XP
   (c) Windows NT and Windows 2000
   (d) Windows 98 and Windows Me

2. What happens if you click and drag a file from drive C to drive A?
   (a) The file is copied to drive A
   (b) The file is moved to drive A
   (c) A menu appears that allows you to choose between moving and copying
   (d) The file is sent to the recycle bin

3. Which of the following is *not* controlled by the Folder Options command?
   (a) Single or double clicking to open a desktop icon
   (b) The presence or absence of Web content within a folder
   (c) The view (e.g., using large or small icons) within My Computer
   (d) Using one or many windows when browsing My Computer

4. What is the significance of a faded (dimmed) command in a pull-down menu?
   (a) The command is not currently accessible
   (b) A dialog box will appear if the command is selected
   (c) A Help window will appear if the command is selected
   (d) There are no equivalent keystrokes for the particular command

5. Which of the following is true regarding a dialog box?
   (a) Option buttons indicate mutually exclusive choices
   (b) Check boxes imply that multiple options may be selected
   (c) Both (a) and (b)
   (d) Neither (a) nor (b)

6. Which of the following is the first step in sizing a window?
   (a) Point to the title bar
   (b) Pull down the View menu to display the toolbar
   (c) Point to any corner or border
   (d) Pull down the View menu and change to large icons

7. Which of the following is the first step in moving a window?
   (a) Point to the title bar
   (b) Pull down the View menu to display the toolbar
   (c) Point to any corner or border
   (d) Pull down the View menu and change to large icons

8. How do you exit from Windows?
   (a) Click the Start button, then click the Shut Down command
   (b) Right click the Start button, then click the Shut Down command
   (c) Click the End button, then click the Shut Down command
   (d) Right click the End button, then click the Shut Down command

9. Which button appears immediately after a window has been maximized?
   (a) The close button
   (b) The minimize button
   (c) The maximize button
   (d) The restore button

10. What happens to a window that has been minimized?
    (a) The window is still visible but it no longer has a minimize button
    (b) The window shrinks to a button on the taskbar
    (c) The window is closed and the application is removed from memory
    (d) The window is still open but the application is gone from memory

11. What is the significance of three dots next to a command in a pull-down menu?
    (a) The command is not currently accessible
    (b) A dialog box will appear if the command is selected
    (c) A Help window will appear if the command is selected
    (d) There are no equivalent keystrokes for the particular command

12. The Recycle Bin enables you to restore a file that was deleted from:
    (a) Drive A
    (b) Drive C
    (c) Both (a) and (b)
    (d) Neither (a) nor (b)

13. The left pane of Windows Explorer may contain:
    (a) One or more folders with a plus sign
    (b) One or more folders with a minus sign
    (c) Both (a) and (b)
    (d) Neither (a) nor (b)

14. Which of the following was suggested as essential to a backup strategy?
    (a) Back up all program files at the end of every session
    (b) Store backup files at another location
    (c) Both (a) and (b)
    (d) Neither (a) nor (b)

ANSWERS

1. d	5. c	9. d	13. c
2. a	6. c	10. b	14. b
3. c	7. a	11. b	
4. a	8. a	12. b	

1. My Computer: The document in Figure 13 is an effective way to show your instructor that you understand the My Computer window, and further that you have basic proficiency in Microsoft Word.

   a. Open My Computer to display the contents of your configuration. Pull down the View menu and switch to the Details view. Size the window as necessary. Press Alt + Print Screen to capture the copy of the My Computer window to the Windows clipboard. (The Print Screen key captures the entire screen. Using the Alt key, however, copies just the current window.)

   b. Click the Start menu, click Programs, then click Microsoft Word.

   c. Pull down the Edit menu. Click the Paste command to copy the contents of the clipboard to the document you are about to create. The My Computer window should be pasted into your document.

   d. Press Ctrl+End to move to the end of your document. Press Enter two or three times to leave blank lines as appropriate. Type a modified form of the memo in Figure 13 so that it conforms to your configuration.

   e. Finish the memo and sign your name. Pull down the File menu, click the Print command, then click OK in the dialog box to print the document.

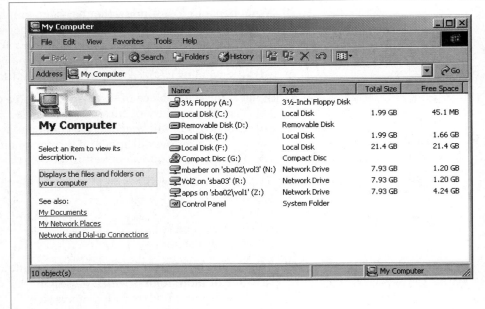

Dear Professor,

Please find the contents of My Computer as it exists on my computer system. I have selected the Folder Options to enable Web content in a folder and to double click an object to open it. I used the View menu to choose the Details view. My system consists of a floppy drive (drive A), three local disks (C, E, and F), a removable disk for backup (drive D), and a CD-ROM drive (drive G). In addition, I have access to three network drives (N, R, and Z).

I enjoyed reading the supplement and look forward to using this information as I learn more about the applications in Microsoft Office.

Sincerely,

Eric Simon

FIGURE 13   *My Computer (exercise 1)*

2. Windows Explorer: Prove to your instructor that you have completed the fourth hands-on exercise by creating a document similar to the one in Figure 14. Use the technique described in the previous problem to capture the screen and paste it into a Word document.

Compare the documents in Figures 13 and 14 that show My Computer and Windows Explorer, respectively. My Computer is intuitive and preferred by beginners, but it is very limited when compared to Windows Explorer. The latter displays a hierarchical view of your system, showing the selected object in the left pane and the contents of the selected object in the right pane. We urge you, therefore, to become comfortable with Windows Explorer, as that will make you more productive.

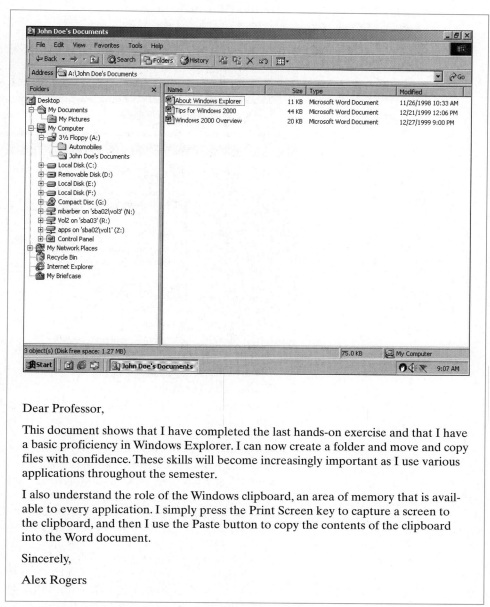

Dear Professor,

This document shows that I have completed the last hands-on exercise and that I have a basic proficiency in Windows Explorer. I can now create a folder and move and copy files with confidence. These skills will become increasingly important as I use various applications throughout the semester.

I also understand the role of the Windows clipboard, an area of memory that is available to every application. I simply press the Print Screen key to capture a screen to the clipboard, and then I use the Paste button to copy the contents of the clipboard into the Word document.

Sincerely,

Alex Rogers

FIGURE 14   *Windows Explorer (exercise 2)*

3. MyPHLIP Web Site: Every text in the *Exploring Office XP* series has a corresponding MyPHLIP (Prentice Hall Learning on the Internet Partnership) Web site, where you will find a variety of student resources as well as online review questions for each chapter. Go to www.prenhall.com/myphlip and follow the instructions. The first time at the site you will be prompted to register by supplying your e-mail address and choosing a password. Next, you choose the discipline (CIS/MIS) and a book (e.g., *Exploring Microsoft Office XP, Volume I*), which in turn will take you to a page similar to Figure 15.

Your professor will tell you whether he or she has created an online syllabus, in which case you should click the link to find your professor after adding the book. Either way, the next time you return to the site, you will be taken directly to your text. Select any chapter, click "Go", then use the review questions as directed.

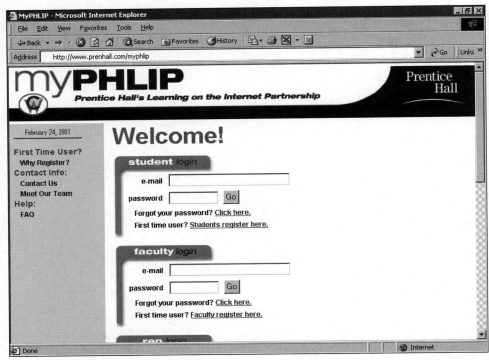

FIGURE 15   *MyPHLIP Web Site (Windows module) (exercise 3)*

4. Organize Your Work: A folder may contain documents, programs, or other folders. The My Classes folder in Figure 16, for example, contains five folders, one folder for each class you are taking this semester. Folders help you to organize your files, and you should become proficient in their use. The best way to practice with folders is on a floppy disk, as was done in Figure 16. Accordingly:
   a. Format a floppy disk or use the floppy disk you have been using throughout the chapter.
   b. Create a Correspondence folder. Create a Business and a Personal folder within the Correspondence folder.
   c. Create a My Courses folder. Within the My Courses folder create a separate folder for each course you are taking.
   d. Use the technique described in problems 1 and 2 to capture the screen in Figure 16 and incorporate it into a document. Add a short paragraph that describes the folders you have created, then submit the document.

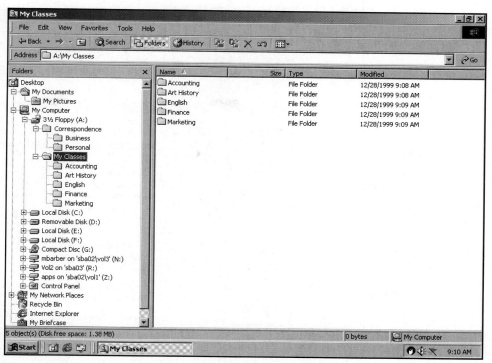

FIGURE 16 *Organize Your Work (exercise 4)*

5. **The Windows Web Site:** The Web is the best source for information on any application. Go to the Windows home page (www.microsoft.com/windows) as shown in Figure 17, then write a short note to your instructor summarizing the contents of that page and the associated links. Similar pages exist for all Microsoft applications such as www.microsoft.com/office for Microsoft Office.

6. **Implement a Screen Saver:** A screen saver is a delightful way to personalize your computer and a good way to practice with Microsoft Windows. This is typically not something you can do in a laboratory setting, but it is well worth doing on your own machine. Point to a blank area of the desktop, click the right mouse button to display a context-sensitive menu, then click the Properties command to open the Display Properties dialog box in Figure 18. Click the Screen Saver tab, click the Down arrow in the Screen Saver list box, and select Marquee Display. Click the Settings command button, enter the text and other options for your message, then click OK to close the Options dialog box. Click OK a second time to close the Display Properties dialog box.

7. **The Active Desktop:** The Active Desktop displays Web content directly on the desktop, then updates the information automatically according to a predefined schedule. You can, for example, display a stock ticker or scoreboard similar to what you see on television. You will need your own machine and an Internet connection to do this exercise, as it is unlikely that the network administrator will let you modify the desktop:
   a. Right click the Windows desktop, click Properties to show the Display Properties dialog box, then click the Web tab. Check the box to show Web content on the Active desktop.
   b. Click the New button, then click the Visit Gallery command button to go to the Active Desktop Gallery in Figure 19 on page 59. Choose any category, then follow the onscreen instructions to display the item on your desktop. We suggest you start with the stock ticker or sports scoreboard.
   c. Summarize your opinion of the active desktop in a short note to your instructor. Did the feature work as advertised? Is the information useful to you?

FIGURE 17 *The Windows Web Site (exercise 5)*

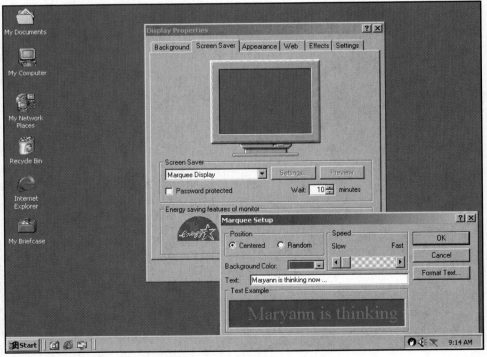

FIGURE 18 *Implement a Screen Saver (exercise 6)*

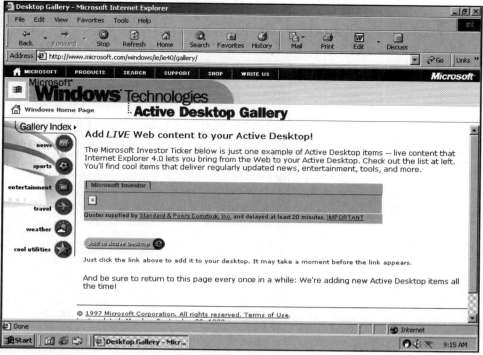

FIGURE 19 *The Active Desktop (exercise 7)*

8. The Control Panel: The Control Panel enables you to change the hardware or software settings on your system. You will not have access to the Control Panel in a lab environment, but you will need it at home if you change your configuration, perhaps by installing a new program. Click the Start button, click Settings, then select Control Panel to display the Control Panel window. Click the down arrow on the Views button to change to the Details view as shown in Figure 20. (The Control Panel can also be opened from My Computer.)

    Write a short report (two or three paragraphs is sufficient) that describes some of the capabilities within Control Panel. *Be careful about making changes, however, and be sure you understand the nature of the new settings before you accept any of the changes.*

9. Users and Passwords: Windows 2000 enables multiple users to log onto the same machine, each with his or her own user name and password. The desktop settings for each user are stored individually, so that all users have their own desktop. The administrator and default user is created when Windows 2000 is first installed, but new users can be added or removed at any time. Once again you will need your own machine:

    a. Click the Start button, click Settings, then click Control Panel to open the Control Panel window as shown in Figure 21. The Control Panel is a special folder that allows you to modify the hardware and/or software settings on your computer.

    b. Double click the Users and Passwords icon to display the dialog box in Figure 20. *Be very careful about removing a user or changing a password, because you might inadvertently deny yourself access to your computer.*

    c. Summarize the capabilities within the users and passwords dialog box in a short note to your instructor. Can you see how these principles apply to the network you use at school or work?

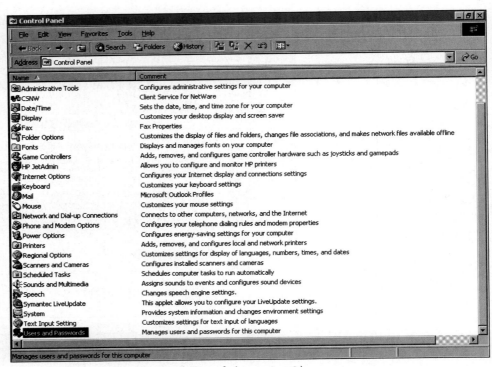

FIGURE 20   *The Control Panel (exercise 8)*

FIGURE 21   *Users and Passwords (exercise 9)*

10. The Fonts Folder: The Fonts folder within the Control Panel displays the names of the fonts available on a system and enables you to obtain a printed sample of any specific font. Click the Start button, click (or point to) the Settings command, click (or point to) Control Panel, then double click the Fonts icon to open the Fonts folder and display the fonts on your system.

    a. Double click any font to open a Fonts window as shown in Figure 22, then click the Print button to print a sample of the selected font.

    b. Open a different font. Print a sample page of this font as well.

    c. Locate the Wingdings font and print this page. Do you see any symbols you recognize? How do you insert these symbols into a document?

    d. How many fonts are there in your fonts Folder? Do some fonts appear to be redundant with others? How much storage space does a typical font require? Write the answers to these questions in a short paragraph.

    e. Start Word. Create a title page containing your name, class, date, and the title of this assignment (My Favorite Fonts). Center the title. Use boldface or italics as you see fit. Be sure to use a suitable type size.

    f. Staple the various pages together (the title page, the three font samples, and the answers to the questions in part d). Submit the assignment to your instructor.

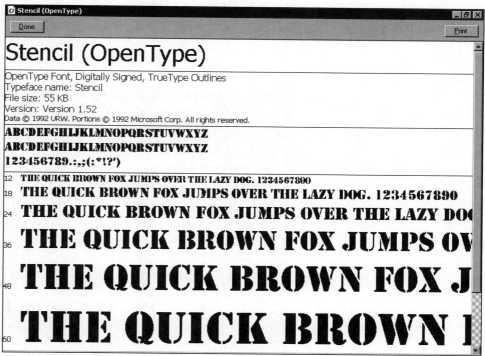

FIGURE 22   *The Fonts Folder (exercise 10)*

11. Keyboard Shortcuts: Microsoft Windows is a graphical user interface in which users "point and click" to execute commands. As you gain proficiency, however, you will find yourself gravitating toward various keyboard shortcuts as shown in Figures 23a and 23b. There is absolutely no need to memorize these shortcuts, nor should you even try. A few, however, have special appeal and everyone has his or her favorite. Use the Help menu to display this information, pick your three favorite shortcuts, and submit them to your instructor. Compare your selections with those of your classmates.

(a)

(b)

FIGURE 23 *Shortcut Keys for Natural Keyboard (Exercise 11)*

Planning for Disaster

Do you have a backup strategy? Do you even know what a backup strategy is? You had better learn, because sooner or later you will wish you had one. You will erase a file, be unable to read from a floppy disk, or worse yet suffer a hardware failure in which you are unable to access the hard drive. The problem always seems to occur the night before an assignment is due. The ultimate disaster is the disappearance of your computer, by theft or natural disaster. Describe, in 250 words or less, the backup strategy you plan to implement in conjunction with your work in this class.

Your First Consultant's Job

Go to a real installation such as a doctor's or attorney's office, the company where you work, or the computer lab at school. Determine the backup procedures that are in effect, then write a one-page report indicating whether the policy is adequate and, if necessary, offering suggestions for improvement. Your report should be addressed to the individual in charge of the business, and it should cover all aspects of the backup strategy; that is, which files are backed up and how often, and what software is used for the backup operation. Use appropriate emphasis (for example, bold italics) to identify any potential problems. This is a professional document (it is your first consultant's job), and its appearance should be perfect in every way.

File Compression

You've learned your lesson and have come to appreciate the importance of backing up all of your data files. The problem is that you work with large documents that exceed the 1.44MB capacity of a floppy disk. Accordingly, you might want to consider the acquisition of a file compression program to facilitate copying large documents to a floppy disk in order to transport your documents to and from school, home, or work. (A Zip file is different from a Zip drive. The latter is a hardware device, similar in concept to a large floppy disk, with a capacity of 100MB or 250MB.)

You can download an evaluation copy of the popular WinZip program at www.winzip.com. Investigate the subject of file compression and submit a summary of your findings to your instructor.

The Threat of Virus Infection

A computer virus is an actively infectious program that attaches itself to other programs and alters the way a computer works. Some viruses do nothing more than display an annoying message at an inopportune time. Most, however, are more harmful, and in the worst case, erase all files on the disk. Use your favorite search engine to research the subject of computer viruses in order to answer the following questions. When is a computer subject to infection by a virus? What precautions does your school or university take against the threat of virus infection in its computer lab? What precautions, if any, do you take at home? Can you feel confident that your machine will not be infected if you faithfully use a state-of-the-art antivirus program that was purchased in January 2001?

The Briefcase

It is becoming increasingly common for people to work on more than one machine. Students, for example, may alternate between machines at school and home. In similar fashion, an office worker may use a desktop and a laptop, or have a machine at work and at home. In every instance, you need to transfer files back and forth between the two machines. This can be done using the Copy command from within Windows Explorer. It can also be done via the Briefcase folder. Your instructor has asked you to look into the latter capability and to prepare a brief report describing its use. Do you recommend the Briefcase over a simple Copy command?

Cut, Copy, and Paste

The Cut, Copy, and Paste commands are used in conjunction with one another to move and copy data within a document, or from one Windows document to another. The commands can also be executed from within My Computer or Windows Explorer to move and copy files. You can use the standard Windows shortcuts of Ctrl+X, Ctrl+C, and Ctrl+V to cut, copy, and paste, respectively. You can also click the corresponding icons on the Standard Buttons toolbar within Windows Explorer or My Computer.

Experiment with this technique, then write a short note to your instructor that summarizes the various ways in which files can be moved or copied within Windows 2000.

Register Now

It is good practice to register every program you purchase, so that the vendor can notify you of new releases and/or other pertinent information. Windows provides an online capability whereby you can register via modem. To register your copy of Windows, click the Start button, click Programs, click Accessories, click Welcome to Windows, then click the Registration Wizard. Follow the directions that are displayed on the screen. (Registering a program does carry the risk of having unwanted sales messages sent to you by e-mail. At the Web site, look for a check box in which you choose whether to receive unsolicited e-mail.) You can do this exercise only if you are working on your own computer.

INDEX

A

Absolute reference, 33, 66–68, 122
  shortcut for, 70, 143
Accounting format, 43
Active cell, 7, 16
Alignment, 44–45
Arguments, 112
Ascending sort, 74
Assumptions (isolation of), 31, 122
AutoComplete, 25
AutoFill capability, 143
AutoFilter command, 142, 152
AutoFit selection, 126
AutoFormat command, 183, 208
AutoSum command, 179, 208
AVERAGE function, 5–6, 134–135

B

Bar chart, 171–172
Border tab, 46, 50
Breakpoint, 138

C

Category label, 168
Cell, 4
Cell reference, 4
Chart, 168
  copying of, 194, 201
Chart sheet, 174
Chart toolbar, 178
Chart type, 169–173, 184, 196
Chart Wizard, 176–177, 180–181
Clipboard, 33
  Office versus Windows, 40,
Close command, 9
Column chart, 171–173, 188–190
Column width, 38
  ##s in, 126

Combination chart, 213
Comments, 68, 75, 152
Common user interface, 200
Conditional formatting, 81
Constant, 5
Copy command, 32–33, 39, 40
COUNT function, 135
COUNTA function, 135
Currency format, 43
Custom format, 43

D

Data disk (*See* Practice files)
Data point, 168
Data series, 168
  formatting of, 187
  viewing of, 193
Date arithmetic, 87, 105
Date format, 43
Default file location, 83
Delete command, 19–20
  cells, 26
  comment, 75
  row, 23
  worksheet, 30
Descending sort, 74
Destination range, 32
Dialog box (shortcuts in), 28
Docked toolbar, 186
Drawing toolbar, 178

E

Edit
  cell content, 5, 24
  comment, 75
E-mail (Excel workbook), 62
Embedded chart, 174, 182
Exit command, 9

Exploded pie chart, 169, 209–210
External Data toolbar, 87

F

File menu, 9–10
File name, 9
    sorting of, 10
File type, 9
Fill handle, 68, 71, 125, 143
Find and Replace command, 125
Find command, 29
Floating toolbar, 186
Folder (creation of), 37
Fonts, 44–45
Footer, 21
Format Cells command, 43–46
Format Painter, 80
Formatting, 42–46
    clearing of, 49
Formatting toolbar, 7–8
Formula, 5
    displaying of, 27, 52
    editing of, 52
    printing of, 120
Formula Auditing toolbar, 27
Formula bar, 7
Fraction format, 43
Freeze Panes command, 139, 145
Function, 5, 112
    searching for, 116
    versus formula, 72, 136
FV function, 112, 118

G

General format, 43
Go To command, 145
Goal Seek command, 114, 117

H

Header, 21
Hiding rows or columns, 139, 151
HLOOKUP function, 138, 157
Horizontal scroll bar, 195
HTML document (*See* Web page)
Hyperlink, 76

I

IF function, 134, 137, 146
Import External Data command, 87, 89
Individual Retirement Account, 132, 160

Insert command, 19–20
    cells, 26
    column, 26
    row, 24
    worksheet, 30
Insert Comment command, 23, 68
Insert Function command, 113, 116
Insert Hyperlink command, 82
Internet Explorer, 76–77
IPMT function, 128, 161–162

L

Landscape orientation, 21, 28
LEFT function, 144, 163
Linked object, 203
Linking (versus embedding), 203

M

MAX function, 134–135
Menus (changing of), 16
Merge and Center command, 44
    horizontal direction, 47
    vertical direction, 129
Microsoft Excel
    starting of, 13
    version of, 18
MIN function, 134–135
Mixed reference, 33, 123, 131
    shortcut for, 143
Move operation, 34–35
Multiple data series, 188–196
Multitasking, 85, 197

N

Name box, 7, 145
Nested If, 148, 163
Noncontiguous range (selection of), 119
Number format, 43

O

Object Linking and Embedding (OLE), 197–204,
    213–214
Office Assistant, 13, 18, 22, 192
Open command, 9–10, 14

P

Page Break Preview command, 139, 150, 210–211
Page Setup command, 21, 28
    with large worksheets, 140

Paste options, 39
Patterns tab, 46
Percent style, 73
Percentage format, 43
Pie chart, 169–171
Places bar, 9–10
PMT function, 112, 121–122
Pointing, 68, 79
Portrait orientation, 21, 28
PPMT function, 128, 161–162
Practice files, 12
Print area, 150
Print command, 9
Print Preview command, 29

R

Range, 32
RANK function, 149, 163
Redo command, 17
Refresh command, 87, 94
Relational operator, 137
Relative reference, 33, 66–68
    shortcut for, 70, 143
Replace command, 29
RIGHT function, 144
Roth IRA, 132, 160
Round trip HTML, 76, 84
Row height, 38

S

Save command, 9–10
Save as command, 9–10, 15
Save as Web Page command, 76
Scientific format, 43
ScreenTip, 7
Scrolling, 139
Select-then-do, 43
Side-by-side column charts, 188–189
Sizing handles, 174
Social Security number (formatting of), 144
Sort command, 74, 134
Source range, 32
Special format, 43
Spell check, 124

Split cells, 44
Spreadsheet (introduction to), 2–5
Stacked column charts, 188–190
Standard toolbar, 7–8
Statistical functions, 134–135
Status bar, 7
SUM function, 72

T

Task pane, 22
Taskbar, 197, 199
Template, 86, 106–107, 110
Text box (creation of), 186
Text format, 43
Three-dimensional column chart, 173
Three-dimensional pie chart, 169
Time format, 43
TODAY( ) function, 88
Toolbars, 7–8
    separation of, 14

U

Undo command, 17
Unfreeze Panes command, 139
Unhiding rows or columns, 139

V

VLOOKUP function, 134, 138, 147

W

Web page, 76, 78–86
Web query, 76, 87–94
Workbook, 6
Worksheet, 6
    linking of, 204, 211
    renaming of, 191
Wrap text, 74

Z

Zoom, 41